The Reconstruction of the Juridico-Political

Hans Kelsen and Max Weber are conventionally understood as the original proponents of two distinct and opposed processes of concept formation generating two separate and contrasting theoretical frameworks for the study of law. *The Reconstruction of the Juridico-Political: Affinity and Divergence in Hans Kelsen and Max Weber* contests the conventional understanding of the theoretical relationship between Kelsen's legal positivism and Weber's sociology of law. Utilizing the conceptual frame of the juridico-political, the contributors to this interdisciplinary volume analyse central points of affinity and divergence in the work of these two influential figures. Thus, the chapters collected in *The Reconstruction of the Juridico-Political* offer a comprehensive reconsideration of these affinities and divergences, through a comparison of their respective reconstruction of the notions of democracy, the State, legal rights and the character of law. From this reconsideration a more complex understanding of their theoretical relationship emerges combined with a renewed emphasis upon the continued contemporary relevance of the work of Kelsen and Weber.

Ian Bryan is Senior Lecturer in Law, Law School, Lancaster University, UK.

Peter Langford is Senior Lecturer in Law, Department of Law and Criminology, Edge Hill University, UK.

John McGarry is Reader in Law, Department of Law and Criminology, Edge Hill University, UK.

The Reconstruction of the Juridico-Political

Affinity and Divergence in
Hans Kelsen and Max Weber

Edited by
Ian Bryan, Peter Langford and
John McGarry

Taylor & Francis Group
a GlassHouse Book

First published 2016
by Routledge
2 Park Square, Milton Park, Abingdon, Oxon, OX14 4RN

and by Routledge
711 Third Avenue, New York, NY 10017

a GlassHouse book.

Routledge is an imprint of the Taylor & Francis Group, an informa business

© 2016 editorial matter and selection: Ian Bryan, Peter Langford and John McGarry; Individual chapters, the contributors

The right of Ian Bryan, Peter Langford and John McGarry to be identified as editors of this work has been asserted by them in accordance with sections 77 and 78 of the Copyright, Designs and Patents Act 1988.

All rights reserved. No part of this book may be reprinted or reproduced or utilised in any form or by any electronic, mechanical, or other means, now known or hereafter invented, including photocopying and recording, or in any information storage or retrieval system, without permission in writing from the publishers.

Trademark notice: Product or corporate names may be trademarks or registered trademarks, and are used only for identification and explanation without intent to infringe.

British Library Cataloguing in Publication Data
A catalogue record for this book is available from the British Library

Library of Congress Cataloging-in-Publication Data
The reconstruction of the juridico-political : affinity and divergence in Hans Kelsen and Max Weber / Edited by Ian Bryan, Peter Langford and John McGarry.
  pages cm
Includes bibliographical references and index.
ISBN 978-0-415-52482-7 (hbk) – ISBN 978-0-203-79878-2 (ebk)
 1. Law–Philosophy. 2. Law–Political aspects. 3. Legal positivism.
 4. Sociological jurisprudence. 5. Kelsen, Hans, 1881–1973 6. Weber, Max, 1864–1920 I. Bryan, Ian. II. Langford, Peter. III. McGarry, John.
 K230.R423 2016
 340'.1–dc23
 2015024624

ISBN: 978-0-415-52482-7 (hbk)
ISBN: 978-0-203-79878-2 (ebk)

Typeset in Baskerville by
Servis Filmsetting Ltd, Stockport, Cheshire

Contents

Acknowledgements vii
Notes on contributors viii

Introduction: affinity and divergence 1
IAN BRYAN, PETER LANGFORD AND JOHN MCGARRY

PART I
Hans Kelsen, Max Weber and democracy **25**

1 *Führerprinzip* and democracy in Weber and Kelsen 27
  ANTONINO SCALONE

2 Democracy within pluralism: Hans Kelsen on civil society
  and civic friendship 44
  ELIF ÖZMEN

PART II
Hans Kelsen, Max Weber and the State **59**

3 Max Weber's conception of the State: the State as *Anstalt*
  and as *validated conception* with special reference to
  Kelsen's critique of Weber 61
  HUBERT TREIBER

4 Kelsen reading Weber: is a sociological concept of the State
  possible? 98
  CATHERINE COLLIOT-THÉLÈNE

5 Kelsen, Weber and the problem of the emergence of the State 110
MICHEL TROPER

PART III
Hans Kelsen, Max Weber and rights 123

6 The State under the rule of law? The relationship of State and law in the work of Hans Kelsen and Georg Jellinek 125
GERHARD DONHAUSER

7 Human rights and subjective rights: affinities in Max Weber and Georg Jellinek 140
KATHRIN GROH

PART IV
Hans Kelsen, Max Weber and the character of law 161

8 Max Weber and Hans Kelsen: formal rationality and legitimacy of modern law 163
MICHEL COUTU

9 Using Weber's and Kelsen's schemas for legal history 179
JEAN-LOUIS HALPÉRIN

Index 195

Acknowledgements

We would like to thank Colin Perrin, Commissioning Editor at Routledge, for his support regarding this contribution and also Rebekah Jenkins and Laura Muir, former and present Editorial Assistants, for their assistance and patience during the preparation and submission of the manuscript. We would also like to express our gratitude to the contributors to this volume, both for their support for our project and for their incisive and original contributions. We would like to thank Edge Hill University for its financial and administrative support which enabled the conference *Hans Kelsen and Max Weber: Convergences and Divergences in Conceptions of the Juridico-Political* to take place in July 2012. Many of the papers contained in this volume were presented at the conference.

In addition to the aforementioned, Peter would like to acknowledge and thank all his friends for their interest and encouragement; and to thank his father for his support throughout this book project. Ian would like to express his profound gratitude to family and friends for their insightful comments and unfailing kindness. John would like to thank his family, Clare, Joe, Joan and Ken for their support and patience.

Ian, Peter and John
June 2015

Notes on contributors

Ian Bryan is Senior Lecturer in Law, Law School, Lancaster University. His teaching, research and publication activities span a wide range of fields, including the administration of criminal justice, criminal law, the laws of evidence, legal history, human rights and legal theory.

Catherine Colliot-Thélène is Professor of Philosophy, Department of Philosophy, University of Rennes 1, France. She has translated a number of Max Weber's works into French, and published widely on the work of Max Weber and in the area of political philosophy. Her books include *Le désenchantement de l'État. De Hegel à Max Weber* (Paris: Éditions de Minuit, 1992); *Etudes wébériennes: Rationalités, histoires, droits* (Paris: Presses Universitaires de France, 2001); *La démocratie sans demos* (Paris: Presses Universitaires de France, 2011); and (editor with F. Guénard) *Peuples et populisme* (Paris: Presses Universitaires de France, 2014).

Michel Coutu is a Full Professor of Labour Law, School of Industrial Relations, Faculty of Arts and Science, University of Montreal, Canada. He has published extensively in the areas of sociology of law (including papers on Max Weber in the *Journal of Law and Society*), labour law theory, human rights and collective bargaining legislation. His books include *Max Weber et les rationalités du droit* (Paris: Librairie générale de droit et de jurisprudence, 1995); a translation of Max Weber, *Rudolf Stammler et le matérialisme historique* (Paris: Editions du Cerf, 2003); (editor with G. Rocher) *La légitimité de l'Etat et du droit: Autour de Max Weber* (Paris: Librairie générale de droit et de jurisprudence, 2006); and (editor with G. Murray) *La citoyenneté au travail: Quel avenir?* (Québec: Les Presses de l'Université Laval, 2010).

Gerhard Donhauser is Senior Lecturer in Philosophy and Law, specializing in legal theory, at the Universities of Innsbruck and Klagenfurt and a Researcher at the Hans Kelsen Institute, Vienna, Austria. He has published widely in the areas of philosophy of law, legal theory and political science. His books include *Türhüter: Wie Recht wird, was es ist* (Vienna: New Academic Press, 2013); *Angst und Schrecken: Beobachtungen auf dem Weg vom Ausnahmezustand zum Polizeistaat in Europa* *und den USA* (Vienna: New Academic Press, 2015); and *Wer hat Recht?: Eine Einführung in die Rechtsphilosophie* (Vienna: New Academic Press, 2015).

Kathrin Groh is Professor of Public Law, Universität der Bundeswehr, Munich, Germany. She has published widely in the areas of constitutional and political theory. Her publications include *Selbstschutz der Verfassung gegen Religionsgemeinschaften: Vom Religionsprivileg des Vereinsgesetzes zum Vereinigungsverbot* (Berlin: Duncker & Humblot, 2004); (with C. Weinbach) *Zur Genealogie des politischen Raums. Politische Strukturen im Wandel* (Wiesbaden: VS Verlag, 2005); (co-editor) *Die Europäische Verfassung – Verfassungen in Europa* (Baden-Baden: Nomos, 2005); and *Demokratische Staatsrechtslehrer in der Weimarer Republik: Von der konstitutionellen Staatslehre zur Theorie des modernen demokratischen Verfassungsstaats (Hugo Preuß, Gerhard Anschütz, Richard Thoma, Hans Kelsen und Hermann Heller)* (Tübingen: Mohr Siebeck, 2010).

Jean-Louis Halpérin is Professor of Law, Department of Social Sciences, l'École Normale Supérieure, Paris, France. He has published extensively in the areas of modern legal history (eighteenth to twentieth centuries), comparative law and legal theory. His books include *L'impossible Code civil* (Paris: Presses Universitaires de France, 1992); *Entre nationalisme juridique et communauté de droit* (Paris: Presses Universitaires de France, 1999); *Histoire des droits en Europe: De 1750 à nos jours* (Paris: Flammarion, 2005); *Histoire du droit des biens* (Paris: Economica, 2008); *Profils des mondialisations du droit* (Paris: Dalloz-Sirey, 2009); and *Histoire du droit privé français depuis 1804*, 3rd edition (Paris: Presses Universitaires de France); *Five Legal Revolutions since the 17th Century. An Analysis of a Global Legal History* (Dordrecht: Springer, 2014).

Peter Langford is Senior Lecturer in Law, Department of Law and Criminology, Edge Hill University, UK. He has published in the areas of human rights and legal theory. In the area of legal theory, he has published a book on the work of the contemporary Italian philosopher, Roberto Esposito, *Roberto Esposito: Law, Community and the Political* (London: Routledge, 2015).

John McGarry is Reader in Law, Department of Law and Criminology, Edge Hill University, UK. He has published in the areas of public law and jurisprudence.

Elif Özmen is Professor of Practical Philosophy, Department of Philosophy, University of Regensburg, Germany. She has published widely in the areas of moral philosophy, ethics and political and social philosophy. Her books include (editor) *Hans Kelsens Politische Philosophie* (forthcoming 2016); (editor) *Über Menschliches. Anthropologie zwischen Natur und Utopie* (Münster: Mentis, 2015); *Politische Philosophie zur Einführung* (Hamburg: Junius, 2013); *Moral, Rationalität und Gelungenes Leben* (Paderborn: Mentis, 2005).

Antonino Scalone is Professor of Public Law, Department of Public, International and Community Law, University of Padua, Italy. He has published widely in the areas of political and legal philosophy. His books include *Rappresentanza politica e rappresentanza degli interessi* (Milan: Franco Angeli, 1996); *Una battaglia contro gli spettri. Diritto e politica nella Reine Rechtslehre di Hans Kelsen (1905–1934)* (Turin: Giappichelli, 2008); (editor with M. Bertolissi and G. Duso) *Ripensare la Costituzione. La questione della pluralità* (Milan: Polimetrica, 2008); (editor with G. Duso) *Come pensare il federalismo? Nuove categorie e trasformazioni costituzionali* (Milan: Polimetrica, 2010); *L'ordine precario. Unità politica e pluralità nella Staatslehre novecentesca da Carl Schmitt a Joseph H. Kaiser* (Milan: Polimetrica, 2011).

Hubert Treiber is Emeritus Professor of Administrative Sciences, Leibniz University, Hannover, Germany. He has published widely on Max Weber and worked on Friedrich Nietzsche and Paul Rée. His publications include (editor with K. Sauerland) *Heidelberg im Schnittpunkt intellektueller Kreise* (1995); (with Leonie Breunung) *Die Vollzugsorganisation als Entscheidungsfaktor des Verwaltungshandelns* (2000); (with G. Grasshoff) *Naturgesetz und Naturrechtsdenken im 17. Jahrhundert* (2002); (editor and commentator) *Paul Rée: Gesammelte Werke 1875–1885* (2004, Supplementa Nietzscheana, vol. 7); (with Heinz Steinert) *Die Fabrikation des zuverlaessigen Menschen. Ueber die 'Wahlverwandtschaft' von Kloster- und Fabrikdisziplin* (2005); (with L. Breunung) *Recht als Handlungsressource kommunaler Industrieansiedlungspolitik. Zum Gebrauch und Verzicht von Recht bei ungleicher Machtverteilung* (2005); 'Der "Eranos" – Das Glanzstück im Heidelberger Mythenkranz?', in W. Schluchter and F. W. Graf (eds), *Asketischer Protestantismus und der 'Geist' des modernen Kapitalismus* (Tübingen: Mohr Siebeck, 2005), pp.75–153; 'Max Weber, Johannes von Kries and the Kinetic Theory of Gases', (2015) 15(1) *Max Weber Studies* 46–68; with Stefan Breuer and Eckart Otto, editor of *Studies in Cultural and Social Sciences* (Wiesbaden: Harrassowitz), recent volumes of which include: S. Breuer, 'Herrschaft' in der Soziologie Max Webers, 2011; H. Tyrell, 'Religion' in der Soziologie Max Webers, 2014; H. Bruhns, Max Webers historische Sozialökonomie, 2014.

Michel Troper is Emeritus Professor of Public Law, l'Université de Paris Ouest-Nanterre-La Défense, Nanterre, France. He has been a member of the Institut Universitaire de France and is founding President of the Société Française de philosophie politique et juridique. He has published widely in the areas of legal theory, constitutional law and legal history. His books include *Pour une théorie juridique de l'Etat* (Paris: Presses Universitaires de France, 1994); (editor with V. Champeil-Desplats and C. Grzegorczyk) *Théorie des contraintes juridiques* (Paris: Librairie générale de droit et de jurisprudence, 2005); *Terminer la Révolution: La Constitution de 1795* (Paris: Fayard, 2006); *Le droit et la nécessité* (Paris: Presses Universitaires de France, 2011); and *La séparation des pouvoirs et l'histoire constitutionnelle française* (Paris: Librairie générale de droit et de jurisprudence, 2014).

Introduction:
affinity and divergence

Ian Bryan, Peter Langford and John McGarry

The comparison of Hans Kelsen (1881–1973) and Max Weber (1864–1920) – the consideration of their affinity and divergence[1] – is furnished with interpretative potential by considering their work as animated by the reconstruction of the juridico-political. From this perspective, the notion of reconstruction is understood to operate at two levels, and to commence, at an abstract level, from the elaboration of a conceptual framework within which to thematize the juridico-political. The determination of the methodology for this thematization is then related to a more concrete level involving conceptions of the legitimacy and effectiveness of political and institutional transformation and the phenomenon of positive law. The combination of these two levels also enables this interpretation of Kelsenian and Weberian reconstructions of the juridico-political to be comprehended as forms of intervention within the existing juridico-political reality.

The notion of the juridico-political, which provides the parameters for this comparative interpretation of Kelsen and Weber, emphasizes the interconnection, rather than the separation, between reflection upon law and politics. The interconnection between law and politics entails that each is part of a methodological unity which acknowledges both their identity and difference. This, in turn, enables the work of Kelsen and Weber, which is designated as 'political',[2] to be encompassed as an integral part of this interpretation. The underlying presumption of a reconstruction the notion of the juridico-political is organized into four analytical parts. Each part concentrates upon a particularly indicative element, within the notion of the juridico-political, through which to trace a theoretical process of reconstruction and, thus, specific aspects of affinity and divergence.

The analytical separation is orientated by an understanding of reconstruction as a distinct process situated between a mere return to, or restoration of, existing juridico-political concepts and the articulation of an entirely new conceptual framework. The distinctive character of this reconstructive process is also shaped by the intensity and extent of the transformation of the existing structures of the juridico-political during the lifetime of both Kelsen and Weber.[3] In particular, it is the transformation produced by the military defeat of Wilhelmine Germany and the Austro-Hungarian Empire, which place Kelsen and Weber at the centre of the creation of a juridico-political framework for the German and Austrian nation States which emerge, respectively, from the Treaty of Versailles and the Treaty of Saint-Germain-en-Laye. The initial affinity of their direct association with these juridico-political frameworks diverges with Weber's withdrawal from Weimar party politics and death, in 1920, and Kelsen's appointment as a judge to the Austrian Constitutional Court, combined with his academic position at the University of Vienna, which continues until his dismissal from the Constitutional Court in 1930.[4] The dismissal of Kelsen is followed by his departure from Austria to take up an academic appointment, in 1930, at the University of Cologne. This was then affected by commencement of the collapse of the Weimar Republic, in 1933, with Hitler's appointment as Reich Chancellor, and the initiation of the National Socialist transformation of the juridico-political structures of the Weimar Republic: The 'Law for the Restoration of the Professional Civil Service' of April 1933, requires, from its definition of Kelsen as a Jew, his dismissal from his position at Cologne.[5]

The disappearance of both the Weimar Republic and the First Austrian Republic is, during and immediately after the Second World War, subject to renewed academic interrogation, and this centres upon the predominant 'positivism', and its empty 'formalism', or 'formalist' analyses of the juridico-political, of the interwar period. It identifies these theoretical characteristics with the essential weakness of its conceptual framework in relation to the justification of a constitutional democracy; and, from this weakness, its potential, if not actual, complicity in the collapse of both constitutional democracies.[6] This critical interrogation is accompanied by the resurgence of theories of natural law, the return to political philosophy and theories of totalitarianism as the origin from which to overcome these fundamental weaknesses.[7] The subsequent developments and modifications of these theoretical approaches, through which the juridico-political is conceived, are marked by either the maintenance of emphatic critical distance or a lack of significant return to the work of Kelsen and Weber.[8] The comparison of the work of Kelsen and Weber, orientated by the reconstruction of the juridico-political, therefore, detaches itself from this predominant perspective. The detachment is based upon a different form of critical engagement in which the work of Kelsen and Weber is regarded as a conceptual resource of continued pertinence for reflection upon the juridico-political.

Kelsen, Weber and democracy

The pertinence arises, in the first path of reflection, through the consideration of the concept of democracy in the work of Kelsen and Weber. If the concept of democracy is related to the question of political representation, the further and more fundamental question of the stability of an order of political representation arises.[9] This manner of introducing the question of democracy indicates the potential repetition of a central question in Hobbes's *Leviathan*: the reconciliation of the requirements of order – the separation between private and public – and participation.[10] The repetition of this question receives a response, by Kelsen and

Weber, in which the reconciliation of order and participation can, however, only be achieved within a constitutional, multi-party democracy. The conception of a constitutional, multi-party democracy is, thus, as a regime or form of rule which determines the parameters of the response to the requirement to reconcile order and participation.

For Weber, the Weimar Republic is a form of rule (*Herrschaft*), which is subject to the wider dynamics of a specifically modern, legal-rational type of domination (*Zweckrationalität*). The Weimar Constitution and multi-party democratic system are the modern political form through which the relationship between the rulers and the ruled is determined. Democracy based upon political parties is distinguished from the previous political form of Wilhelmine monarchy[11] and a democracy based upon a more direct relationship between rulers and ruled. Political representation through the election of members of political parties becomes the sole medium for the reconciliation of the requirements of order and participation.[12]

The wider dynamics of a specifically modern, legal-rational type of domination manifest themselves in a series of contradictions within the Weimar system. At the level of the ruler, the contradiction is between the political party and the leader. The contradiction is not merely that between the group and the individual, but between an institution, subject to the logic of bureaucratization, and the individual, as its leader.[13] Here, the contradiction centres upon the capacity of a party and a leader to render compatible the general and particular interest. The political party, as the representative of a particular element of society, seeks, through election, to become the majority party. The leader of the majority party is then required, once a government is formed, to determine in whose interests the party will govern. This, in turn, opens the question of the degree to which the leader, as an individual personality, is shaped by the general bureaucratization and professionalization of political parties. The discussion and advocacy, by Weber, of a directly elected President within the Weimar system[14] is the attempt to install a permanent source of individual leadership outside the contradictions of the political parties and their leaders: the personification of *Führerdemokratie*.[15]

At the level of the ruled, the contradiction is between two understandings of their political representation. The decision to vote for a political party entails that they have an interest which is only represented by a particular party. The particularism of this position is in contradiction with an understanding of their belonging to a people of a nation State; and the contradiction is exacerbated by the contradiction between the political party and the leader. The addition of a directly elected President is intended to overcome these contradictions, at the level of the ruled, by introducing a principle of unity beyond, but as an integral supplement to, the system of political parties.[16]

The Kelsenian consideration of democracy thinks with and beyond the Weberian conceptual framework. The Constitution of the Republic of Austria, within which the multi-party democracy operates, is drafted by Kelsen pursuing an explicit process of transforming political discussion and compromise into a normative framework of positive law.[17] The multi-party democracy is situated within a federal system accompanied by the inclusion of a Constitutional Court conferred with authority to review legislation at both federal and State level.[18] The position of the Constitutional Court, within a federal system, is the corollary of a parliamentary system based upon 'a strict *principle of legality*, according to which the entire administration—including the government—may act only on the basis of parliamentary statutes'.[19]

The distinct legal form of the Austrian Republic introduces the initial difference of the Kelsenian conception of democracy.[20] The difference in legal form retains the Weberian limitation of democracy to party democracy and the rejection of direct democracy,[21] while furnishing it with a distinct justification. The distinctiveness relates to Kelsen's engagement with, and critique of, Marx and the tradition of political philosophy, in particular, the work of Rousseau.[22] From this engagement, the question of representation, as the relationship between ruler and ruled within a multi-party democracy, centres upon the 'meaning of freedom'.[23] For Kelsen, the meaning 'has changed from the idea that the individual should be free from State rule to the idea that he should be able to participate in that rule'.[24] The questions of the character of participation, of the rule by majority and of the distinction between formal and social democracy flow directly from this alteration in the meaning of freedom.

The response to these questions diverges further from the Weberian framework due the subsequent emergence of a form of rule, which Kelsen terms dictatorship or autocracy,[25] which overturns the constitutional, multi-party democratic system, and replaces it with a form of personal rule through a single party. In place of a single process of democratization, Kelsen considers the emergence of dictatorship or autocracy, after the First World War, to constitute an opposed principle of political rule to democracy. The reconstruction of the juridico-political has, therefore, to comprehend the basis for the emergence of this principle of political rule.

The comprehension involves the introduction of an analysis which indicates a parallel between forms of rule and philosophy. The parallel, for Kelsen, is between forms of rule, political ideals and a wider philosophical perspective or worldview (*Weltangschauung*). Democracy is then intimately associated with the analysis of a personality structure which is no longer grasped in terms of Weberian concepts. Rather, the influence of Freudian psychoanalysis is evident in combination with the identification of a specifically democratic personality. The Kelsenian analysis indicates the interconnection of epistemological relativism, pluralism of values, discussion, compromise and the political form of rule of democracy in the formation of a democratic personality.[26]

Kelsen's intervention within the existing juridico-political reality of the 1920s and 1930s is the attempt to reinforce democracy, as constitutional, multi-party democracy, in confrontation with the emergence and encroachment of dictatorship and autocracy. The continued pertinence of Kelsen's analysis relates to the distinct methodological reflection upon democracy within a situation of pluralism. The Kelsenian approach provides an alternative basis upon which to respond to the dilemmas of 'modern, disenchanted democracies'[27] designated by the contemporary Anglo-American tradition of political theory.

Kelsen, Weber and the state

The constitutional, multi-party democracies, instituted by the Weimar Republic and the Austrian Republic, exist as forms of representation and rule. The character of that rule involves, beyond the process of elections, the installation of a majority political party as the government. The capacity to govern and, thus, to rule, rests upon other institutions and logics which have permanence beyond the cycle of elections. This, in turn, leads to the second path of reflection, the reconstruction of the notion of the State.

The reconstruction involves Kelsen and Weber in a fundamental and complex reflection upon the method through which the State is to be conceptualized. The initial, underlying affinity between Kelsen and Weber in the process of reconstruction is the insistence upon the State as a notion produced through an operation of cognition. It is the subsequent definition and character of this operation of cognition which generates the divergence between Kelsen and Weber: the methodological separation, through Kelsen's critique of Weber, of legal science from a sociological science, and, in this demarcation, the purported demonstration of the superiority of the methodology of legal science.[28]

For Weber,[29] the reflection upon the notion of the State is an aspect of the wider methodological consideration of the character, regularity and meaning of human action.[30] This is accompanied by the differentiation of different types of domination, and it is in the process of differentiation that Weber both utilizes and modifies legal categories.[31] The methodological approach commences from the meaning to be attributed to social action – the action of individuals in relation to other individuals – and subsequently introduces the notion of the State. The primacy accorded to the meaning of social action entails that the State is understood as a type of organization which orientates and co-ordinates social action. The notion of the State, as a notion of organization, is placed together with two other notions – association (*Verein*) and organization (*Verband*) – in relation to which the State (*Anstalt*) is the final and most comprehensive form of organization. The three terms – *Verein, Verband* and *Anstalt* – are originally legal terms, but Weber modifies their content in order to utilize them as terms to denote and distinguish between forms of orientation of social action.

The State, as *Anstalt*, is both the most comprehensive form of organization and the expression of a process of rationalization. Social action is orientated and co-ordinated through a generalized form of compulsion – positive law – which directs human action through legal norms. The Weberian conception of a legal norm is one which retains its obligatory character – the expression of an 'ought-to-be' (*Sollen*) – while situating it within a broader evaluation of social action. The capacity to designate human action as orientated by the State depends upon the degree to which human action adheres to the obligations contained in legal norms.

At the level of human action, adherence to legal norms is evaluated in accordance with the degree of an individual's internal and external conformity. The combination of inner and outer conformity expresses the Weberian insistence upon adherence to legal norms as more than the mere observance of external conformity.[32] The requirement for external conformity to be complimented by inner conformity is the counterpart of the Weberian notion of legitimacy: the acceptance, by the ruled, of rule through legal norms which attests to both its validity and effectiveness.[33]

At the level of the State, as *Anstalt*, the character of this organization of human action through positive law rests upon a monopoly of both the capacity to enact positive law and the capacity to enforce obedience to obligations contained in legal norms. This, in turn, defines a further element of the State (*Anstalt*), namely, the existence of a permanent apparatus and staff – the bureaucracy – to ensure the application and enforcement of legal norms.[34] The compulsory character of the comprehensive organization of human action by the State (*Anstalt*) is the fundamental element which distinguishes it from the other Weberian terms for collective association of *Verein* and *Verband*. The recognition of the essential presence of compulsion is shaped by the same dependence of this modern form of domination upon legitimacy. The application and enforcement of legal norms, through the permanent apparatus of a bureaucracy, has to maintain both the individual's inner and outer compliance with rule through the normative framework of positive law. The bureaucratic procedures through which the application and enforcement of legal norms are undertaken thereby presuppose their adherence to validity and efficiency.[35] Hence, the Weberian methodological reconstruction, commencing from the meaning of social action, establishes a notion of the State (*Anstalt*) whose compulsory orientation of social action is limited to procedures which maintain legitimacy.[36]

The Weberian conception of the State, in contrast to the Kelsenian conception, contains an implicit transformation of the German tradition of *Staatslehre/ Staatswissenschaft*.[37] The methodological orientation to the meaning of social action precludes attributing to the State, in opposition to German tradition of *Staatslehre/ Staatswissenschaft*, the role of the primary object in a sociological theory of the State. This has the effect of introducing a distance between the Weberian approach and the preceding tradition of *Staatslehre/ Staatswissenschaft*, and it is this distance which enables Weber to develop a distinctive reconstruction of the State.

Kelsen's explicit analysis and critique of the German tradition of *Staatslehre/ Staatswissenschaft*, commencing from the *Hauptprobleme der Staatsrechtslehre entwickelt aus der Lehre vom Rechtssatze* (1911), is accompanied by an engagement with Weber.[38] The *Hauptprobleme* contains Kelsen's initial discussion of Weber, centred upon Weber's essay 'The "Objectivity" of Knowledge in Social Science and Social Policy' (1903–4). The critique of the *Staatslehre/ Staatswissenschaft*[39] is then accompanied by the development of a critique of Weber, which is elaborated in *Der Soziologische und der Juristische Staatsbegriff* (1922, 2nd edn, 1928).[40] Here, Kelsen offers a sustained analysis of sections of Weber's posthumously published

Wirtschaft und Gesellschaft (*Economy and Society*) (1922), through which a Kelsenian legal science of positive law is methodologically separated from a Weberian sociology of law.

A Kelsenian legal science of positive law is predicated upon the insistence that the meaning of legal norms, as the content of a system of positive law, can only be generated from legal norms themselves. This insistence guides and shapes the Kelsenian critique of both the tradition of *Staatslehre/Staatswissenschaft* and the critique of Weber. In relation to the tradition of *Staatslehre/Staatswissenschaft*, it is the underlying primacy accorded to the notion of the State which is the concerted focus of the Kelsenian critique. For this, primacy is presented, by Kelsen, as the attribution of a pre-existing substance to the meaning of the notion of the State. This, in turn, creates an enduring dualism between the notion of the State and the notion of law which is reflected in a series of contradictions within the tradition of *Staatslehre/Staatswissenschaft*. The resolution of these contradictions requires Kelsen to break with the conceptual foundations of this tradition by asserting the primacy of positive law and the meaning of legal norms.

The break is effected by recasting the dualism between State and law as the expression of a hypostatization: the attribution of real, independent existence to a concept – the State – whose origin is the product of a purely cognitive activity. The possibility of hypostatization is continually present, but the methodological clarity provided by a science of positive law demonstrates that this possibility is accompanied by an alternative possibility. The notion of the State is understood as a heuristic device – the conscious and deliberate product of the mind – in order to facilitate an enhanced understanding of a system of positive law.[41]

The critique of Weber centres upon the dissolution of the specifically legal meaning of a legal norm into a theory of social action and, with this dissolution, the disappearance of a distinct legal science of positive law. Kelsen considers that the Weberian reconstruction of the State, as a specific form of organization and co-ordination of social action, is unable to recognize and combine a conception of validity and effectiveness. Rather, flowing from the initial placement of legal norms within a theory of social action, validity disappears without remainder into the conception of the effectiveness of the State.[42]

Kelsen's concern is to preserve the distinctive character which a science of positive law attributes to legal norms. This requires that the obligation lodged in a legal norm – the 'ought-to-be' (*Sollen*) – can only be grasped through a process of imputation which derives from legal norms themselves. It is to be strictly demarcated from the realm of nature (*Sein*) and from all conceptions of obligation based upon psycho-physiological models, which themselves rest upon notions of natural causation derived from empirical observation. For, in the absence of this separation of a realm of legal, as opposed to psycho-physiological, normativity, the capacity to identify a conception of legal validity is removed. This, in turn, prevents the Kelsenian methodological progression to the notion of the *Grundnorm* (Basic norm) as the fundamental prerequisite for a coherent legal science of positive law.

The textual critique of Weber's *Wirtschaft und Gesellschaft*, in *Der Soziologische und der Juristische Staatsbegriff*, thus, rests upon the demonstration of the methodologically deficient approach of a Weberian reconstruction of the State. Kelsen places into question the Weberian procedure of utilizing legal concepts – *Verein*, *Verband* and *Anstalt* – and according them a modified content. The questioning concerns the methodological pertinence of this procedure which, for Kelsen, merely detaches these concepts from the level of a legal system, and its associated normative validity, and accords them a purely factual or empirical existence. The interrogation then extends to the central Weberian methodological device, the Ideal type, as these legal concepts are transformed into idealized organizational forms through which to interpret the degree of collective direction and co-ordination of human action.

The initial affinity between Kelsen and Weber regarding the essentially cognitive character of the notion of the State is also, through Kelsen's critique of Weber, an instance of intense divergence. Beyond the question of the interpretative fidelity of Kelsen's analysis of the sections of Weber's *Wirtschaft und Gesellschaft*,[43] the challenge of the Kelsenian critique to Weberian sociology leads to the interrogation of the methodological coherence and purported superiority of a Kelsenian science of positive law. The interrogation can retain the combination of affinity and divergence between Kelsen and Weber in relation to the reconstruction of the notion of the State by adopting the alternatives of a methodological reinforcement of the Weberian ideal type[44] or the demonstration of the requirement for an essential sociological supplement to a Kelsenian science of positive law.[45]

A further possibility is to retain the affinity and divergence between Kelsen and Weber through a transposition of both approaches into an alternative framework. This involves an overt reconfiguration of both the Weberian and Kelsenian notions of the State. The reconfiguration presupposes that neither the Weberian nor the Kelsenian notions of the State are able to generate a coherent notion of the State unless they are situated as complementary elements of a 'general theory of the State which is not a theory which describes the State, but which constitutes it'.[46] The general theory arises from the French tradition initiated by the critical engagement of Raymond Carré de Malberg (1861–1935) with the German tradition of *Staatslehre/Staatswissenschaft*,[47] and centres upon Carré de Malberg's *Contribution à la Théorie générale de l'Etat* (1920–22).[48] The methodology of Carré de Malberg, in particular, the understanding of a theory of the State as an integral part of a legal science of positive law is, however, replaced with a theory of discourse. The general theory of the State considers the particular juridical concepts, which have emerged to describe the State, as forms of legal argumentation utilized to justify the exercise of a monopoly of power.[49]

This theory of the State encompasses both the Weberian conception and the Kelsenian conception. The Kelsenian theory of the identity of the State and law is retained, but related to the Weberian theory of the monopoly of legitimate violence: the State exercises its monopoly of power through the legal form of a hierarchy of norms. From this presentation of the complementary character of the Weberian and Kelsenian conceptions, the legal form of a hierarchy of norms can be utilized as both a theory of legal norms and as a theory of the historical origin of the State.[50] Here, the hierarchy of norms, as the historical origin of the State, facilitates the advent of a juridical discourse of sovereignty as the justification for this hierarchy.[51] The reconfiguration produced by this general theory of the State, however, requires the reintroduction, through the discourse of sovereignty, of the notion of a will, and, thus, confronts the emphatic Kelsenian opposition, until the final, posthumous *General Theory of Norms* (1979),[52] to any presence of either a notion of a will or a juridical concept of sovereignty within a theory of positive law. In this confrontation, the central question becomes the degree to which the discourse of sovereignty is capable of replacing the Kelsenian theory of the *Grundnorm* (Basic norm) as the essential theoretical compliment to a hierarchy of norms.[53]

Kelsen, Weber and legal rights

The reconstruction of the notion of the State evident in the Weberian and Kelsenian projects leads to the question of the degree to which this is associated with a specific conception of the legal relationship of the individual to the State. The Weberian reconstruction, through the modification of the legal concepts of *Verein*, *Verband* and *Anstalt*, recognizes differing types of collective co-ordination and direction of individual human action. This is combined with the notion of rule (*Herrschaft*) to indicate a relationship between ruler and ruled, which, within the State as *Anstalt*, is undertaken through the formal legal norms of positive law. The Kelsenian reconstruction, through the methodological reduction of the State to law, renders a hierarchically structured system of legal norms as the exclusive framework within which to consider the obligation to conform to legal norms. The realm of *Sollen* – the 'ought-to-be' – which is demarcated by a legal science of the legal norms of positive law represents a legal order as an order of constraint (*Rechtsordnung als Zwangsordnung*).

The affinity of Weber and Kelsen regarding the primacy of positive law, as either constraint (Kelsen) or compulsory co-ordination of human action (Weber), opens the question of the extent to which the individual has an independent or autonomous legal existence. The response to this question leads to the definition of the foundation and character of the individual's legal existence which, in turn, becomes the question of the status and character of legal rights in relation to the State. Weber and Kelsen offer divergent responses in accordance with their different approaches to one of the central representatives of the German tradition of *Staatslehre*, Georg Jellinek (1851–1911).[54]

For Weber, the influence of Jellinek relates to the initial stimulus and subsequent distance from Jellinek's *Die Erklärung der Menschen und Bürgerrechte* (1895) (*The Declaration of the Rights of Man and the Citizen*).[55] It is the emphasis upon the religious origin of the Rights of Man, in particular, the freedom of conscience, which Weber indicates as this initial stimulus. However, the removal of this earlier acknowledgement of Jellinek's work indicates the lack of enduring influence or orientation from Jellinek.[56]

The stimulus leads to the detailed historical investigation of Protestantism contained in *The Protestant Ethic and the Spirit of Capitalism*.[57] The oblique rather than direct connection between Weber and Jellinek in *The Protestant Ethic* is indicative of the lack of an abiding interest in, or orientation to, the juridical relationship between the individual and the State which underpins Jellinek's corpus of work.[58] This is can be held to derive from the early legal formation and publication of Weber in the area of civil law,[59] which is then reinforced by the subsequent concentration and critical engagement with the German tradition of historical economics.[60] Hence, one of the guiding concerns for Weber is that of the relationship between the State and the economy, and the question of rights, insofar as it arises, is limited to those which arise between individuals and their economic transactions with the notion of the State as the background guarantor.[61]

The limited importance of the question of rights is reinforced by Weber's subsequent work on the Russian Revolutions of 1905 and 1917. The connection, in the development of Occidental capitalism, between the emergence of a capitalist economy and a particular bearer of a 'spirit of capitalism' and its associated freedoms was absent from the Russian context.[62] From this understanding and analysis, the distinctive character of Occidental capitalism is reinforced, and combined with the rejection of a necessary causal connection between the development of capitalism and a bearer of a 'spirit of capitalism'. The distinctive character of the development of Occidential capitalism is itself an aspect of the broader processes of disenchantment and rationalization which, for Weber, require that one relinquish any remnants of the earlier Enlightenment conception of progress. Here, the distance between Jellinek and Weber is further extended as, for Jellinek, who remains shaped by an ethical understanding of Neo-Kantianism,[63] the juridical differentiation of the legal personality of the State is accompanied by its self-limitation through a series of progressively more autonomous legal statuses for individuals. The statuses express both the possibilities within a theory of positive law and a potential history of progress towards the most autonomous legal status.[64]

The Kelsenian legal science of positive law engages in a sustained and enduring critique of Jellinek's legal theory of positive law.[65] The critique centres upon the methodological incoherence of Jellinek's dual conception (*Zwei-Seiten-Lehre*) of the State as both a juridical concept of public law (legal institution) and a social reality (a collective organization). For Kelsen, the dual conception, by the preservation of the social conception of the State, continually displaces the origin of the State beyond a hierarchy of legal norms. Hence, both the operations of self-attribution of legal personality to the State and its subsequent juridical self-limitation arise, within Jellinek's theory, from an origin which is external to law and its specific realm of normative obligation (*Sollen*). This, in turn, affects the pertinence of the derivation and delineation of the legal statuses of the individual in relation to the State.

For Kelsen, a legal science of positive law involves a methodological reconstruction of the State and the individual in which both are defined as purely cognitive operations – legal fictions – conferring conceptual unity on the realm of legal norms (*Sollen*). Thus, the question of the relationship between the State and the individual is replaced with the question of legal imputation: the ascription of an action to a legal order composed of a system of legal norms. The operation of imputation is assisted by the heuristic device of legal fictions which create points of unity within a hierarchy of legal norms in the form of the State and the legal person. The effect is a conscious, methodological dissolution of 'the concept of subjective right', from which 'what will always emerge are, quite simply legal connections between human beings, more precisely, between material facts of human behaviour which are linked together by – that is, as the content of – the legal norm'.[66] The methodological dissolution then extends to encompass the dualism between private and public law as it 'relativizes the opposition between private and public law, transforming it into an intra-systemic opposition, from the absolute, extra-systemic opposition of traditional legal theory, that is, from the difference between law and non-law, between law and state'.[67]

The presence of the question of rights is effectively transformed, through Kelsen's critique of Jellinek, into the question of the internal regulation of the legal order through the concept of a constitution. In this transformation, it is possible to consider the continuing influence of Jellinek derived from two shorter works devoted to proposals for the legal reform within the Austro-Hungarian Empire. These proposals, which relate to the establishment of a Constitutional Court[68] and the legal recognition and protection of minorities,[69] initiate a juridical mode of thought which can be argued to be a stimulus for the development of certain aspects of the Kelsenian conception of a legal science and the conception of democracy. The Kelsenian transformation of the question of rights, thus becomes the question of the status and character of a *Rechtstaat* within a legal science of positive law.[70]

Kelsen, Weber and the character of law

The common absence of a theory of legal rights in Weber and Kelsen is the methodological counterpart of the concentration upon a more general analysis of law. The character of this level of analysis reveals both affinity and divergence in the approach of Kelsen and Weber. The comparison of their respective analyses establishes its initial affinity in the recognition of positive law. However, the degree of affinity is qualified by the divergence in the methodological conception of positive law.

The Weberian approach, contained in the section entitled 'Sociology of Law' in *Wirtschaft and Gesellschaft* (*Economy and Society*),[71] situates positive law as the distinctively modern form of Occidental law composed of a formalized system of general legal norms. The modern form of Occidental law is considered to result from wider processes of disenchantment and rationalization, and is also placed within a wider historical and comparative analysis of other systems of law.

The Kelsenian approach appears, in contrast, to be resolutely ahistorical in orientation.[72] The legal science of positive law is predicated upon conferring methodological coherence to a hierarchical system of law composed exclusively of general norms of positive law. The conferral of methodological coherence is accompanied by the rejection of any characterization of the development of law other than that occurring *within* a hierarchy of legal norms of positive law. These internal developmental tendencies are themselves the conceptualization, by legal science, of the general systemic dynamics of this hierarchy.

The initial impression of significant divergence and incompatibility between the Weberian and Kelsenian approaches leads to their reaffirmation as the separate fields of legal analysis of legal positivism and sociology of law. The potential for this simple reaffirmation is, however, reduced once it is acknowledged that a greater complexity is evident in the relationship of affinity and divergence. This increased complexity emerges at the level of both the analysis of positive law and the comparative and historical analysis of other legal regimes or forms of law.

At the level of the method of analysis of positive law, the appearance of the significant comparative sophistication of the Weberian framework, predicated upon the combinations derived from the analytical categories of formal, substantive, rational and irrational,[73] is rendered less stark with the acknowledgment that Kelsenian analysis identifies the same 'essential characteristics of formal legal rationality'.[74] The reduction in the degree of divergence has the effect of shifting the discussion to the capacity of the Kelsenian framework to conceive of the potential challenges to formal legal rationality flowing from the Weberian analytical categories. Here, questions of methodology are potentially intertwined with the continued influence of the original legal formation of Weber (civil law) and Kelsen (public law). For the central Weberian concern with the return of the combination of substantive rationality, irrational law-making and irrational law-finding, within a sphere of formal legal rationality, is accorded a different form of recognition by Kelsen.[75]

At the level of the comparative and historical analysis of other legal regimes or forms of law, the assumption of the fundamentally ahistorical Kelsenian framework requires reconsideration.[76] For the Kelsenian notion of centralization presupposes, as its necessary corollary, the decline in the importance and predominance of custom as a source of law-making and law-application.[77] This, in turn, indicates an affinity between the Kelsenian position and the Weberian concentration upon the historical invention of legal techniques and the development of rationalizing processes. From this potential affinity, the further question of the relationship in Kelsen and Weber between legal techniques, doctrinal developments and law emerges. The further question enables the possible reconception of the preceding stark opposition between legal positivism and sociology of law as a difference in the degree of emphasis upon, and the form of conceptualization of, the connection between law and culture.[78] This reconception would, however, entail the return to the explicit Kelsenian consideration of law and culture, represented by *Society and Nature. A Sociological Inquiry* (1943),[79] which would appear to produce further divergence rather than enhanced affinity with the Weberian position.

The affinity generated by the question of the connection between legal technique, doctrinal developments and law could, however, be extended by the recognition that it is itself the expression of a methodological precaution. The Kelsenian and Weberian approaches are both founded upon the introduction of a critical methodological distance from the direct identification of legal theory and legal order. The critical distance thereby detaches analysis of the connection between legal technique, doctrinal developments and law from conceptions of simple cause and effect. In this detachment, there is the possibility for a more nuanced historical and comparative analysis of the character of law.[80]

The comparison of Kelsen and Weber, orientated by the four paths of reflection of this volume, indicate a multiplicity of elements of affinity and divergence in their respective reconstructions of the juridico-political. This reveals that the conventional categorization of the work of Kelsen and Weber as the origin of the clear separation between legal positivism and the sociology of law is open to productive reconsideration. Each of the notions – democracy, State, legal rights and law – which have provided the specific analytical focus for the comparison of their work indicate the continued pertinence of their reconstructions of the juridico-political for critical legal thought.

Notes

1 For alternative discussions of the affinity and divergence between Kelsen and Weber, see N. Bobbio, 'Max Weber und Hans Kelsen', in M. Rehbinder and R. Tieck (eds), *Max Weber als Rechtssoziologe*, Berlin: Dunkler & Humblot, 1987, pp. 109–26 (French translation 'Hans Kelsen et Max Weber', in N. Bobbio, *Essais de Théorie du Droit*, Paris: Bruylant, 1998, pp. 255–70; Italian original, 'Max Weber e Hans Kelsen', *Sociologica del dritto* (1981), 8, 135–54); A. Carrino, 'Weber e la sociologia del dritto nella critica di Kelsen', *Sociologica del dritto* (1987), 14, 31–49; and W. Gephart, *Law, Culture and Society. Max Weber's Comparative Cultural Sociology of Law*, Frankfurt am Main: Klostermann, 2015, pp. 30–2 (the English translation of the introduction to M. Weber, *Wirtschaft und Gesellschaft. Die Wirtschaft und die gesellschaftlichen Ordnungen und Mächte. Nachlaß. Recht*, Tübingen: Mohr, 2010).

2 In English, the central texts of Weber are collected in Max Weber, *Political Writings*, P. Lassman and R. Spiers (eds), Cambridge: Cambridge University Press, 2003; and Max Weber, *The Russian Revolutions*, G. C. Wells and P. Baehr (trans and eds), Cambridge: Polity Press, 1997 (the English translation offers a truncated version of the 1905–6 essays, but the full version of the 1917 essays). However, these would now need to be supplemented, as a result of the progress of the *Max Weber Gesamtausgabe*, Vol. 1/22, 4, *Wirtschaft und Gesellschaft. Herrschaft*, E. Hanke (ed), Tübingen: Mohr, 2005 (*Economy and Society. Unpublished Works. Domination*); Vol. III/7, *Allgemeine Staatslehre und Politik (Staatssoziologie)* unvollendet. Mit- und Nachschriften, 1920, G. Hübinger (ed), Tübingen: Mohr, 2009 (*General Theory of the State and Politics (Sociology of the State)* – unfinished lecture course of 1920). For Kelsen, apart from the recent collection and translation of the exchanges between Carl Schmitt over the question of the character of a constitution, L. Vinx, *The Guardian of the Constitution: Hans Kelsen and Carl Schmitt on the Limits of Constitutional Law*, Cambridge: Cambridge University Press, 2015, and the translations of *Vom Wesen und Wert der Demokratie* (1920/2nd edn, 1929) (*The Essence and*

Value of Democracy), B. Graf (trans), N. Urbinati and C. Invernizzi Accetti (eds), Lanham: Rowman and Littlefield, and of *Staatsform und Weltanschauung* (1933) ('State-Form and World-Outlook'), in H. Kelsen, *Essays in Legal and Moral Philosophy*, P. Heath (trans) and selected by O. Weinberger, 1973, Dordrecht: Springer, pp. 95–113, the majority of his German political writings remain untranslated in English. For the major works in German, see H. Kelsen, *Sozialismus und Staat. Eine Untersuchung der politischen Theorie des Marxismus*, Leipzig: C. H. Hirschfeld, 1920 (2nd edn, 1923); 'Marx oder Lassalle? Wandlungen in der politischen theorie des Marxismus', *Archiv für Geschichte des Sozialismus und der Arbeiterbewegung* (1924), 11, 261–89; *Allgemeine Staatslehre*, Berlin, Springer: 1925; *Das Problem des Parlamentarismus*, Vienna/Liepzig: Wilhelm Braumüller, 1925; 'Staatsform als Rechtsform', *Zeitschrift für öffentliches Recht* (1926), 5, 73–93; 'Zur Soziologie der Demokratie', *Der oesterreichische Volkswit* (1926), 19, 209–11, 239–42; 'Das Wesens des Staats', *Internationale Zeitschrift für Theorie des Rechts* (1926), 1, 5–17; *Der Staat als Übermensch. Eine Erwiderung*, Vienna: Springer, 1926; 'Vortrage über die "Demokratie" und Schlusswort in der Diskussion über "Demokratie"', in *Verhandlungen des fünften Deutschen Soziologentages vom 26. bis 29. September 1926 in Wien Vorträge und Diskussionen in der Hauptversammlungl und in den Sitzungen der Untergruppen*, Tübingen: Mohr, 1927, pp. 37–68, 113–18; *Der Staat als Integration. Eine prinzipielle Auseinandersetzung*, Vienna: Springer, 1930.

3   For Kelsen, there is the collapse of the Austro-Hungarian Empire, participation in the establishment of the juridico-political foundation of the post-First World War democratic, constitutional nation State of the Republic of Austria, the formation of the newly independent States of the former Austro-Hungarian Empire, the weakening and collapse of the institutions of the Austrian State into the political project of National Socialism, the defeat of National Socialism and the establishment of the post-Second World War European and international juridico-political structures (this is combined with Kelsen's move to Cologne, initial exile in Geneva and Prague and then the subsequent exile, residence and academic positions in the United States. Kelsen died, in the United States, in 1973). For Weber, there is the collapse of Wilhelmine Germany, participation in the German delegation at the Treaty of Versailles and participation in the establishment of the post-First World War democratic, constitutional nation State of the German Weimar Republic and initial membership, and then resignation from, the German Democratic Party (*Deutsche Demokratische Partei*) (Weber died in 1920).

4   This marks the first stage in the authoritarian transformation of the juridico-political system of the First Austrian Republic, which is comprehensively instituted, in 1934, with 'the so-called authoritarian-corporate constitution which abolished the idea of elections. It attributed legislative powers to a Federal Diet (*Bundestag*) consisting of delegates, which were nominated by "councils" – a State Council (*Staatsrat*), a Federal Council of Culture (*Bundeskulturrat*), a Federal Council of Commerce (*Bundeswirtschaftsrat*) and a council representing the States (*Länderrat*). Members of these councils were either appointed by the Federal President or by various corporations (*Berufsstände*) and churches. These councils had to pre-discuss all laws which were to be passed by the Federal Diet. This system was only partly effective – many laws were just pronounced by the government' (M. Stelzer, *The Constitution of the Republic of Austria: A Contextual Analysis*, Oxford: Hart Publishing, 2011, pp. 11–12). The authoritarian form of the First Republic disappeared, in 1938, in the *Anschluss* by the German National Socialist Regime.

5   See, O. Lepsius, 'Hans Kelsen und der Nationalsozialismus', in R. Walter, W. Ogris and T. Olechowski (eds), *Hans Kelsen: Leben – Werke – Wirksamkeit*, Vienna: Manz, 2009, pp. 271–88.

6   See, for example, the work of Emil Brunner, Jacques Maritain, Reinhold Niebuhr and Leo Strauss, against which Kelsen explicitly defends himself, in the 1955 article, 'The

Foundations of Democracy', *Ethics* (1955), 66, 1, Part 2, 1–101. It is Leo Strauss who, while not identifying Weber with this collapse, in the second chapter of *Natural Right and History*, considers Weber both as the exemplary figure of social science, whose positivism descends into historicism and nihilism and as the central obstacle to the return to political philosophy.

7   For initial theories of totalitarianism, see, for example, H. Arendt, *The Origins of Totalitarianism*, New York: Schocken Books, 1951; C. J. Freidrich and Z. K. Brzezinski, *Totalitarian Dictatorship and Autocracy*, Cambridge, MA: Harvard University Press, 1956; J. Talmon, *The Origins of Totalitarian Democracy*, Vol. 1, London: Secker & Warburg, 1952; Vol. 2, 1960.

8   For example, the emergence, within the Anglo-American tradition, and the wider dissemination from the 1970s onwards, of the work of Ronald Dworkin, Michael Waltzer, Robert Nozick and John Rawls. The increasing reception, within the European academic tradition, particularly in French and German, of these developments in the Anglo-American tradition, is combined with a critical reinterpretation of the existing theoretical methods and approaches of the European tradition. This is exemplified, though expressed in distinct and different forms, in the work of Dieter Grimm, Jürgen Habermas, Luc Ferry, Marcel Gauchet, Pierre Manent, Ulrich K. Preuß and Alain Renaut.

9   This is the position from which Scalone commences his analysis in Chapter 1 of the present volume. This builds upon and develops his distinctive work in *Rappresentanza politica e rappresentanza degli interessi*, Milan: Franco Angeli, 1995; and *L'ordine precario: Unita' politica e pluralita' nella Staatslehre novecentesca da Carl Schmitt a Joseph H. Kaiser*, Monza: Polimetrica, 2011

10 The Hobbesian question was initially introduced in Noberto Bobbio's 'La teoria dello Stato e del potere', in P. Rossi (ed), *Max Weber e l'analisi del mondo*, Turin: Einaudi, 1981, pp. 215–46. For alternative approaches to Weber, see D. Beetham, *Max Weber and the Theory of Modern Politics*, 2nd edn, Cambridge: Polity Press, 1991; P. Breiner, *Max Weber and Democratic Politics*, New York: Cornell University Press, 1996; M. Cacciari, 'Weber and the Critique of Socialist Reason', in M. Cacciari, *The Unpolitical On the Radical Critique of Political Reason*, M. Verdicchio (trans), A. Carrera (ed), New York: Fordham University Press, 2009, pp. 104–21 (Italian original, 1978); M. Cacciari, 'Weber and the Politician as Tragic Hero', in Cacciari, *The Unpolitical On the Radical Critique of Political Reason*, ibid., pp. 206–38 (Italian original, 2006); D. D'Andrea, *L'incubo degli ultimi uomini. Etica e politica in Max Weber*, Rome: Carroci, 2005; F. Ghia, *Ascesi e gabbia d'acciaio. La teologia politica di Max Weber*, Soveria Mannelli: Rubbettino, 2010; A. Kalyvas, *Democracy and the Politics of the Extraordinary: Max Weber, Carl Schmitt, and Hannah Arendt*, Cambridge: Cambridge University Press, 2009; P. Lassman, 'The rule of man over man: politics, power and legitimation', in S. Turner, *The Cambridge Companion to Weber*, Cambridge: Cambridge University Press, 2000, pp. 83–98; W. Mommsen, *Max Weber and German Politics 1890–1920*, M. S. Steinberg (trans), 2nd edn, Chicago: Chicago University Press, 1990 (German original, 1959; 2nd edn, 1974); W. Mommsen, *The Age of Bureaucracy: Perspectives on the Political Sociology of Max Weber*, Oxford: Blackwell, 1974; W. Mommsen, *The Political and Social Theory of Max Weber: Collected Essays*, Cambridge: Polity Press, 2007 (original publication 1989); G. Rebuffa, *Nel crepuscolo della democrazia. Max Weber tra sociologia del diritto e sociologia dello stato*, Bologna: Il Mulino, 1991; A. Scaglia, *Max Weber e la città democratica. Idealtipo del potere non legittimo*, Rome: Carroci, 2007; F. Tuccari, *Il pensiero politico di Weber*, Rome: Laterza, 1995; J.-M. Vincent, *Max Weber: Ou la démocratie inachevée*, Paris: Editions du Félin, 2009; S. S. Wolin, 'Max Weber: Legitimation, Method, and the Politics of Theory', *Political Theory* (1981), 9, 3, 401–24.

11 It should be noted that the Wilhelmine monarchical system undergoes a significant modification, if not transformation, during the First World War, with the increasing

role and control of the army over the economy and State institutions. See G. Feldman, *Army, Industry and Labour in Germany, 1914–1918*, London: Bloomsbury, 1992 (original publication 1966), and the references to further developments, since 1966, of this original analysis in the Bibliography.

12 See, the critique of the Wilhelmine system in 'Suffrage and Democracy in Germany' (1917) and 'Parliament and Government in Germany under a New Political Order' (1918) together with the essay 'The Profession and Vocation of Politics' (1919), in Max Weber, *Political Writings*, P. Lassman and R. Spiers (eds), Cambridge: Cambridge University Press, 2003.

13 Here, one should note the effect of the analyses of Robert Michels on Max Weber, in particular, the *Zur Soziologie des Parteiwesens in der modernen Demokratie. Untersuchungen über die oligarchischen Tendenzen des Gruppenlebens* (1911), as well as the earlier articles, in the *Archiv für Sozialwissenschaft und Sozialpolitik*, from 1905 onwards. On the relationship between Weber and Michels, see W. J. Mommsen, 'Robert Michels and Max Weber: Moral Conviction versus the Politics of Responsibility', in W. J. Mommsen and J. Österhammel (eds), *Max Weber and his Contemporaries*, London: Routledge, 1987, pp. 121–38; L. A. Scaff, 'Max Weber and Robert Michels', *American Journal of Sociology* (1981), 86, 6, 1269–86; F. Tuccari, *I dilemmi della democrazia moderna: Max Weber e Robert Michels*, Rome: Laterza, 1993. On Michels, see the recent collection, H. Bluhm and S. Krause (eds), *Robert Michels' Soziologie des Parteiwesens: Oligarchien und Eliten – Die Kehrseiten Moderner Demokratie*, Wiesbaden: Springer, 2012. However, as Treiber emphasizes, in his review of recent work on Weber's theory of domination (H. Treiber, 'La "sociologie de la domination" de Max Weber à la lumière de publications récentes', *Revue française de sociologie* (2005), 46, 4, 871–82), as a result of the work of Portinaro (P. P. Portinaro, 'Amerika als Schule de politischen Entzauberung: Eliten und Parteien bei Max Weber', in E. Hanke and W. J. Mommsen (eds), *Max Webers Herrschaftssoziologie: Studien zur Entstehung und Wirkung*, Tübingen: Mohr, 2001, pp. 285–302), the influence of Michels has now to be considered in relation to the influence of Moisei Ostrogorsky (1854–1921) and James Bryce (1838–1922).

14 See, Max Weber, 'The President of the Reich', in Weber, *Political Writings*, op. cit., pp. 304–8 (German original, 1919).

15 Scalone, in Chapter 1 of this volume, insists upon the centrality of this notion for Weber.

16 Here, as Scalone emphasizes, in Chapter 1 of this volume, one should avoid situating Weber as the simple precursor to the later analyses of Carl Schmitt in *Der Hüter de Verfassung* (1930). For the earlier German debate, flowing from the original German edition of Mommsen, *Max Weber and German Politics*, op. cit., see the debate between Loewenstein and Mommsen (K. Loewenstein, 'Max Weber als "Ahnherr" des "plebiszitäre Fürhrerstaats"', *Kölner Zeitschrift für Soziologie und Sozialpsychologie* (1961), 13, 2, 274–89 and W. J. Mommsen, 'Zum Begriff Der "Plebiszitaren Fuehrerdemokratie" Bei Max Weber', *Kölner Zeitschrift fur Soziologie und Sozialpsychologie* (1963), 15, 2, 295–322). See, also, F. Tuccari, *Carisma e leadership nel pensiero di Max Weber*, Milan: Franco Angeli, 1991.

17 Compare the statement by Weber to Hugo Preuß ((1860–1925) who drafted the Weimar Constitution), cited by Mommsen, *Max Weber and German Politics*, op. cit., p. 356, in which Weber, when discussing the question of whether the State should be centralized or federal in character, considers that the Weimar Constitution should arise 'as little as possible from legal considerations and as much as possible from practical considerations'. One should also note that Weber's discussions regarding the federal system of the Weimar Republic centre upon questions of political power and unity, see Mommsen, *Max Weber and German Politics*, op. cit., pp. 355–62.

18 See T. Öhlinger, 'The Genesis of the Austrian Model of Constitutional Review of Legislation', *Ratio Juris* (2003), 16, 2, 206–22; G. Schmitz, 'The Constitutional Court

of the Republic of Austria 1918–1920', *Ratio Juris* (2003), 16, 2, 240–65; G. Schmitz, *Die Vorentwürfe Hans Kelsens für die österreichische Bundesverfassung*,Vienna: Manz, 1981; and S. Lagi, 'Hans Kelsen and the Austrian Constitutional Court (1918–1929)', *Co-herencia*, (2012), 9, 16, 273–95, online at: www.redalyc.org/articulo.oa?id=77424078010 (accessed 1 June 2015). For the situation of the Weimar Republic, see M. Stolleis, 'Judicial Review, Administrative Review, and Constitutional Review in the Weimar Republic', *Ratio Juris* (2003), 16, 2, 266–80.
19 Öhlinger, 'The Genesis of the Austrian Model of Constitutional Review of Legislation', ibid., 208.
20 For approaches to the Kelsenian theory of democracy, see S. Baume, *Hans Kelsen and the Case for Democracy*, Colchester: ECPR Press, 2011 (French original, 2007); R. De Capua, *Hans Kelsen e il problema della democrazia*, Rome: Carrocci, 2003; Horst Dreier, *Rechtslehre, Staatssoziologie und Demokratietheorie bei Hans Kelsen*, Baden-Baden, Nomos, 2nd edn, 1990; C.-M. Herrera, *Théorie juridique et politique chez Kelsen*, Paris: Editions Kimé, 1997; S. Lagi, *Il pensiero politico di Hans Kelsen*, Genoa: Name, 2008; O. Lepsius, 'Kelsens Demokratietheorie', in T. Ehs (ed), *Hans Kelsen. Eine politikwissenschaftliche Einführung*, Vienna: Facultas, 2009, pp. 67–89; O. Lepsius, 'Kelsen, théoricien du droit', in O. Jouanjan (ed), *Hans Kelsen. Forme du droit et politique de l'autonomie*, Paris: Presses Universitaires de France, 2010, pp. 135–70; F. Lijoi, *La positività del diritto. Saggio su Hans Kelsen*, Rome: Arcane, 2011; F. Lijoi, *Scienza giuridica, democrazia e diritto. Interpretazioni costituzionali in Austria dall'Impero alla Repubblica*, Rome: Arcane, 2012; R. C. van Ooyen, *Der Staat de Moderne: Hans Kelsens Pluralismustheorie*, Berlin: Dunkler and Humblot, 2003; R. C. van Ooyen, *Hans Kelsen Und Die Offene Gesellschaft*, Wiesbaden: Springer, 2010; and L. Rizzi, *Legittimità e democrazia. Studio sulla teoria politica di Hans Kelsen*, Milan: Giuffrè, 1990.
21 As emphasized by Scalone, in Chapter 1 of this volume.
22 See, Kelsen, *Sozialismus und Staat. Eine Untersuchung der politischen Theorie des Marxismus*, op. cit.; 'Marx oder Lassalle? Wandlungen in der politischen theorie des Marxismus', op. cit.; and *The Essence and Value of Democracy*, op. cit., p. 29ff. See, also, R. Baumert, 'Kelsen, lecteur critique de Rousseau: de la volonté générale à la volonté collective', *Jus Politicum* (2013), 10, online at: www.juspoliticum.com/Kelsen-as-a-critique-of-Rousseau.html (accessed 1 June 2015); and C.-M. Herrera, 'Le problème de la contractualité sociale chez Hans Kelsen', in J.-F. Kervégan and H. Mohnhaupt (eds), *Liberté sociale et lien contractual dans l'histoire du droit et la philosophie*, Frankfurt am Main: Klostermann, 1999, pp. 367–94. See, for a comparison with Weber's conception and analysis of the contract, C. Colliot-Thélène, 'Solidarité et contrat dans la sociologie du droit de Max Weber', in Kervégan and Mohnhaupt (eds), *Liberté sociale et lien contractual dans l'histoire du droit et la philosophie*, ibid., pp. 349–65.
23 Kelsen, *The Essence and Value of Democracy*, op. cit., p. 30.
24 Ibid.
25 For Kelsen, ibid., and the essay, 'State From and World-Outlook'(1933), the term includes both the Fascist regime in Italy and the Union of Soviet Social Republics. The year 1933 also marks the emergence of the National Socialist regime in Germany.
26 This is developed by Özmen in Chapter 2 of this volume
27 The phrase is that of Özmen. Scalone, in Chapter 1 of this volume, emphasizes the continued pertinence of Kelsen's critique of sovereignty, theory of the primacy of international law and theory of federalism in relation to a contemporary situation '*beyond* the nation State' (the phrase is that of Scalone). See also, A. Scalone, *Una battaglia contro gli spettri. Diritto e politica nella Reine Rechtslehre di Hans Kelsen (1905–1934)*, Turin: Giappichelli, 2008.
28 Here, Kelsen's earlier critique of Hermann Kantorowicz and Eugen Ehrlich, developed between 1912 and 1917, is less central than the *Der soziologische und der juristische*

Staatsbegriff (1922; 2nd edn, 1928) which contains an extended commentary and critique of Weber. Kelsen's *Reine Rechtslehre* (1934) reaffirms the distinction between legal science and sociology of law, see H. Kelsen, *Introduction of the Problems of Legal Theory*, S. L Paulson and B. L. Paulson (trans), Oxford: Oxford University Press, 2002, pp. 13–14. There is a final, more positive discussion of Weber in Kelsen's *General Theory of Law and State* (1945), in which the coherence of Weber's sociology of law is held to presuppose 'the juristic concept of law, the concept of law defined by normative jurisprudence' (i.e. Kelsen's pure theory of positive law) (H. Kelsen, *General Theory of Law and State*, New Brunswick/London: Transaction Publishers, 2006, p. 178).

29 For approaches to the notion of the State in Weber, see A. Anter, *Max Weber's Theory of the Modern State: Origins, Structure, Significance*, K. Tribe (trans), London: Palgrave Macmillan, 2014; A. Anter and S. Breuer (eds), *Max Webers Staatssoziologie: Positionen und Perspektiven*, Baden-Baden: Nomos, 2007; S. Breuer, *Bürokratie und Charisma, zur politischen Soziologie Max Webers*, Darmstadt: Wissenschaftliche Buchgesellschaft, 1994; S. Breuer, *Max Webers tragische Soziologie: Aspekte und Perspektiven*, Tübingen: Mohr Siebeck, 2006; S. Breuer, '*Herrschaft*' in der Soziologie Max Webers, Wiesbaden: Harrassowitz, 2011; François Chazel, 'Communauté politique, Etat et droit dans la sociologie wébérienne: grandeur et limites de l'entreprise', *L'Année sociologique* (2009), 59, 2, 275–301; and François Chazel, 'La sociologie wébérienne de la domination revisitée. À propos d'un ouvrage de Stefan Breuer', *L'Année sociologique* (2014), 64, 1, 171–90; C. Colliot-Thélène, *Le désenchantement de l'État. De Hegel à Max Weber*. (Paris: Éditions de Minuit, 1992); G. Hübinger, 'Max Weber's "Sociology of the State" and the Science of Politics in Germany', *Max Weber Studies* (2009), 1–2, 17–32; and G. Hübinger, 'Die "Staatssoziologie" Max Webers', in F.-J. Peine and H. A. Wolf (eds), *Nachdenken über Eigentum, FS für Alexander v. Brünneck*, Baden-Baden: Nomos, 2011, pp. 443–52.

30 As Treiber emphasizes in Chapter 3 of this volume, the position that one adopts in relation to Weber's approach depends upon an interpretation of the chronology and influence of Weberian texts, in particular the Basic Sociological Concepts (1913), on the formulation of this reflection. For Treiber, the Basic Sociological Concepts should be considered to have a direct relationship with the relevant paragraphs of *Wirtschaft und Gesellschaft (Economy and Society)*. This is further supported by reference to the recently published final, unfinished lecture course of Weber on a Sociological Theory of the State (M. Weber, *Allgemeine Staatslehre und Politik (Staatssoziologie)*, *Max Weber Gesamtausgabe* III, 7, G. Hübinger and A. Terwey (eds), Tübingen: Mohr Siebeck, 2009). One should also note that the course is reconstructed from the comprehensive notes of two students who attended the lecture course.

31 This emphasized by Treiber in Chapter 3 of this volume.

32 This emphasized by Treiber in Chapter 3 of this volume.

33 This is emphasized by Breuer, '*Herrschaft*' in der Soziologie Max Webers, op. cit. See, also, S. Breuer, 'Rationale Herrschaft', *Politische Vierteljahresschrift* (1990), 31, 4–32 (French translation in *Trivium* (2010), 7, online at: http://trivium.revues.org/3758 (accessed 1 June 2015)).

34 On this question of the relationship between the modern State and bureaucracy in Weberian thought, see H. Treiber, 'État moderne et bureaucratie moderne chez Max Weber', *Trivium* (2010), 7, online at: http://www.trivium.revues.org/3831 (accessed 1 June 2015).

35 This is emphasized by Treiber in Chapter 3 of this volume.

36 The possibility, within the Weberian framework of illegitimate domination, is discussed by W. J. Mommsen, 'Politik und politische Theorie bei Max Weber', in J. Weiß (ed), *Max Weber heute. Erträge und Probleme der Forsung*, Frankfurt am Main: Suhrkamp, pp. 515–42; and S. Breuer, 'Nichtlegitime Herrschaft', in H. Bruuns and W. Nippel (eds), *Max Weber und die Staat in Kulturvergleich*, Göttingen: Vandenhoeck and Ruprecht, pp. 63–76.

37 Treiber, in Chapter 3 of this volume, provides the potential sources of this Weberian transformation. On the genesis and development of this tradition, see M. Fioravanti, *Giuristi e costituzione politica nell'Ottocento tedesco*, Milan: Giuffrè, 1979; D. F. Lindefeld, *The Practical Imagination. The German Sciences of State in the Nineteenth Century*, Chicago: Chicago University Press, 1997; O. Jouanjan, *Une histoire de la pensée juridique en Allemagne 1800–1914*, Paris: Presses Universitaires de France, 2005; P. Schiera, *Laboratorium der bürgerlichen Welt Deutsche Wissenschaft im 19. Jahrhundert*, Berlin: Suhrkamp, 1992; C. Schönberger, '"L'État" de la théorie générale de l'État. Remarques comparatives sur une discipline spécifiquement allemande', in A. Chatriot and D. Gosewinkel (eds), *Figurationen des Staates in Deutschland und Frankreich. Les figures de l'État en Allemagne et en France, 1870–1945*, Munich: Oldenburg, 2006, pp. 257–75; C. Schönberger, 'Vom Staat als Überperson zur Staatslehre ohne Staat. Psychologische Argumentationsmuster in der deutschen Staatsrechtswissenschaft von Laband bis Kelsen', in M. Schmoeckel and H. Schott (eds), *Psychologie als Argument in der juristischen Literatur des Kaiserreichs*, Baden-Baden: Nomos, 2009, pp. 225–36; M. Stolleis, *Public Law in Germany, 1800–1914*, Oxford: Berhahn Books, 2001; and W. Wilhelm, *Zur juristischen Methodenlehre im 19. Jahrhundert*, Frankfurt am Main: Klostermann, 1958.
38 See, for a discussion of the limitations of this initial critical analysis in the *Hauptprobleme*, C. Schönberger, 'Hans Kelsens "Hauptprobleme der Staatsrechtslehre". Der Übergang vom Staat als Substanz zum Staat als Funktion', in M. Jestaedt (ed), *Hans Kelsen Werke*, Vol. 2/I, Tübingen: Mohr, 2008, pp. 23–35 (French translation in O. Joujan (ed), *Hans Kelsen. Forme du droit et politique de l'autonomie*, Paris: Presses Universitaires de France, 2010, pp. 47–70). For a comprehensive examination of Kelsen's relationship to the German tradition of *Staatsrechtslehre*, see M. Jestaedt (ed), *Hans Kelsen und die deutsche Staatsrechtslehre: Stationen eines wechselvollen Verhältnisses*, Tübingen: Mohr, 2013.
39 It is also arguable that the drafting of the Constitution of the Austrian Republic represents not merely a break with the previous juridical form of the Austro-Hungarian Empire, but also with the German tradition of *Staatsrechtlehre*. This is emphasized by G. Bongiovanni, 'Rechtsstaat and Constitutional Justice in Austria: Hans Kelsen's Contribution', in P. Costa and D. Zolo (eds), *The Rule of Law: History, Theory and Criticism*, Dordrecht: Springer, 2007, pp. 293–319. See, also, G. Bongiovanni, *Reine Rechtslehre e dottrina giuridica dello Stato. H. Kelsen e la Costituzione austriaca del 1920*, Milan: Giuffrè, 1998.
40 H. Kelsen, *Der Soziologische und der Juristische Staatsbegriff*, Tübingen: Mohr, 1922 (2nd edn, 1928).
41 This methodological procedure is most evident in Kelsen's essays 'Zur Theorie der juristischen Fiktionen. Mit besonderer Berücksichtigung von Vaihingers Philosophie des Als-ob', *Annalen der Philosophie* (1919), 1, 630–58; 'Gott und Staat', *Logos* (1922/1923), 261–84; and *Das Problem der Souveränität und die Theorie des Völkerrechts. Beitrag zu einer reinen Rechtslehre*, Tübingen: Mohr, 1920 (2nd edn, 1928).
42 This is contained in the exemplary presentation and analysis of Colliot-Thélène in Chapter 4 of this volume.
43 This is emphasized by Colliot-Thélène in Chapter 4 of this volume.
44 This is a central element of Colliot-Thélène's interrogation of the Kelsenian critique in Chapter 4 of this volume.
45 This a central element of Treiber's interrogation of the Kelsenian critique in Chapter 3 of this volume.
46 M. Troper, *Pour une théorie juridique de l'Etat*, Paris: Presses Universitaires de France, 1994, p. 7.
47 On this critical engagement, see C. Schönberger, 'De la souveraineté nationale à la souveraineté populaire. Mutations et continuité de la théorie de l'Etat de Carré de Malberg', *Revue Française d'Histoire des Idées Politiques* (1996), 4, 297–316; C. Schönberger,

'Penser l'État dans l'Empire et la République. Critique et réception de la théorie juridique de l'État de Laband dans l'oeuvre de Carré de Malberg', in O. Beaud and P. Wachsmann (eds), *La science juridique française et la science juridique allemande de 1870 à 1918*, Strasbourg: Presses Universitaires de Strasbourg, 1997, pp. 255–71; and E. Maulin, *La théorie de l'État de Carré de Malberg*, Paris: Presses Universitaires de France, 2003.

48 R. Carré de Malberg, *Contribution à la Théorie générale de l'Etat*, Paris: Sirey, 1920–22.
49 This is emphasized by Troper in Chapter 5 of this volume. It is developed in M. Troper, *Pour une théorie juridique de l'Etat*, Paris: Presses Universitaires de France, 1994; M. Troper, *Le droit, la théorie du droit, l'Etat*, Paris: Presses Universitaires de France, 2001; and M. Troper, *Le droit et la nécessité*, Paris: Presses Universitaires de France, 2011. It is further extended in P. Brunet, *Vouloir pour la nation: Le concept de représentation dans la théorie de l'Etat*, Paris: LGDJ, 2004.
50 This is an integral aspect of Troper's analysis in Chapter 5 of this volume.
51 This, as Troper emphasizes in Chapter 5 of this volume, necessitates that Carré de Malberg's three senses of sovereignty in *Contribution à la Théorie générale de l'Etat*, op. cit., is supplemented with a fourth sense, namely, imputation: the attribution of sovereignty.
52 H. Kelsen, *A General Theory of Norms*, M. Hartney (trans), Oxford: Oxford University Press, 1991.
53 This, in turn, involves the question of the relationship between the separation of powers and sovereignty. On this, see M. Troper, *La séparation des pouvoirs et l'histoire constitutionnelle française*, Paris: LGDJ, 2014.
54 On Jellinek, see S. Amato, 'Centralismo e federalismo nel Kaiserreich guglielmino: il Gesetzentwurf di Jellinek sulla responsabilità del cancelliere imperiale (1909)', in, L. C. Boralevi (ed), *Challenging centralism. Decentremento e Autonomie nel pensiero politico europeo*, Florence: Florence University Press, 2011, pp. 193–202; A. Anter (ed), *Die normative Kraft des Faktischen: Das Staatsverständnis Georg Jellineks*, Baden-Baden: Nomos, 2004; O. Jouanjan, 'Preface. Georg Jellinek ou le juriste philosophe', in G. Jellinek, *L'Etat modern et son droit. Première Partie. Théorie Générale de l'Etat*, Paris: Editions Panthéon Assas, 2005, pp. 5–85, which develops the initial analysis in O. Jouanjan, *Une historie de la pensée juridique en Allemagne*, Paris: Presses Universitaires de France, 2005, pp. 287–341; D. Kelly, 'Revisiting the Rights of Man: Georg Jellinek on Rights and the State', *Law and History Review* (2004), 22, 3, 493–529; J. Kersten, *Georg Jellinek und die klassische Staatslehre*, Tübingen: Mohr Siebeck, 2000; S. Lagi (trans and ed), *Georg Jellinek, Storico Del Pensiero Politico (1883–1905)*, Firenze: Centro Editoriale Toscano, 2009; S. Lagi, 'Georg Jellinek, A Liberal Political Thinker Between the Habsburg Empire and Germany 1885–1898', *Hungarian Academy of Sciences Working Papers in Philosophy*, 2015, 1, online at: http://fi.btk.mta.hu/index.php/en/esemenyek-3/proramelozetes/450-seminar-series-sara-lagi (accessed 1 June 2015); S. L. Paulson and M. Schulte (eds), *Georg Jellinek: Beiträge zu Leben und Werk*, Tübingen: Mohr Siebeck, 2000; and C. Schönberger, *Das Parlament im Anstaltsstaat: Zur Theorie parlamentarischer Repräsentation in der Staatsrechtslehre des Kaiserreichs (1871–1918)*, Frankfurt am Main: Klostermann, 1997.
55 G. Jellinek, *Die Erklärung der Mensch en- und Bürgerrechte*, Leipzig: Dunkler and Humblot, 1895; 2nd edn, 1904; 3rd edn, Munich: Dunkler and Humblot, 1919.
56 This is the starting point for P. Ghosh's investigation of the intellectual dynamics of the relationship between the projects of Weber and Jellinek, see P. Ghosh, 'Max Weber and Georg Jellinek: two divergent conceptions of law', *Saeculum* (2008), 59, 2, 299–348. The initial acknowledgement and subsequent removal are contained in the first journal format of publication (1904/5) and the subsequent book (1920) of Max Weber's *The Protestant Ethic and the Spirit of Capitalism*. See also, for alternative presentations of the relationship between Weber and Jellinek, S. Breuer, *Georg Jellinek und Max Weber von der sozialen zur soziologischen Staatslehre*, Nomos: Baden-Baden, 1999; G. Hübinger,

'Staatstheorie und Politik als Wissenschaft im Kaiserreich: Georg Jellinek, Otto Hintze, Max Weber', in H. Maier, U. Matz, K. Sontheimer and P.-L. Weinacht (eds), *Politik, Philosophie, Praxis. Festschrift für Wilhelm Hennis*, Stuttgart: Klett-Cotta, 1988, pp. 143–61; R. Marra, *La religione dei diritti. Durkheim – Jellinek – Weber*, Turin: Giappichelli, 2006.

57 M. Weber, *The Protestant Ethic and the Spirit of Capitalism and Other Writings*, P. Baehr and G. Wells (trans), Oxford: Oxford University Press, 2002 (contains the 1905 version with the original paragraph reference to Jellinek); M. Weber, *The Protestant Ethic and the Spirit of Capitalism*, S. Kalberg (trans and ed), New York: Oxford University Press, 2011 (the 1920 version with the reference to Jellinek removed).

58 This is emphasized by Groh in Chapter 7 of this volume.

59 Weber's doctoral thesis concerned the legal development of commercial partnerships in medieval Italy, and his Habilitation concerned agrarian history and law in Ancient Rome.

60 On this engagement, see P. Ghosh, *Max Weber and 'The Protestant Ethic': Twin Histories*, Oxford: Oxford University Press, 2014.

61 This question becomes more complex once the labour contract becomes the subject of specific attention, see Weber's review of Lothmar's *Der Arbeitsvertrag*, Berlin: Dunkler and Humblot, 2001 (originally published in two volumes, 1902 and 1908), in M. Weber, 'Rezension von: Philipp Lothmar, Der Arbeitsvertrag', in M. Weber, *Wirtschaft, Staat und Sozialpolitik: Schriften und Reden 1900–1912*, MWG I, 8, W. Schluchter, P. Kurth and B. Morgenbrod (eds), Tübingen: Mohr, 1999, pp. 37–61. On this, see M. Coutu, 'Max Weber and the Labour Contract: Between Realism and Formal Legal Thought', *Journal of Law and Society* (2009), 36, 4, 558–78.

62 This is emphasized by Groh in Chapter 7 of this volume. It is also the orientation from which Chazel commences his extended review of the French translation of Weber's political writings. See, F. Chazel, 'Les *Écrits politiques* de Max Weber: un éclairage sociologique sur des problèmes contemporains', *Revue française de sociologie* (2005), 46, 4, 841–70.

63 This is emphasized in different ways by Groh in Chapter 7 of this volume and by Ghosh, *Max Weber and 'The Protestant Ethic': Twin Histories*, op. cit.

64 The statuses refer to Jellinek's *System der subjektiven öffentliche Rechte* (1895) and the *Allgemeine Staatslehre* (1900). On the statuses, see W. Pauly, 'Le droit public subjectif dans la doctrine de Georg Jellinek', in O. Jounjan (ed), *Figures de l'Etat de droit. Le Rechtstaat dans l'histoire intellectuelle et constitutionelle de l'Allemagne*, Strasbourg: Presses Universitaires de Strasbourg, 2001, pp. 293–312; and W. Pauly and M. Siebinger, 'Staat und Individuum', in A. Anter (ed), *Die normative Kraft des Faktischen. Das Staatsverständnis Georg Jellineks*, Baden-Baden: Nomos, 2004, pp. 135–51. For Groh, in Chapter 7 of this volume, both Weber and Jellinek remain within the confines of a pre-First World War German liberalism.

65 This is emphasized by Donhauser in Chapter 6 of this volume. The critique commences with the *Hauptprobleme* (1911), op. cit., and is further developed in Kelsen, *Das Problem der Souveränität und die Theorie des Völkerrechts. Beitrag zu einer reinen Rechtslehre*, op. cit.; Kelsen, *Der soziologische und der juristische Staatsbegriff. Kritische Untersuchung des Verhältnisses vom Staat und Recht*, op. cit.; Kelsen, *Allgemeine Staatslehre*, op. cit.; H. Kelsen, *Grundriss einer allgemeinen Theorie des Staates*, Vienna: R. M. Rohner, 1926; and H. Kelsen, *Reine Rechtslehre. Einleitung in die rechtswissenschaftliche Problematik*, Vienna: Franz Deuticke, 1934 (Paulson and Paulson (trans), *Introduction to the Problems of Legal Theory*, op. cit.).

66 Kelsen, *Introduction to the Problems of Legal Theory*, op. cit., p. 52 (*Reine Rechtslehre*, 1934).

67 Ibid., p. 94. See, also, O. W. Lembcke, 'Staats(rechts)lehre oder Rechts(staats)lehre? Zum Rechtspositivismus bei Jellinek und Kelsen', in R. Schmidt (ed), *Rechtspositivismus: Ursprung und Kritik*, Baden-Baden: Nomos, 2014, pp. 83–134.

68 G. Jellinek, *Ein Verfassungsgerichtshof in Österreich*, Vienna: Hölder, 1885.

69 G. Jellinek, *Das Recht der Minoritäten*, Vienna: Hölder 1898. See, also the introduction to the modern reprint, by W. Pauly, 'Majorität und Minorität', in G. Jellinek, *Das Recht der Minoritäten*, W. Pauly (ed), Berlin: Keip, 1996, pp. vii–xx.
70 This emphasized by Donhauser in Chapter 6 of this volume. See, also, G. Bongiovanni, *Reine Rechtslehre e dottrina giuridica dello Stato. H. Kelsen e la Costituzione austriaca del 1920*, Milan: Giuffrè, 1998.
71 It should be noted that, as a result of the editorial process of the Max Weber Gesamtausgabe, this part of the former composite of Weber's work, entitled *Wirtschaft and Gesellschaft*, has now been subdivided. The German edition of this part, is now entitled *Wirtschaft und Gesellschaft. Die Wirtschaft und die gesellschaftlichen Ordnungen und Mächte. Nachlaß. Recht* (2010), and contains, in addition to 'The Sociology of Law' another text entitled 'The Economy and the Orders'. The English translation of the section on 'The Sociology of Law' is contained in M. Weber, *Economy and Society*, G. Roth and C. Wittich (eds), Berkeley: University of California Press, 1978, pp. 641–900.
72 This is emphasized as part of the analysis by Coutu in Chapter 8 of this volume.
73 On this, see the exemplary analysis by H. Treiber, 'Max Weber and Eugen Ehrlich: On the Janus-headed Construction of Max Weber's Ideal Type in the Sociology of Law', *Max Weber Studies* (2008), 8, 2, 225–46. See, also the further precisions in H. Treiber, 'Insights into Weber's Sociology of Law', in K. Andenoes, S. Machura and K. Papendorf (eds), *Understanding Law in Society: Developments in Socio-legal Studies*, Berlin/Zurich: Litt Verlag, 2011, pp. 21–79.
74 The phrase is from Coutu's analysis in Chapter 8 of this volume.
75 See, for example, Kelsen's conclusion to the discussion and rejection of the dualism of private and public law, 'What we call private law, seen from the standpoint of its function – *qua* part of the legal system – in the fabric of the law as a whole, is simply a particular form of law, the form corresponding to the capitalistic economic system of production and distribution; its function, then, is the eminently political one of exercising power. Another form of law would suit a socialistic economic system, not the autonomous, democratic form represented by present private law, but – presumably – a heteronomous, autocratic form closer to our present administrative law. Whether that would be a more satisfying or more just form of regulation remains an open question here. The Pure Theory of Law does not aim to decide the question, nor can it decide it', *Introduction to the Problems of Legal Theory*, op. cit., p. 96.
76 This is one of the central emphases of Halpérin in Chapter 9 of this volume.
77 This is emphasized by Halpérin in Chapter 9 of this volume.
78 It is this connection between law and culture, and the continued contemporary relevance of Weber's analyses of law, which informs the approach of the editors of Max Weber's writings on Law in the *Max Weber Gesamtausgabe* (M. Weber, *Wirtschaft und Gesellschaft. Die Wirtschaft und die gesellschaftlichen Ordnungen und Mächte. Nachlaß. Recht*, Tübingen: Mohr, 2010), see Gephart, *Law, Culture and Society*, op. cit. For the initial interpretative development of this position, see W. Gephart, 'Das Collagenwerk. Zur so genannten "Rechtssoziologie" Max Webers', *Rechtsgeschichte* (2003), 3, 111–27; S. Hermes, 'Das Recht einer Soziologischen Rechtslehre. Zum Rechtsbegriff in Max Webers Soziologie des Rechts', *Rechtstheorie* (2004), 35, 195–231; and S. Hermes, 'Vom Aufbau der sozialen Welt. Zur Genese, Genealogie und Kategorienlehre von Max Webers Soziologie des Rechts', *Rechtstheorie* (2007), 38, 419–49. For the qualifications of the pertinence of this approach to Weber, see H. Treiber, 'On Max Weber's Sociology of Law, now known as The Developmental Conditions of the Law. A Review Essay on *Max Weber Gesamtausgabe* I/22-3: Recht', *Max Weber Studies* (2012), 1, 121–38; and F. Chazel, 'La "sociologie du droit" de Max Weber à la lumière de l'édition critique de la *Max Weber Gesamtausgabe*', *Droit et Société* (2012), 81, 475–97.
79 H. Kelsen, *Society and Nature. A Sociological Inquiry*, Chicago: Chicago University Press,

1943. See the highly critical review of Talcott Parsons in which Kelsen's analysis is held to be seriously deficient as a purported sociological theory (T. Parsons, 'Book Review of Hans Kelsen, Society and Nature. A Sociological Inquiry', *Harvard Law Review* (1944–45), 58, 140–44). On the position of this work within the periodization of Kelsen's work, see C. Jablonner, 'Bemerkungen zu Kelsens Vergeltung und Kasualität, besonders zur Naturdeutung der Primitiven', in W. Krawietz, E. Topitsch and P. Koller (eds), *Ideologiekritik und Demokratietheorie bei Hans Kelsen*, Berlin: Dunkler and Humblot, 1982, pp. 47–62.

80 This is emphasized by Halpérin in Chapter 9 of this volume. See, J.-L. Halpérin, *Profils des mondialisations du droit*, Paris: Dalloz, 2009, for the development of this form of analysis through the notion of a number of globalizations of law. This is to be contrasted with the position of Coutu in Chapter 8 of this volume, for whom, it is the phenomenon of legal pluralism which marks the difficulty of any deeper affinity between the Weberian and Kelsenian approaches.

Part I

Hans Kelsen, Max Weber and democracy

Chapter 1

Führerprinzip and democracy in Weber and Kelsen

Antonino Scalone

The modern political order is not natural, but artificial. This means that it is a human order, built *ex nihilo* from a human decision. Hobbes gives the best explanation of the mechanism that produces the political order; this is constructed – Hobbes writes in Chapter XVI of the *Leviathan* – through the principle of representation:

> A Multitude of men, are made One Person, when they are by one man, or one Person, Represented; so that it be done with the consent of every one of that Multitude in particular. For it is the Unity of the Representer, not the Unity of the Represented, that maketh the Person One. And it is the Representer that beareth the Person, and but one Person: And Unity, cannot otherwise be understood in Multitude.[1]

Political representation produces a very strong power concentrated in the hands of the sovereign, and this fact ensures peace among citizens. However, for Hobbes, citizens and their associations cannot participate in political life: the role of citizens is limited to private life, where they can express their own opinions; political associations are forbidden.[2] It is noteworthy that this prohibition is confirmed at the time of the French Revolution, particularly by the so-called *loi Le Chapelier*:[3] this means that it is not only connected to the so-called absolutist State, but is a peculiarity of the modern State itself. This assertion may appear problematic to those who are used to distinguishing and opposing the concepts of absolute, liberal and democratic States. The purpose here is not to claim that there is no difference among these forms of State, but simply that they are comprehensible, in their common and diverging features, only by assuming them as different expressions of the same logical structure: the Hobbesian one. In his fundamental concepts we find this underlying logic based on the representative principle and, one based on the mechanism of authorization within Locke's political thought, which is usually ascribed to the liberal field[4] within the political conception of the French Revolution. Within Kant's thought, even, one can find one of the most cogent demonstrations of the impossibility of the right of resistance, due to the fact that there is no people and their representatives, there are only subjects.[5]

How can we reconcile the requirement for order and internal peace, based on the clear distinction between public and private, with the right to participate in political life which would seem to radically question that distinction? This is probably the most important political question of the twentieth century. This question is already present in Hobbes, at least *in fieri*. It initially appears in Chapter XXVII of the *Leviathan*, and also in Chapter XXXVII, where Hobbes deals with miracles and leaves to the individual the liberty to believe in them or not. Hobbes writes:

> A private man has always the liberty, because thought is free, to believe or not believe in his heart those acts that have been given out for miracles, according as he shall see what benefit can accrue, by men's belief, to those that pretend or countenance them, and thereby conjecture whether they be miracles or lies.[6]

Schmitt incisively highlights that, although Hobbes makes the sovereign the 'lieutenant of God', in the moment he recognizes the subject's liberty to believe or not, he introduces the decisive 'rupture' within the 'otherwise so complete, so overpowering unity' of his system.[7] According to Schmitt, here we already find the principles of individual liberty that will then give birth to liberal constitutionalism:

> The distinction between private and public, faith and confession, *fides* and *confessio*, is introduced in a way from which everything else was logically derived in the century that ensued until the rise of the liberal constitutional state. The modern 'neutral' State, derived from agnosticism and not from the religiosity of Protestant sectarians, originated at this point.[8]

The crisis of the State is, therefore, included *ab origine* in its logic structure, which cannot clearly distinguish between public and private, and cannot clearly define the field of sovereign competence. The more distant the memory of civil wars of religion, the less motivated the absolutist pretence of the State appears to the private conscience and, then, to the general public, and the request to participate in public life more cogent.[9]

It is the approach of Max Weber and Hans Kelsen to the question of how the distinction between public and private – which, as we have seen, is considered necessary for order and internal peace – may be accommodated with the right to participate in political life that is the focus of this chapter.

Weber never discusses or cites Hobbes, but we can affirm (agreeing with Bobbio) that the two concepts of sovereignty are very similar:[10] Weber's *Herrschaft* is Hobbes' sovereignty, and the *Herrschaftsverband* is the *societas civilis* of Hobbes, characterized by the monopoly of the power of coercion. There is also a narrow connection between the concept of representation explained in Chapter XVI of the *Leviathan* and the *freie Repräsentation* explained in *Wirtschaft und Gesellschaft*;[11] it is not accidental that Weber writes of the free representative in the Parliament '*wie der Monarch unverantwortlich ist*': he is a *Herr* without mandated responsibility.

However, Weber knows that the political situation is characterized by parties, too, which are mass organizations; for the masses, the modern parties in the twentieth century represent the most important instrument to participate in political life and to accede to the power, '*Every* party strives for *power*, which is to say to share in the *administration*.'[12] But every party voices a certain interest, a certain idea of the world, a particular *Weltanschauung*; at the same time it is strongly hierarchized and bureaucratized,[13] and, at the summit, there is a political leader. For Weber, in fact, the modern party is formed by:

> a permanent core of people with a vested interest in the party who are grouped together under the direction of a leader or a group of notables; the structure of this core varies greatly in its stability and often has a fully developed bureaucracy nowadays.[14]

Weber re-emphasizes the importance of bureaucracy in *Politik als Beruf* (1919), where he describes the contemporaneous developments in the American political system:

> To win over the masses it was necessary to call into being an enormous apparatus of associations which were democratic in appearance, so as to create a voting association in each district of the town, to keep the organisation in constant operation, and to subject everything to tight bureaucratic control.[15]

Weber's *Parliament and Government* extends this analysis further, for '[f]inally, the same progress towards bureaucratisation as it is taking place in economic life and in State administration is now also to be found in the *parties*'.[16]

For Weber, the political leader is fundamental; he is at the same time: (a) a party-chief, bound by the party-interest; and (b) a member of the Parliament or a government-chief, and, as such, the representative of the whole people (we cannot forget that, according to Weber, the Parliament is the most important site for the training of the politicians): theoretically he has to engage in decision making, expressing not the particular interest of his party, but the general interest, the *Gemeinwohl*. In reality, political decisions are taken by party-leaders and resolutions are the result of compromises agreed in Parliament, but the legitimation of the decision depends, from the formal and logical point of view, on the representative bond: the representative (every representative) can (and has to) decide in name of the people because the people have authorized him to do so. For this reason, Weber is against the *referendum*, 'The *referendum* knows nothing of compromise, and yet it is inevitable that the majority of laws must be based on compromise in a mass State with an internal structure characterized by powerful regional, social, religious and other oppositions'.[17]

Obviously, it is necessary that citizens believe that the representative decides in conformity with the *Germeinwohl*. Here is the most important reason for the fragility of the legitimacy of contemporary political systems; citizens need the parties to be represented, in their particularity, as a 'part', but at the same time they consider that the party's representation is to the detriment of the *Gemeinwohl*: they inhabit this contradiction between two images, two representations of themselves, bearers of particular interests and members of the people. This contradiction is exacerbated by a lack of trust in the party-leaders, because they view this role as an unsatisfactory combination of personal and party-interest. The virtuous political-chief knows, with his own personal charisma, how to rule the difficult balance between these opposite interests. It is significant that Weber portrays the political chief like a modern hero:

> Politics means slow, strong drilling through hard boards, with a combination of passion and sense of judgment. It is of course entirely correct, and a fact confirmed by all historical experience, that what is possible would never have been achieved if, in this world, people had not repeatedly reached for the impossible. But the person who can do this must be a leader; not only that, he must, in a very simple sense of the word, be a hero.[18]

However, Weber thinks that the *Führerdemokratie* is the destiny of the contemporary State; the contemporary democracy is by necessity *Führerdemokratie*:

> But the only choice lies between a leadership democracy with a 'machine' and democracy without a leader, which means rule by the 'professional politician' who has no vocation, the type of man who lacks precisely those inner, charismatic qualities which make a leader.[19]

This is the necessary consequence of the supremacy of the small number in complex societies, 'The "principle of the small number" (that is the superior manoeuvrability of *small* leading groups) always rules political action. This element of "Caesarism" is ineradicable (in *mass states*).'[20]

The specific focus devoted to the 'parts' is not accompanied by support for corporativist representation. On the contrary, the proposals for corporate representation are defined as 'amateurish pipe-dreams'[21] by Weber: he means that politics is only a specialist activity of professional people, by *leaders*, who will never emerge from the *berufständische Interessenvertretung* (corporativist representation). Moreover, it is very difficult to translate the weight and the importance of every profession into a professional-representative system.[22] This is in contrast to the mutable and adaptable character of the modern capitalistic economy.[23] The *Verbände* (associations) are accorded the possibility to carry out an important role in the political and economic system, but they must organize as free associations in the same form as the political parties. These *Verbände* are 'suitable organizations for *fighting* and *compromise*',[24] founded on free recruitment, 'Any attempt to compel them to unite on the model of an official department of state would be a purely mechanical compulsion which would put an end to their inner life.'[25]

Lastly, politics is characterized by political struggle, whose goal is power. In this context, Parliament has no certain, institutional monopoly over political decision making: it is merely the site where political decisions made elsewhere are recorded, and for the formation and training of politicians. In spite of his particular focus upon parties, *Verbände* and political compromises, Weber does not minimize the need for national unity and its power-politics.[26] Consequently, his position appears complex and contradictory: on the one hand, he affirms the necessity of organized political parties competing without the possibility of corporatist regulation; on the other, he affirms the necessity of a political leader, in the role of President, to be chosen by plebiscite and the awareness that, in modern mass society, there is no alternative to the *Führerdemokratie*.

From this perspective, one may suggest that there is a significant similarity between the Weberian concept of *Führerdemokratie* and some aspects of Schmittian thought. In the essay *Der Reichspräsident*, for example, Weber adopts theses that may seem to anticipate the views that Carl Schmitt will express, in particular, in *Der Hüter der Verfassung*. In that essay, Weber proposes the direct election of the President of the *Reich*, who he identifies as the 'head of the executive, of official patronage' and 'possessor of a delaying veto, and the power to dissolve Parliament and to consult the people', and at the same time, the real and only 'palladium of genuine democracy'.[27] Indeed, the issue is more complicated than it seems. From a constitutional point of view, the Weberian president of the *Reich*, as head of government, cannot be identified with the President of the *Reich* foreseen in the Weimar Constitution, in Article 49, whom Schmitt refers to, and considers as a *pouvoir neutre* (following its original definition by Benjamin Constant) or *pouvoir preservateur* (as *per* Schmitt[28]). The theoretical framework, in which that figure fits, is completely different: in Weber there is a complete acceptance of the system of parties (whose modernization the president may be the guarantee):

> Only the election of the president of the Reich by the people will provide an opportunity and occasion to *select leaders* and hence also to reorganise the parties along lines which will supersede the completely antiquated system of management by notables that has existed up till now.[29]

Moreover, there is an awareness of the central and irreplaceable role of Parliament, 'Whether one loves or hates the whole parliamentary business, it is *not* to be got rid of'.[30] The President of the Reich would interact with it as a counterweight, but not be an alternative to it.[31] His power would be further justified by the need to overcome tendencies towards territorial particularism[32] and balance the excessive weight of Prussia, 'Only *a President elected by the people* can have a role that is more than merely tolerated in Berlin *alongside the Prussian head of the State*'.[33]

In contrast, in Schmitt, the presidential orientation is combined with a deep mistrust of the parties and of political pluralism, which he even comes to view as the potential for civil war,[34] being convinced that the parliamentary institution is completely outmoded and claiming that 'homogeneity' is the prerequisite for a stable political unity (this statement complements the need for eliminating the heterogeneous) and, finally, the preference – that will lead to his support for the National Socialist regime – for a political system which is not based on election, but on the *acclamatio* of the head of State by the people.[35]

The connections and the similarities between Weber and Kelsen's theory are well-known. As stated by Bobbio we can say that they concern the difference between the science of law and the sociology of law, the concept of coercion, the question of *Wertfreiheit* and concept of the State's monopoly of the power.[36] Kelsen himself acknowledges the intellectual debt to Weber in the *Introduction* to the first edition of the *Hauptprobleme*[37] and the sociology of law, in particular, in *Der soziologische und der juristische Staatsbegriff*.[38] The similarities between Weber and Kelsen in the theory of democracy are extremely important.

For Kelsen, democracy is not the direct expression of the power of the people: it is impossible to realize direct democracy (*unmittelbare Demokratie*) in contemporary societies, characterized by highly developed complexity and specialization of work.[39] Indeed, Kelsen generalizes the uncertainty of the *unmittelbare Demokratie* to the simplest political organizations too:

> Even when the popular assembly makes decisions by majority, direct democracy is only possible for a small community and little differentiated cultural relations. This form of state is therefore hardly ever taken into consideration nowadays. In places where it still exists, at least in its essential features – as in some little cantons of Switzerland – the constitution cannot renounce [. . .] an indirect organ of legislation.[40]

The concept of impossible direct democracy is reaffirmed in *Wesen und Wert der Demokratie*,[41] and renders necessary the use of a parliamentary system:

> But, since in the modern State the application of a direct democracy is practically impossible, nobody can seriously doubt that the parliament is the only real form for the modern current society to create democracy. Therefore a decision on parlamentarianism is also a decision on democracy.[42]

In a similar manner, in the first edition of *Sozialismus und Staat*, there is a statement, which is not included in the second edition, where Kelsen, confirming the limits of parliamentary democracy, however re-states the impossibility of direct democracy:

> The mass, that never moves automatically, never by itself, cannot enact the initially creative, specific function of will. The decisive stage for the direction and content of the 'popular will' is mainly before the democratic procedure, where the popular will – or rather its political expression, the will of the State – is formed and has an absolutely autocratic feature: the will of a single person to lead is imposed upon the will of the many.[43]

In this argument, there are other important concordances with Weber's analysis of the modern organization of State and society, characterized by instrumental rationality and professional specialization. Politics itself is characterized by this principle for both Kelsen and Weber: it is a specifically reserved sphere for professional politicians. Also, according to Kelsen, Parliament is the place where politicians are trained and selected, and the place where political compromises between parties and interest or pressure groups are formed. Political compromise is the goal of parliamentary activity; Kelsen writes, 'The entire parliamentary procedure indeed, with its technique based on speeches and replies, arguments and counter-arguments tends to a compromise.'[44] Parliamentarianism itself is the best compromise between the individual liberty and the necessities of the modern social organization, 'Parliamentarianism is therefore a compromise between the democratic need for liberty and the principle of the differentiating division of labour that influences every technical-social progress.'[45]

Kelsen considers that society is characterized by social conflicts between political and economic interests: he speaks openly of class struggle,[46] and presents the *Gemeinwohl* as only an illusion. He had already criticized this idea in his earlier *Wählerlisten und Reklamationsrecht* of 1906, where he states that the deputies represent only social interests. The modern idea that the deputies represent the *Gemeinwohl*, Kelsen writes, 'is completely in contrast with the concrete relationships, because deputies are never organs of the overall State, of the unitary State, but as well as the representatives of the social classes, they always represent partial interests.'[47] In the *Hauptprobleme der Staatsrechtslehre*, Kelsen emphasizes that each voter is only interested in choosing the representative of his own interests and not the representative of the common good, 'The essential element residing in the act of will of the voter [. . .] is the determined person of the parliamentarian that the voter wants to have in parliament as a representative of its interest!'[48] The *Gemeinwohl* is a mere appearance, or rather, a dangerous illusion, 'There is no "general interest", but always only groups' interests that take the State power, the will of the state for themselves by any possible means.'[49] Finally, Kelsen writes in *Wesen und Wert der Demokratie*:

> By the way, the ideal of a higher general interest that goes beyond the group's interest and is therefore 'supra-party', of a solidarity in the interest of all members of the society, without distinction of religion, nationality, class and so on, is a metaphysical illusion, or rather a metapolitical one.[50]

For this reason, Kelsen maintains that the parties are not a pathological side of the political life (that is the meaning attributed to them by Carl Schmitt and by Heinrich Triepel, against whom Kelsen polemicizes in *Wesen und Wert der Demokratie*), and he defends an electoral mechanism based upon proportional representation.[51] In a majority system, large minorities are continually at risk of an absence of effective representation in Parliament and 'it is believed that it is not unfair that the election of the president is lost to a party by one vote.'[52] In contrast, the system of proportional representation, is imbued with the 'individual principle of liberty', with the 'principle of radical democracy.'[53]

The formal character of law has the (political) function of guaranteeing political compromises between parties and special interest groups; for this reason Kelsen defends the principle of legality and professionalism in the administration: only the professional bureaucrat, selected by competition, can guarantee the correct and impersonal application of the law. The legality of the administration is the best guarantee for democracy, and there is a narrow bond between democracy and bureaucracy:

> The legality of the execution – and in the legislative process this means the popular will and therefore democracy itself – is without any doubt better guaranteed in the intermediate and lower resorts [. . .] by an autocratic organisation than by an autonomous administration.[54]

In this respect, it is possible to consider that, for Kelsen, there is a certain developmental destiny for the State and western civilization. It is a destiny composed of the combination of the process of bureaucratization and the representation of the State in the legal form of a *Rechtsstaat*. From this perspective, there seems to be a certain consonance between the Kelsenian concept of the rule of law and the Weberian concept of legal power. The main characteristic of the latter is that of being equipped with bureaucratic and judicial 'specialised apparatuses' that act within the limits of general and abstract rules that constitute its system.[55]

However, this is the limit of Kelsen's 'juridical Spinozism'.[56] As with Weber, he cannot completely relinquish the idea of political unity. The State is a '*Herrschaftsverband*' (political association) characterized by the element of power, which Kelsen expresses in *Sozialismus und Staat*,[57] substantially agreeing with Weber – and this belief is the main critical element against the Marxian political conception: in his opinion the Marxian idea of the extinction of the State is unacceptable and utopian. He rather thinks that it is only a coercive apparatus which is indifferent to the goals it is aiming at. In fact, in his thoughts on Austrian Social Democracy, and, particularly, on Kautsky, Kelsen highlights and shares not only a substantial lack of interest towards the prospect of the extinction of the State, but also recognizes how unavoidable its role is.[58]

The possible democracy, that obviously has nothing to do with the absence of leaders typical of an abstract democracy, which Kelsen deems completely unattainable, cannot be without leaders; as he clearly states, 'The reality of society is essentially power and leadership'.[59] The possible democracy consists, rather, in the voters' participation in selecting their leaders through an election,[60] and in attributing those leaders with a precise political responsibility.[61] This is the possibility for everybody to ascend, without restriction, to the role of leader.[62]

This marks a significant difference from Weber's *Führerdemokratie*, as, for Kelsen, it is inadvisable to directly elect the head of State and government on the model of the United States. He considers that a single person cannot adequately represent the various opinions and interests of the people; moreover, a directly elected leader tends to be independent from Parliament and from the electorate's control.[63]

Kelsen also thinks that it is not possible to completely renounce the idea of a single person who, as the president of the republic, *embodies* political unity: on the contrary, he considers that the idea is necessary for political and social cohesion, for *Integration*, in conformity with Smend's well-known expression.[64] If a legal theory can, or, rather, must renounce the idea of a *höchste Organ* (highest organ), the people, as a collective mass, are still in need of this idea:

> In the same way in which the theory of law is based on the awareness that you are subject, and therefore bound, to obey only to provisions, but not to the people making them, the vast majority of people, being against abstract thought, needs a clearly identifiable symbol of authority. This is the symbolic meaning, more than everything else, of the institution of the head of State.[65]

This is not all. Certainly Kelsen criticizes the idea of political representation, which he defines as a *nackte Fiktion*, a simple invention with an ideological and political role.[66] The theory of representation serves only to justify the independence of Parliament with respect to the people, independence that, for Kelsen, can be explained only with the requirement of the division of labour in a modern society, 'From a legal-political point of view, the parliament's independence from the people can only be justified with a number of reasons that essentially derive from the technical-social advantages of the division of labour [. . .]'.[67] The necessities of this division of labour are as pressing as the representative mechanism that, according to Hobbes, produces political unity. This necessity is accompanied by the impossibility of direct political participation in political life for the single individual; he has indeed to submit to a double restriction or mediation: the first is constituted by the political parties; the second is constituted by Parliament. If the individual has not political existence without the parties, then '[c]learly the isolated individual does not have any real existence from a political point of view' because he cannot have any influence on the formation of will of the State,[68] the people, as a whole, represent a dumb mass.[69]

Kelsen is as ambiguous as Weber in the underlying orientation of his theoretical reflection. Both acknowledge that the existence of political parties and of organized interests are the expression of non-pathological phenomena. For Kelsen and Weber, in contrast to Schmitt, Leibholz, Triepel and a significant proportion of German theorists of the State, political and social pluralism is a necessary presupposition of modern political existence. This contrast is exemplified in the comparison between Kelsen and Triepel; in particular, between Triepel's *Die Staatsverfassung und die politischen Parteien*,[70] and Kelsen's critique in the second edition of *Das Wesen der Demokratie*. Triepel states that mass parties diverge significantly from the liberal concept of Parliament based on the principle of independence and freedom of conscience of the deputy. He considers that the increasing influence of parties in public life is the result of a radical change of the very form of parliamentarianism, which is primarily the result of the introduction of proportional election systems, as well as the development of mass parties in place of the parties of opinion of the liberal age.[71] However, he has to admit that there is a difference between legal theory, which generally does not attribute any role to parties, and the sociological reality which acknowledges their growing significance.[72] He emphasizes that a failure to acknowledge this sociological reality is comparable to burying one's head in the sand.[73] His work, therefore, concludes with a completely outmoded reference to a possible future organic concept of State that can overcome the atomistic and individualistic one whose extreme form is represented by the despicable State of parties.[74]

Kelsen's critical approach is able to reveal the underlying political orientation of Triepel's position: the continual contradiction of reality in order to confirm his ideological convictions.[75] Kelsen states that Triepel contradicts himself because, on the one hand, he postulates the extra-institutional feature of the parties and, on the other, he emphasizes the many provisions of positive right through which the parties are acknowledged to play a role in the process of formation of will.[76] Kelsen concludes that this, together with his inclination for organicism, reveals the '*Abneigung* (reluctance)' as a hostility towards democracy under the cover of a façade of scientificity.[77] This comparison is indicative of the wider ambiguity of the approach of Schmitt, Leibholz, Triepel and others in their acceptance of the necessity of political and social pluralism. The ambiguity of their acceptance of this necessity contains the contemporary relevance of their considerations: the problems that Kelsen and Weber deal with retain a contemporary validity and underlie a specifically modern reflection upon politics.

While this determines the continued pertinence of their respective theoretical frameworks, one should also emphasize a divergence between them. Weber's thought still appears limited by its connections to the idea of the national State.[78] Kelsen appears to be more contemporary in at least three respects, whose full complexity cannot be considered here, though their main outlines can be indicated. First, his criticism of the theory of sovereignty which is closely linked to the central belief in the supremacy of international law over the State, and the prospect of a coming *civitas maxima*[79] strongly characterized by a cosmopolitan natural law.

Second, his effort in transcending the language of power which, in his opinion, was completely filled with 'politics' and was, therefore, essentially unscientific. This effort resulted in the text of the Austrian Constitution of 1920 where the term 'law' is used instead of the term 'power'. In Article 1, for example, it is stated that Austria is a democratic republic and its '*law*' (not its '*power*' as it is written in the Weimar Constitution) comes from the people.[80]

Third, in his analysis of the concept of federalism:[81] according to Kelsen, in its correct meaning, federalism is not characterized by a bipolar structure (central State and single member States), but by a *tripolar* structure where the partial system of the single member States and the overall partial system are on the same level (and, therefore, the overall central system is wrongly defined as an *Oberstaat* (souzerain)), and they are both equally subject to the federal Constitution.[82] As far as the so-called *Bundesexekution* (federal enforcement) is concerned, this whole structure entails that, not only can the latter can be performed in the case of breaches by the member States, but also where breaches are carried out *both* by member States and by the so called *Oberstaat*, all partial expressions, *Teilordnungen*, of the only *Gesamtverfassung*[83] (entire Constitution) in force.

One may argue with particular aspects of the above analyses, as well as question their compatibility with other aspects of Kelsenian thought (e.g. the definition of the State as *Herrschaftsverband*, mentioned above: it seems to keep, despite all efforts, some residual traditional concepts of State and some hints of the classic notion of sovereignty with it, which was so harshly criticized by the jurist from Vienna). However, these analyses are still of topical interest and offer important theoretical resources to comprehend a political reality which emerges *beyond* the nation State.

Notes

1 T. Hobbes, *Leviathan* (1651), Oxford: Oxford University Press, 1996, p. 109.
2 I leave out, intentionally, the complicated problem of the political role of the associations which Hobbes considers in Chapter XXII of the *Leviathan*. On this topic and for further bibliography, see A. Scalone, 'Le società parziali in Hobbes', in *Lo Stato. Rassegna di diritto costituzionale, dottrina dello Stato e filosofia del diritto*, Vol. 1, Torino: G. Giappichelli Editore, 2012, pp. 185–203.
3 Compare J. H. Kaiser, *Die Repräsentation organisierter Interessen*, 2nd edn, Berlin: Duncker & Humblot, 1978.
4 For a criticism on this ascription, see Q. Skinner, 'Meaning and understanding in the history of ideas', in Q. Skinner, *Visions of Politics*, Vol. 1, Cambridge: Cambridge University Press, 2002, pp. 57–89.
5 See, further, I. Kant, *Methaphysische Anfangsgründe der Rechtslehre*, *Werke*, Vol. VI, hrsg. von der Königlichen Preussischen Akademie der Wissenschaften, Berlin und Leipzig (Akademische Ausgabe), p. 318. The following, both published in 1928, re-introduce the representative principle in its Hobbesian conception as pivotal in the modern concept of State: G. Leibholz, *Das Wesen der Repräsentation, und der Gestaltwandel der Demokratie im 20. Jahrhundert*, 3rd edn, Berlin: Duncker & Humblot, 1966 and C. Schmitt, *Verfassungslehre*, Berlin: Duncker & Humblot, 1928. On this topic, see the classic H. Hofmann, *Repräsentation. Studien zur Wort und Begriffsgeschichte von der Antike bis ins 19. Jahrhundert*, Berlin: Duncker & Humblot, 1974; and, also, G. Duso, *La rappresentanza politica. Genesi e crisi del concetto*, Milano: Franco Angeli, 2003, esp. pp. 22–23, A. Biral, *Storia e critica della filosofia politica moderna*, Milano: Angeli, 1999.
6 Hobbes, *Leviathan*, II, XXXVII, op. cit., p. 296.
7 C. Schmitt, *The Leviathan in the State Theory of Thomas Hobbes: Meaning and Failure of a Political Symbol* (1938), Westport, CT and London: Greenwood Press, 1996, pp. 55–56.
8 Ibid., p. 56.
9 On this topic, see R. Koselleck, *Kritik und Krise. Ein Beitrag zur Pathogenese der bürgerlichen Welt*, Freiburg-München: Verlag Karl Alber, 1959. On the difficulty in distinguishing between public and private, see, also, R. Schnur, *Individualismus und Absolutismus*, Berlin: Duncker & Humblot, 1963. On the role of the public, the classic reference is J. Habermas, *Strukturwandel der Öffentlichkeit*, Neuwied: Luchterland Verlag, 1962.

10 Compare N. Bobbio, 'La teoria dello Stato e del potere', in P. Rossi (ed), *Max Weber e l'analisi del mondo moderno*, Torino: Einaudi, 1981, p. 220.
11 Compare Duso, op. cit., pp. 142–43 and A. Scalone, *Rappresentanza politica e rappresentanza degli interessi*, Milano, Franco Angeli, 1996.
12 M. Weber, 'Parliament and Government in Germany under a New Political Order', in M. Weber, *Political Writings*, Cambridge: Cambridge University Press, 1994, p. 167 ('*Jede* Partei erstrebt als solche: *Macht*, das heißt: Anteil an der Verwaltung', M. Weber, 'Parlament und Regierung im neuordneten Deutschland' (1918), in M. Weber, *Gesammelte politische Schriften*, 5th edn, Tübingen: J.C.B. Mohr (Paul Siebeck), 1988, p. 341).
13 Ibid., p. 212, 'The party apparatus is growing in importance and the significance of notables is declining correspondingly' ('Der Parteiapparat steigt an Bedeutung, und entsprechend sinkt die Bedeutung der Honorationen', ibid., p. 385); there is a strong connection between bureaucracy and democracy too, 'Bureaucratization and the rational management of finances are concomitants of democratization here as they are everywhere else', ibid., p. 214 ('So sind doch hier wie überall Bürokratisierung und rationale Finanzwirtschaft Begleiterscheinungen der Demokratisierung', ibid., p. 387).
14 Ibid., p. 149 ('Ein dauernder, unter einem Führer oder einer Honoratiorengruppen vereinigter Kern von Parteiinteressenten mit sehr verschieden fester Gliederung, heute oft mit entwickelter Bürokratie', ibid., p. 324).
15 Weber, *Political Writings*, op. cit., p. 341 ('Zur Massengewinnung wurde es notwendig, einen ungeheuren Apparat von demokratisch aussehenden Verbände ins Leben zu rufen, in jedem Stadtquartier einen Wahlverband zu bilden, unausgesetzt den Betrieb in Bewegung zu halten, alles straff zu burokratisieren', Weber, *Gesammelte politische Schriften*, op. cit., p. 535).
16 Weber, *Parliament and Government*, op. cit., p. 149 ('Nicht anders als in Wirtschaft und staatlicher Verwaltung steht es schließlich mit dem Fortschritt zur Bürokratisierung nun auch: in den *Parteien*', Weber, *Parlament und Regierung*, op. cit., p. 324).
17 Ibid., p. 225 ('Das Referendum kennt eben nicht: das Kompromiß, auf welchem in jedem Massenstaat mit starken regionalen, sozialen, konfessionalen und anderen Gegensätzen der inneren Struktur unvermeidlich die Mehrzahl aller Gesetze beruht', ibid., p. 398).
18 Weber, 'The profession and vocation of Politics', in *Political Writings*, op. cit., p. 369 ('Die Politik bedeutet ein starkes langsames Bohren von harten Brettern mit Leidenschaft und Augenmaß zugleich. Es ist ja durchaus richtig, und alle geschichtliche Erfahrung bestätigt es, daß man das Mögliche nicht erreichte, wenn nicht immer wieder in der Welt nach dem Unmögliche gegriffen worden ware. Aber der, der das tun kann, müß ein Führer und nicht nur das, sondern auch – in einem sehr schlichten Sinn – ein Held sein', *Politik als Beruf*, op. cit., p. 560).
19 Ibid., p. 351 ('Aber es gibt nur die Wahl: Führerdemokratie mit "Maschine" oder führerlose Demokratie, das heißt: die Herrschaft der "Berufspolitiker" ohne Beruf, ohne die inneren, charismatischen Qualitäten, die eben zum Führer machen', ibid., p. 544).
20 Weber, *Parliament and Government*, op. cit., p. 174 ('Stets beherrscht das "Prinzip der kleinen Zahl", d.h. die überlegene politische Manövrierfähigkeit *kleiner* führender Gruppen, das politische Handeln. Dieser "cäsaristische" Einschlag ist (in *Massenstaaten*) unausrottbar', *Parlament und Regierung*, op. cit., p. 348).
21 M. Weber, 'Suffrage and Democracy in Germany', in *Political Writings*, op. cit., p. 88 ('dilettantischen Seifenblase', Weber, *Wahlrecht und Demokratie in Deutschland*, in *Gesammelte politische Schriften*, op. cit., p. 252).
22 Compare ibid., pp. 92–93 (ibid., p. 256).
23 Ibid., p. 93, 'For these purely economic reasons there is nothing objectively more untruthful than the attempt to create *organic* structures (in the sense of the old social estates) as electoral corporations in the political sphere in an age of constant technical

and commercial restructuring and the progressive growth of economical and social ties based on *single-purpose associations*' ('Etwas objektiv Unwahrhaftigeres als der Versuch, in einem Zeitalter beständiger technischer und kommerzieller Umschichtungen und fortschreitender zweckverbandsmäßiger ökonomischer und sozialer Bindungen "*organische*" Gliederungen im altem ständischen Sinn als politische Wahlkörper schaffen wollen, gibt es schon aus diesen rein ökonomischen Gründen in aller Welt nicht', ibid.).
24 Ibid., p. 98 ("Organisationen für *Kampf* und *Kompromiß*", ibid., p. 261).
25 Ibid., p. 99 ('Der Versuch, sie nach Art einer staatlichen Behörde zwangmäßig zusammenschliessen, ware ein rein mechanischer Zwang, der ihrem inneren Leben ein Ende bereiten würde', ibid., p. 262).
26 Compare M. Weber, 'Der Nationalstaat und die Volkswirtschaftspolitik' (1985), in *Gesammelte politische Schriften*, op. cit., pp. 1–25.
27 M. Weber, 'The President of the Reich', in *Political Writings*, op. cit., p. 308 (M. Weber, 'Der Reichspräsident', in *Gesammelte politische Schriften*, op. cit., p. 501, 'Ein volksgewählter Präsident als Chef der Exekutive, der Amtspatronage und (eventuell) Inhaber eines aufschiebenden Vetos und des Befugnisses der Parlamentsauflösung ist der Palladium der echten Demokratie').
28 C. Schmitt, *Der Hüter der Verfassung*, Tübingen: J.C.B. Mohr (Paul Siebeck), 1930.
29 Weber, *The President of the Reich*, op. cit., p. 306 ('Nur die Wahl eines Reichspräsidenten durch das Volk gibt Gelegenheit und Anlaß zu einer Führerauslese und damit zu einer Neuorganisation der Parteien, welche das bisherige ganz veraltete System der Honoratiorenwirtschaft überwindet', Weber, *Der Reichspräsident*, op. cit., p. 499).
30 Weber, *Parliament and Government*, op. cit., p. 166 ('Man mag den parlamentarichen Betrieb hassen oder lieben . beseitigen wird man ihn *nicht*', Weber, *Parlament und Regierung*, op. cit., p. 340).
31 Cf. Weber, *The President of the Reich*, op. cit., p. 306.
32 Cf. ibid., p. 307.
33 Ibid. ('Nur ein volks gewählter Reichpräsident kann in Berlin neben der preußischen Staatsspitze eine andere als eine rein gedudete Rolle spielen', ibid., p. 500). On this topic, see the convincing arguments of L. Cavalli, 'Il carisma come potenza rivoluzionaria', in P. Rossi (ed), *Max Weber e l'analisi del mondo moderno*, op. cit., pp. 161–88 and A. Bolaffi, 'Max Weber o dell'ambiguità', in M. Weber, *Scritti politici*, Roma: Donzelli, 1999, pp. XIV–XV.
34 See C. Schmitt, 'Staatsethik und pluralistischer Staat' (1930), in C. Schmitt, *Positionen und Begriffe im Kampf mit Weimar-Genf-Versailles*, Hamburg: Hanseatische Verlaganstalt, 1940, pp. 133–45.
35 See C. Schmitt, *Die geistesgeschichtliche Lage des heutigen Parlamentarismus*, 2nd edn, München-Leipzig: Duncker & Humblot, 1926.
36 Compare N. Bobbio, *Max Weber e Hans Kelsen* (1981), in N. Bobbio, *Diritto e potere. Saggi su Kelsen*, Napoli: Esi 1992, pp. 159–77. See, also, M. Stockhammer, 'Hans Kelsen Rechtstheorie und Max Webers Soziologie im Spiegel der Erkenntnistheorie', *Österreichische Zeitschrift für öffentliches Recht* (1953), 5, 3, 410–27.
37 H. Kelsen, *Hauptprobleme der Staatsrechtslehre, entwickelt aus der Lehre vom Rechtsatze*, Tübingen: J.C.B. Mohr (Paul Siebeck), 1911.
38 H. Kelsen, *Der soziologische und der juristische Staatsbegriff. Kritische Untersuchung des Verhältnisses zwischen Staat und Recht*, Tübingen: J.C.B. Mohr (Paul Siebeck), 1922.
39 Compare H. Kelsen, *Allgemeine Staatslehre*, Wien: Springer, 1925, p. 344, 'The progressive differentiation of social relationships necessarily leads to a division of labour in every field, as well as in the formation of will or production of right. Legislative and executive functions go from the mass of subordinate people to single people or groups. The desire of political liberty or self-determination is only limited to subordinate people designating state organs acting through division of labour' ('Fortschreitende Differenzierung der

soziale Verhältnisse führt notwendig wie auf allen Gebieten so auch auf dem der staatlichen Willensbildung oder Rechtserzeugung zur Arbeitsteilung. Die Funktion der Gesetzgebung und Vollziehung geht von der Masse der Normenunterworfenen auf einzelne Individuen oder Gruppen über. Die Wille zur politischen Freiheit oder Selbstbestimmung beschränkt sich auf die Berufung der arbeitsteilig funktionierenden Staatsorgane durch die Normenunterworfenen').

40 Ibid., pp. 333–44 ('Auch wo die Volksversammlung mit Stimmenmehrheit ihre Beschlüsse faßt, ist unmittelbare Demokratie nur für kleine Gemeinswesen und wenig differenzierte Kulturverhältnisse möglich. Daher kommt diese Staatsform auch heute kaum mehr praktisch in Betracht. Wo sie heute wenigstens grundsätzlich besteht – wie in einzelnen kleinen Schweizer Kantonen – kann die Verfassung nicht auf ein [. . .] Organ mittelbarer Gesetzgebung verzichten').

41 H. Kelsen, *Wesen und Wert der Demokratie*, 2nd edn, Tübingen: J.C.B. Mohr (Paul Siebeck), 1929, p. 27.

42 Ibid. ('Allein da für den modernen Staat die unmittelbare Demokratie praktisch unmöglich ist, darf man wohl nicht ernstlich daran zweifeln, daß der Parlamentarismus die einzige reale Form ist, in der die Idee der Demokratie innerhalb der sozialen Wirklichkeit von heute erfüllt werden kann').

43 H. Kelsen, *Sozialismus und Staat. Eine Untersuchung der politischen Theorie des Marxismus*, Leipzig: Verlag von C.L. Hirschfeld, 1920, p. 128 ('Die niemals automatisch, niemals aus sich selbs bewegliche Masse die dem Wollen specifische, iniziativ schöpferische Funktion, nicht zu leisten vermag. Das für die Richtung und den Inhalt des "Volkswillens" entscheidende Stadium liegt meist vor dem demokratischen Verfashren, in dem der Volkswille – vielmehr seine politische Ausdrucksform: der Staatswille – gebildet wird, und hat durchaus autokratischen Charakter: der Führerwille eines einzelnen wird dem Willen der vielen aufgezwungen').

44 H. Kelsen, *Wesen und Wert der Demokratie*, Tübingen: J.C.B. Mohr (Paul Siebeck), 1929, p. 57 ('Denn das ganze parlamentarische Verfahren mit seiner dialektisch-kontradiktorischen, auf Rede und Gegenrede, Argument und GegenargumeGegenargument abgestellten Technik ist gerichtet auf die Erzielung eines Kompromisses'). A complete and radically opposed thesis upon parliamentarianism is sustained in the same period by C. Schmitt, *Die geistesgeschichtliche Lage der heutigen Parlamentarismus*, 2nd edn, Berlin: Duncker & Humblot, 1926. Concerning the distinct interpretations of parliamentarianism by Kelsen and Schmitt, I refer to my *L'ordine precario. Unità politica e pluralità nella Staatslehre novecentesca da Carl Schmitt a Joseph H. Kaiser*, Monza: Polimetrica, 2011, pp. 135–37 and 209–42.

45 Ibid., p. 29 ('Der Parlamentarismus stellt somit sich als ein Kompromiß zwischen der demokratischen Forderung der Freiheit und dem allen sozialteknischen Fortschritt bedingenden Grundsatz differenzierender Arbeitsteilung dar').

46 Compare H. Kelsen, *Über Grenzen zwischen juristischer und soziologischer Methode*, Tübingen: J.C.B. Mohr (Paul Siebeck), 1911.

47 H. Kelsen, 'Wählerlisten und Reklamationsrecht', *Juristische Blätter* (1906), 35, 25, 304 ('im krassen Widerspruch zu den konkreten Verhältnisse steht, weil die Abgeordneten niemals als Organe des Gesamtstaates, des Einheitsstaates, sonder immer nur, gerade so wie die ständischen Verteter, Vertreter gesellschaftlicher Teilinteressen sind').

48 H. Kelsen, *Hauptprobleme der Staatsrechtslehre, entwikelt aus der Lehre vom Rechtsatze*, Tübingen: J.C.B. Mohr (Paul Siebeck), 1923, p. 487 ('Das Wesentliche, das im Willensakte der Wahl des einen Wählers [. . .] liegt, ist die bestimmte Person des Abgeordneten, die der Wähler als Vertreter seiner Interessen im Parlamente haben will!').

49 Ibid., p. 479 ('Es gibt eben überhaupt kein "Gesamtinteresse", sondern immer nur Gruppeninteressen, die auf irgendeine Weise die staatliche Macht, den Staatswillen für sich gewinnen').

50 Kelsen, *Wesen und Wert der Demokratie*, op. cit., pp. 21–22 ('Im übrigen ist das Ideal eines über den Gruppeninteressen und jenseits derselben stehenden und sohin "überparteilichen" Gesamtinteressen, einer Interessensolidarität aller Gemeinschaftsglieder ohne Unterschied der Konfession, Nation, Klassenlage usw., eine metaphysische, oder besser: eine metapolitische Illusion').
51 On this question, compare A. Scalone, 'La società rispecchiata: Kelsen e il diritto elettorale', *Leviathan* (2010), 1, 1, 43–66.
52 Kelsen, *Allgemeine Staatslehre*, op. cit., p. 348 ('man glaubt kein Unrecht zu erleiden, wenn man bei der Wahl der Präsidenten mit einer Partei unterliegt, die nur eine Stimme weniger hat als die siegreicher Gegner').
53 Ibid., p. 349 ('individualistische Prinzip der Freiheit'; 'Prinzip der radikalen Demokratie').
54 Kelsen, *Wesen und Wert*, op. cit., p. 73 and *Allgemeine Staatslehre*, op. cit., p. 366 ('Die Gestzmäßigkeit der Vollziehung – und das bedeutet bei demokratischer Gesetzgebung: der Volkswille und sohin: die Demokratie selbst – wird in der Mittel- und Unterinstanz zweifellos besser als durch Selbstverwaltung durch eine autokratische Organisation [. . .] gewahrt').
55 Bobbio, *Max Weber e Hans Kelsen*, op. cit., p. 176. According to Bobbio, the difference between Kelsen and Weber, is rather the fact that the former 'proposes to develop a theory of State' of general validity, whereas the latter 'describes an ideal type of State that is historically identified' (ibid.).
56 A. Carrino, 'Vita e forme in Kelsen', in H. Kelsen, *Dio e Stato. La giurisprudenza come scienza dello spirito*, A. Carrino (ed), Napoli: Edizioni scientifiche italiane, 1988, p. 35. This expression means a totally immanent and monistic concept of the law and of policy.
57 Kelsen, *Sozialismus und Staat*, op. cit., p. 6. The similarity of the Weberian concept of State and the Kelsenian is stated by U. Schmill Ordónez, *El concepto del derecho en las teorías de Weber y de Kelsen*, in Ó. Correas (ed), *El otro Kelsen*, Mexico: Universidád autónoma de México, 1989, p. 193.
58 Compare Kelsen, *Sozialismus und Staat*, op. cit., p. 58.
59 Kelsen, *Wesen und Wert der Demokratie*, op. cit., p. 79 ('Denn soziale Realität ist Herrschaft und Führerschaft').
60 Cf. ibid., p. 84.
61 Ibid., pp. 87–88, 'The leaders' responsibility is a specific feature of the real democracy' ('Die Verantwortlichkeit der Führer ein spezifisches Merkmal der realen Demokratie ist').
62 Ibid., p. 88.
63 Cf. ibid., p. 82.
64 By that, I do not mean to neglect or underestimate Kelsen's harsh criticisms of Smend, whose theory he considered in a dedicated essay entitled, *Der Staat als Integration*, Wien: Springer 1930. However, I merely mean to suggest that, with Schmitt, there are some similarities beyond the seemingly radically different theoretical and political positions. In particular, what is striking is the similarity between the symbolic role accorded to the head of State, by Kelsen, in the *Allgemeine Staatslehre*, and the notion of 'personal integration' in Smend's *Verfassung und Verfassungsrecht*, München-Leipzig: Duncker & Humblot, 1928. For further consideration of Kelsen's criticism of Smend, see A. Scalone, 'Kelsen critico di Smend', *Diritto e cultura* (1999), 1–2, 169–98, now in *L'ordine precario*, op. cit., pp. 171–208.
65 Kelsen, *Allgemeine Staatslehre*, op. cit., p. 305 ('In demselben Maße, als die Rechtstheorie auf der Erkenntnis bestehen muß, das man nur den Normen, nicht aber dem die Normen setzenden Menschen, unterworfen, d.h. gehorsampflichtig ist, in eben demselben Maße scheint die große Menge der Menschen, weil abstraktem Denken abgeneigt, eines sinnlich wahrnehmbaren Autoritätssymboles bedürftig. In diesem Symbolfunktion liegt mehr als in allen anderen die Bedeutung des Institutes eines

Satatsoberhauptes'). Paradoxically, given the particularly harsh controversy between the two jurists concerning the President of the *Reich*, Kelsen, here, appears to agree with some Schmittian arguments. This perhaps indicates how difficult it is, even for Kelsen's rigorously immanent and formalized thoughts, to completely renounce the necessity for the idea of a representative person, which is one of the most typical features of the modern conception of politics. On the controversy between Schmitt and Kelsen concerning the President of the *Reich*, see my *L'ordine precario*, op. cit., pp. 135-70 and the bibliography therein.

66 Ibid., p. 315. For a more detailed analysis of the concept of representation in Kelsen and Leibholz, see A. Scalone, 'Gerhard Leibholz e Hans Kelsen sul principio rappresentativo', in Gruppo di ricerca sui concetti politici, *Concordia discors: Scritti in onore di Giuseppe Duso*, Padova: Padova University Press, 2012, pp. 179-95.

67 Ibid., p. 314 ('Rechtspolitisch ist die Unabhängigkeit des Parlaments vom Volk durch mannigfache Gründe zu rechtfertigen, die im wesentlichen auf die sozialtechnischen Vorteile der Arbeitsteilung hinauslaufen').

68 Kelsen, *Wesen und Wert*, op. cit., p. 20 ('Daß das isolierte Individuum politisch überhaupt keine existenz hat, da es keinen wirklichen Einfluß auf die Staaatswillensbildung gewinnen kann, [. . .] das ist offenkundig').

69 Kelsen, *Allgemeine Staatslehre*, op. cit., p. 315 ('Das ganze Wolk aber ist stumm').

70 H. Triepel *Die Staatsverfassung und die politischen Parteien*, Berlin: Liebmann, 1927.

71 Cf. ibid., p. 25.

72 Cf. ibid., pp. 19-20.

73 Cf. ibid., p. 31.

74 Cf. ibid., pp. 36-37.

75 Kelsen, *Wesen und Wert der Demokratie*, op. cit., pp. 107-8.

76 Cf. ibid., p. 109; Triepel, *Die Staatsverfassung*, op. cit., pp. 15-16.

77 Kelsen, *Wesen und Wert*, op. cit., p. 112.

78 Compare, for example, M. Weber, 'The Nation State and Economic Policy', in *Political Writings*, op. cit., pp. 16-17, 'For us the nation state is not something vague, as some believe, is elevated ever higher, the more its nature is shrouded in mystical obscurity. Rather, it is the worldly organization of the nation's power. In this nation state the ultimate criterion for economic policy, as for all others, is in our view "reason of state"' ('Und der *Nationalstaat* ist uns nicht ein unbestimmtes etwas, welches man um so höher zu stellen glaubt, je mehr man sein Wesen in mystisches Dunkel hüllt, sondern die weltliche Machtorganisation der Nation, und in diesem Natrionalstaat ist für uns der letzte Wertmaßstab auch der volkswirtschaftlichen Betrachtung die *Staatsräson*', Weber, *Gesammelte politische Schriften*, op. cit., p. 14). On this topic, see A. Scalone, *Rappresentanza politica e rappresentanza degli interessi*, op. cit., pp. 66-69.

79 Compare H. Kelsen, *Das Problem der Souveranität und die Theorie des Völkerrechtes: Beitrag zu einer reinen Rechtslehre*, Tübingen: J.C.B. Mohr (Paul Siebeck), 1920; A. Carrino, *Presentazione* to the Italian translation of Kelsen's book, Milano: Giuffré 1989, pp. V-XLVI.

80 See. H. Kelsen, *Österreichisches Staatsrecht: Ein Grundriss entwicklungsgeschichtlich dargestellt Österreichisches Staatsrecht*, Tübingen: J.C.B. Mohr (Paul Siebeck), 1923, p. 164, 'The fact that it is spoken of "law" and not of "power", as usual, was consciously done to refuse the "power-terminology". For this reason the Constitution in general does not even speak of legislative, executive, judicial power etc [. . .] but of legislation, execution, jurisdiction' ('Daß von "Recht" und nicht, wie üblich, von "Gewalt" gesprochen ist, geschah in bewußter Ablehnung der "Gewalt" terminologie. Daher denn auch die Verfassung nicht von gesetzgebender, vollzihender, richterlicher "Gewalt" usw., sondern von Gesetzgebung, Vollziehung, Gerichtsbarkeit usw. Spricht').

81 Compare Kelsen, *Allgemeine Staatslehre*, op. cit., pp. 164-225, H. Kelsen, 'Die

Bundesexekution: Ein Beitrag zur Theorie und Praxis des Bundesstaates, unter besonderer Berücksichtigung der deutschen Reichs- und der österreichisches Bundes-Verfassung', in Z. Giacometti and D. Schindler (eds), *Festgabe für Frits Fleiner zum 60. Geburstag*, Tübingen: J.C.B. Mohr (Paul Siebeck), 1927, pp. 127–87. About the federalism in Kelsen's thought, compare O. Pfersmann, 'Hans Kelsen et la théorie de la centralization et de la decentralization: le cas de la supranationalité', *Revue d'Allemagne et des pays de langue allemande* (1996), avril-juin, esp. pp. 178–79; E. Wiederin, 'Kelsens Begriff des Bundesstaates', in S. L. Paulson and M. Stolleis (eds), *Hans Kelsen. Staatsrechtslehrer und Rechtstheoretiker des 20. Jahrhundert*, Tübingen: J.C.B. Mohr (Paul Siebeck), 2005, p. 242; O. Beaud, *Théorie de la Fédération*, Paris: Presses Universitaires de France, 2007, p. 146; A. Scalone, 'Federalismo e decentramento fra Schmitt e Kelsen', in G. Duso and A. Scalone (eds), *Come pensare il federalismo? Nuove categorie e trasformazioni costituzionali*, Monza: Polimetrica, 2010, pp. 233–52.

82 Compare Kelsen, *Allgemeine Staatslehre*, op. cit., pp. 199–200. On this topic, see Scalone, 'Federalismo e decentramento fra Schmitt e Kelsen', ibid., pp. 233–52.

83 Compare H. Kelsen, 'Die Bundesexekution. Ein Beitrag zur Theorie und Praxis des Bundesstaates, unter besonderer Berücksichtigung der deutschen Reichs- und der österreichischen Bundesverfassung', op. cit., pp. 127–87.

Chapter 2

Democracy within pluralism: Hans Kelsen on civil society and civic friendship

Elif Özmen

Introduction: the fact of pluralism and the problem of unity

Hans Kelsen's work is comprehensive: it reaches from the project of a 'pure' theory of law to a formal concept of law and State to an analysis of the epistemological requirements of political theories and systems, particularly of democracy. His work is in many respects original. Kelsen argues for a normativistic legal positivism, law without justice, a theory of the State without a State, democracy without *demos*, society without a common good or *Volkswille* – and he insists on the obligatory character of democratic decisions given an unavoidable value relativism. His work is entirely modern – it is post-metaphysical, post-traditional and, to paraphrase a term by Max Weber, *entzaubert*.[1] However, in the contemporary Anglo-American and German debates within political philosophy and philosophy of law, it plays, at most, a marginal role. This is regrettable, particularly because Kelsen's defence of democracy is based on a radically pluralistic conception of society.

The character of this defence represents a genuine alternative to predominant perspectives in contemporary political theory. Pluralism is conventionally seen as a political, social and even moral problem since it leads to a fragmentation of values, erosion of the substance of civil society and dissolution of social bonds. Contemporary political philosophy is increasingly challenged by the problem of the vitality and stability of liberal and pluralistic democracies. The main question here concerns the willingness of citizens to endorse the political, legal and social norms that they hypothetically have good reasons to consent to. Are the means of law and force adequate to guarantee not only political, but also social stability and unity? Is public agreement, or at least some shared values, needed – despite the factual heterogeneity and the pluralism of beliefs, values, conceptions of the good and of ways of life in democracies? Are civic or even friendship-like relations necessary or constitutive for a legitimate, stable and ethical democratic society? If we answer these questions in the affirmative, what are the sources of the community's shared norms and commitments if adherence to the law alone is not sufficient, and civic virtues and affirmative political identification are necessary but, at the same time, cannot be imposed?

These questions play a major role in the work of John Rawls – probably the most influential philosophical defender of constitutional liberal democracy during the last 40 years. In the 1980s, they led to a *consensual turn* in his thinking. In *A Theory of Justice* from 1971, Rawls presents a typical contractarian justification of a political order where self-interested individuals make rational choices. In his later justification of a *political (not metaphysical) liberalism*, the novel idea of an overlapping consensus is added.[2] According to Rawls himself, it was 'a serious internal problem that forced those changes':[3]

> Now the serious problem is this. A modern democratic society is characterized not simply by a pluralism of comprehensive religious, philosophical, and moral doctrines but by a pluralism of incompatible yet reasonable comprehensive doctrines. No one of these doctrines is affirmed by citizens generally.[4]

This *fact of pluralism* constitutes a *stability problem*, especially for societies in which the equal freedom of its members is superior to questions of social cohesion or collective identity. The question of what the citizens have in common, despite all of their differences, becomes particularly pressing in these societies:

> How is it possible that there may exist over time a stable and just society of free and equal citizens profoundly divided by reasonable though incompatible religious, philosophical, and moral doctrines? Put another way: How is it possible that deeply opposed though reasonable comprehensive doctrines may live together and all affirm the political conception of a constitutional regime?[5]

The core of the problem is captured in the formulations 'to live together' and 'to affirm'. For the later Rawls, the abstract philosophical justification of a well-ordered society is not as important as the conditions for its realization. Hence, 'the point of the idea of an overlapping consensus on a political conception is to show how, despite a diversity of doctrines, convergence on a political conception of justice may be achieved and social unity sustained in long-run equilibrium.'[6]

Social unity and sustainability via factual consensus within a liberal framework of justice is Rawls' proposed solution for the problem of stability that arises from the fact of pluralism. For others, namely the proponents of communitarianism and civic republicanism, this political, not metaphysical, but still liberal approach is far too thin to sustain a democratic polity.[7] For creating unity and cohesion within a pluralistic society, no 'principles of justice' or other abstract and theoretical concepts are required; rather, what is necessary are concrete concepts and activities of civic importance, i.e. shared values and purposes, common goods and civic virtues such as solidarity, fraternity, sociability, trust and deep citizenship.[8]

During the course of the debate about the socio-moral conditions for democracy, the notions of *civil society* and *civic* or *political friendship* have also become prominent. The concept of civil society originated from the non-governmental structures of solidarity and communication within dissident and democracy movements in Central and East European socialist States, which supported the revolutions of the 1990s.[9] However, it is not a new insight that there is – and has to be – a form of *civic* engagement between State, market and one's own family in order for the public spirit and community to flourish. It is already central to ancient political philosophy, where the notion of *philia politike* was developed. The current renaissance of this Aristotelian notion in political philosophy is not obvious,[10] because it is based on a concept of associational membership that assumes a common ground of all citizens – a homogenous community of equal people – and not a pluralism of incompatible 'deeply opposed though reasonable comprehensive doctrines',[11] as claimed by Rawls and most contemporary political philosophers.

In order to situate Hans Kelsen's theory of democracy within this discussion, on the presupposition of pluralism and the alleged problem of stability, I begin by explaining two contrasting conceptions of the relation between the individual and the State and community. This enables an understanding of the idea of political friendship as a source of solidarity (second section). Then, I present Kelsen's theory of democracy in relation to its epistemological, ontological and ethical assumptions. The task of demythologizing the concepts of the State, authoritative power and absolute political values places Kelsen's political theory in the tradition of individualism, proceduralism and ethos-free politics that underlie the modern concept of associational membership (third section). Lastly, I return to the problem of social and political unity, stability and solidarity, and I clarify in which sense these questions are relevant for Kelsen. To conclude, I discuss whether his remarks on the 'democratic type of personality' and the 'principle of tolerance' can offer an alternative solution to the alleged serious internal problem of modern democratic societies (fourth section).

Two concepts of associational membership[12]

The concept of associational membership, which influenced contemporary communitarian and civic republican contributions to civil society and civic friendship, arises from the ancient idea of the political that is realized in citizenship. This can already be seen in the meaning of the Greek term *politikos* (civil) and *ta politika* (not so much 'affairs of the state', as it is often translated, but rather 'affairs and things that have to do with the public life in the polis'). Hence, something that only affects an individual person is a private matter. The political, public sphere is the place for discussing, negotiating, deciding and practising the concerns of *all* citizens. The difference between *oikos* and *polis* – between human and citizen – is not a matter of categories, however. These are two factually and spatially different aspects of human life, but they refer to each other and are both natural. Hence, neither a transformation from individual to political freedom, nor a metamorphosis of self-regarding individuals to other-regarding citizens is necessary. According to the normative anthropology of the *zoon politikon*, it is essential to humans – as social and political animals – that they want to live together with others, for their own good. So, there is no strict contrast between self-interest and common interest. This explains the normality of political order and political life. Its ontological priority is obvious for Aristotle (among others), 'Hence it is evident that the state is a creation of nature, and that man is by nature a political animal. And he who by nature and not by mere accident is without a state, is either a bad man or above humanity.'[13]

The good human life is only conceivable in community with others. Here, the purpose of humans and the State is realized in equal measure. *Politeia*, as a political order that fulfills the purpose of *ta politika*, and aims at the well-being of all, thus means 'just constitution' *and* 'citizenship'. The common striving for the good enables a common measure of the just and good human life. Furthermore, it has an integrative and binding effect: the community (*koinōnia*) of equal citizens is unified, harmonized and stabilized by virtuous practice. Part of this practice is the fact that the communal web of roles, relationships, expectations and duties – in which everyone is involved – is held together by justice and friendship, 'Friendship and justice seem [. . .] to be concerned with the same objects and exhibited between the same persons. For in every community there is thought to be some form of justice, and friendship too.'[14] Friendship provides a stronger bond between the members of the community than the commitment to the common, but abstract, good of justice. The more members of an association have in common, the more intense the friendship between them will be. According to various forms of *philia politike*, Aristotle distinguishes between constitutions. The best one is the polity – mutual friendship between equal, virtuous citizens – because it fulfills the purpose of *ta politika*. The worst one is tyranny – the tyrant has no friends.[15] Political friendship is thus constitutive of civil harmony, political unity, stability and justice. It is the social bond that determines the relationship between the citizens as well as the citizens' relationship to the political order:

> Friendship seems to hold states together, and lawgivers to care more for it than for justice; for unanimity seems to be something like friendship, and this they aim at most of all, and expel faction as their worst enemy; and when men are friends they have no need of justice, while when they are just they need friendship as well, and the truest form of justice is thought to be a friendly quality.[16]

For the second concept of associational membership, which was influential for modern theories of democracy and liberalism, the anthropology of the *zoon politikon* has ceased to have any normative power. The task is now to first find a justification for political order and a legitimization of political authority. They are not given by nature and are not ends in themselves, but are *artificial* and *useful* and are created by contracts and arrangements. The State, and its purpose, depends on a process of justification, for which the interests and agreements of the relevant individuals are decisive. Anarchy is, hence, a (hypothetical) option.

From a systematic point of view, the justification or constitution of the political order is rooted in a pre-political, pre-social and pre-ethical situation of decision making: the state of nature. The latter does not assume common values or common civil concerns of individuals, but, rather, irresolvable differences between their interests, expectations and values. These differences lead to serious conflicts that cannot be settled. Thomas Hobbes radically interprets them as a civil war, a *bellum omnium contra omnes*.[17] The question of how to respond to such escalating conflicts in a *civil*, i.e. non-violent, way, leads to the notion of the State. The central task of the State is to avoid an escalation of the differences between individuals, e.g. by making laws, and implementing them, by force if necessary. The point is to prevent each subject from pursuing her self-interest by means that would endanger the stability of the community. From this perspective, politics is not a virtue, but a technique for solving conflicts, through the use of law and its associated sanctions to maintain order. Politics does not create a virtue in the sense of a community following some ethos. Its central idea is a voluntary, rational agreement of individuals committing themselves to a co-operative community with mutual benefits. Notions of values are not part of this co-operation.

The State has to remain neutral and detached from what people consider to be good, right and desirable, how they want to live and what they take a good life to be. This normative individualism leads to a pluralism within society, in which the only common obligation for all citizens is to obey the political institutions and legal norms. This obligation claims to be valid independently of traditions, conventions, customs and commitments. At this point, the citizen's life seems to be split into two parts: the private and the public, or political, part. The political relationships between the citizens themselves, and between the citizens and the government, are solely legal in nature. The idea of a friendship between citizens plays no role here and fulfils no integrative function. The State's legitimate monopoly of force ensures that citizens obey the law, which creates a sufficiently strong bond between them – at least that is the hope.[18]

Hans Kelsen's project of demythologizing the political

Kelsen has made numerous critical remarks about ancient political philosophy. Plato's philosophy, in particular, represents the paradigm of a *philosophical absolutism* for Kelsen. This 'is the metaphysical view that there is an absolute reality, i.e., a reality that exists independently of human cognition. Hence its existence is beyond space and time, to which human cognition is restricted.'[19] This absolutism is the basis for an ontological, epistemological and ethical dualism which manifests itself in the opposition between transcendent reality and illusory irreality, the divine and the human, between knowledge and mere opinion, truth and falsehood, and between good and evil.[20] This dualism applies to Plato's (and every other absolutist) political theory, if political and juridical principles are directly inferred, objectified and legitimized from a metaphysical world of ideas (or nature, reason or God). It removes the sphere of politics from the sphere of human volitions, deliberations and judgments.[21] This interpretation also applies to Aristotle, since – according to Kelsen – Aristotle's ethics and politics are, in almost the same manner as Plato's, essentially connected with his metaphysics, and therefore with the ideas of a God and of one absolute good. He glorifies the contemplative life of man removed from all political activity and regards monarchy as the best possible constitution.[22] This blending of the spheres of metaphysics, ontology and religion and the spheres of law and politics is, according to Kelsen, characteristic of all 'metaphysico-religious and pseudo-rationalistic theories of justice' based on a justificatory absolutism and an absolutism of truth and values.[23]

The corresponding concept of associational membership, hence, has to appear questionable to Kelsen, the critic of philosophical absolutism, because it implies that man can only count as a political animal if one believes in a cosmological order, which comprises an essential 'human nature'. A categorical difference between private and public, individual and collective, private and public welfare does not exist if human life and fortune is only realized in a community. Politics is 'natural' only if it has a prior ontological reality, that is to say if 'the state is an entity different from the mass of individual human beings, a superindividual, somehow a collective reality, a mystic organism, and as such, a supreme authority, the realization of absolute value.'[24] What could be wrong with a political order that is legitimized by truth – that is, knowledge (*episteme*) of the absolute good and of categorical justice? What would be the reasons for doubting its legitimacy and for refusing to comply with it? Mere opinions (*doxa*) or individual interests would not count as good reasons, since those do not, by definition, belong to the *ta politika*. The virtue of friendship can only become political, within this concept of associational friendship, and develop its integrative power, by declaring the differences between the citizens, their opinions and interests, to be politically irrelevant.

Kelsen's political theory is the exact opposite of this conception and agrees with the central points of the second, modern conception of associational membership. This can already be seen by the author Kelsen has chosen as his starting point: Jean-Jacques Rousseau. For Kelsen, he is, despite all criticism, 'one of the most efficient ideologists of democracy', and Kelsen cites Rousseau's *Contrat Social* several times concerning what is considered as the *problème fondamental*, the problem of the best constitution – or the problem of democracy:

> To find a form of association which may defend and protect with the whole force of the community the person and the property of every associate, and by means of which each, coalescing with all, may nevertheless obey only himself, and remain free as before. Such is the fundamental problem of which the social contract furnishes the solution.[25]

First, for Rousseau as well as Kelsen, 'the state is a human artifact, made by men for men.[26] *Der Staat, das sind wir!*'[27] However, Kelsen departs more radically from the *étatist* notions of the State as a monistic unity, sovereign entity and *Naturkörper* than the classic liberals and contractarians. He demythologizes the State to a

Staatslehre ohne Staat,[28] in which the concept of State is reduced to a mere *form* of positive law, an *Einheit der Rechtsordnung*.

Second, for both Rousseau and Kelsen the fundamental problem with the State arises from the problem of justifying a concept of freedom that is reasonable and acceptable for individuals and, at the same time, appropriate for defining the social position of the individual within society. How can 'the freedom of anarchy become [. . .] the freedom of democracy?'[29] How can the political order and the State be justified to individuals who have an instinctive desire for freedom and equality? Is there an appropriate response to the question of someone who feels the burden of a foreign will, and thus asks, 'he is a man like me; we are equal; where is his right to dominate me?'[30] Kelsen shares Rousseau's critical distance towards contractualist and natural law traditions, but he explicitly does not agree with Rousseau's solution to the *problème fondamental*. He opposes the *aliénation totale* of the individual in order to form a body politic as a *moi commun*, and also the conception of the *volonté générale* as an expression of everyone's concurrent will and interests.

The reason for this criticism of Rousseau has affinities with Rawls' diagnosis of society: reasonable pluralism is an inevitable fact of modern societies. This means, in the end, that a *volonté générale* would only be possible in an autocracy. For Kelsen, a democratic constitution is hence the only constitution of liberty. Only under these conditions can the *Metamorphose der Freiheit* succeed. The meaning of freedom changes from an individual category to a social and political category. With this transformation, the original negation of any social order also changes, 'if we want to remain equal in social reality, we must allow ourselves to be dominated.'[31] Without a normative order regulating the behaviour of people, i.e. without the accepted domination of human over human through a *Rechtsordnung*, society and the State are not possible. But, and this is crucial, if 'domination is inevitable, if we cannot help being dominated, we want to be dominated by ourselves.'[32] That is the appealing promise of democracy: freedom in the sense of being subject only to one's own will and not that of others through: (a) specific methods of establishing social order (i.e. political self-determination via participation in procedures of creating and applying the social law); and (b) a specific type of government (i.e. government by the people, the rule of law, the guarantee of certain intellectual freedoms).

Third, the starting point of Kelsen's defence of democracy is not only the equal freedom of individuals, but also a notion of inevitable pluralism. If everyone is equally free, individual opinions and interests – and also differences and conflicts – are not only possible, but also very likely. To some extent, these conflicting interests are prior to concepts of justice, of a common good, of political obligation, and other political values and judgments. The reason is that the latter result from the former idea of:

> a social order protecting certain interests socially recognized by the majority as worthy of being protected. But which human interests are worthy of being satisfied and, especially, what is their proper order of rank? That is the

question which arises when conflicting interests exist, and it is with respect to the possible conflict of interests that justice within a social order is required. Where there is no conflict of interests, there is no need for justice.[33]

Hans Kelsen's project of demythologizing the political is most clearly expressed at this point: the rational reason for politics is not the *bonum commune*, justice, society (*Gesellschaft*), community, nature or some other superhuman standard; it is the interests of individuals:

> From the point of view of rational cognition, there are only interests of human beings and hence conflicts of interests. The solution of these conflicts can be brought about either by satisfying one interest at the expense of the other, or by a compromise between the conflicting interests.[34]

Democracy allows for such a compromise while coordinating plural and conflicting interests by means of deliberate and decisive procedures which secure the highest degree of political freedom that is possible within society. Thus, democracy allows for social peace within pluralism. Rawls sought to show how the fact of pluralism is compatible with the central tenets of the liberal theory of justice, Kelsen proceeds one step further. For him, pluralism is not only compatible with democracy, but is also the deeper reason for the priority of democracy over alternative political orders. His remarkably original claim is that arguments lead directly, although not compellingly, from pluralism to democracy, without any need for a specific theory of justice (e.g. a liberal interpretation of democracy).

One part of this argumentation is an epistemological and ethical relativism. For Kelsen, theories of justice are hopelessly subjective, because they are committed to the problem of values and value conflicts. In contrast to most proponents of the modern concept of associational membership, for Kelsen:

> this problem cannot be solved by means of rational cognition. The answer to these questions is a judgment of value, determined by emotional factors, and, therefore, subjective in character – valid only for the judging subject, and therefore relative only.[35]

The subjectivity of value judgments is due to an epistemological or *philosophical relativism*, which initially 'advocates the empirical doctrine that reality exists only within human cognition, and that, as the object of cognition, reality is relative to the knowing subject.'[36] For Kelsen, the world is constituted by the knowledge of human subjects. This anti-metaphysical position also:

> insists on a clear separation of reality and value and distinguishes between propositions about reality and genuine value judgments, which, in the last analysis, are not based on a rational cognition of reality, but on the emotional factors of human consciousness, on people's wishes and fears.[37]

The alleged relativism of judgments about values, namely justifications of justice, stands in stark contrast to the mainstream of contemporary, mainly Kantian and, therefore, universalistic political philosophy (of which John Rawls is the most prominent defender). At the same time, Kelsen's political theory seems to be more pertinent in one respect: by acknowledging the fact of pluralism, it abandons the demand for a non-relativistic, monist justification of political order. This does not, however, leave everything to political caprice or amoralism, because even a relativistic philosophy has a moral:

> The view that moral principles constitute only relative value does not mean that they constitute no value at all; it means that there is not one moral system, but that there are several different ones, and that, consequently, a choice must be made among them.[38]

One way of making authoritative choices is by means of democracy, i.e. constitutionalism, parliamentarianism, law-making, law-applying organs, elections and publicity.

Hence, epistemology can have practical consequences, since, for Kelsen, 'the antagonism between philosophical absolutism and philosophical relativism [...] is analogous to the antagonism between autocracy and democracy.'[39] The consequence of an epistemological relativism – understood politically – is democracy (although, because of philosophical relativism, this cannot be a necessary, deductively gained consequence). Democracy has to prove its worth under the conditions of relativism. The latter is the other aspect of pluralism, i.e. conflicting interests and opinions. What does that mean for the reality of democracy? What does it mean if democracy is now understood as a mere form or method? Kelsen's answer is:

> Because the permanent tension between majority and minority, government and opposition, results in the dialectical process so characteristic of the democratic formation of the will of the state, that one rightly may say: democracy is discussion. Consequently the will of the state, that is to say, the content of the legal order, may be the result of a compromise.[40]

The practice of democracy is discussion – and not insight or coming to know what is true without any argument. The progress of democracy is compromise – and not the exposure of truths. Therefore, the ethical precondition of democracy, its fundamental principle from which other principles such as tolerance, minority rights, freedom of speech and freedom of thought are deduced, 'is that everybody has to respect the political opinion of everybody else, since all are equal and free.'[41]

But how can a pluralist democracy, based on discussion and compromise instead of common values, shared conceptions of the good or, at least, a consensus about a liberal framework of justice, provide or reproduce the socio-moral resources for its stability and continued existence?

How to honour the claim of the *tu*

The analysis so far allows us to classify Kelsen's theory of democracy with respect to the contemporary debates about pluralism and civil society, political integration and civic friendship. His theory of State and law seems to provide no basis for the idea of political unity through the integration into civil society and the practices of civic virtues, i.e. political friendship. It is, rather, based on a conception of pluralism, social heterogeneity and reasonable advantageous co-operation. In a similar manner to State, law, sovereignty, *Wille, Volk* and *Einheit*, citizenship is reduced from a qualified collective identity to a merely *formal* concept:

> Is Citizenship a Necessary Institution? [...] The existence of the state is dependent upon the existence of individuals that are subject to its legal order, but not upon the existence of 'citizens' [...]. In a radical democracy the tendency to enlarge, as far as possible, the circle of those who possess political rights may have the result of granting these rights – under certain circumstances – to aliens.[42]

Owing to the fact that there cannot be a common interest (*volonté générale*) over and above individual and group interests, excluding even a consensus in the sense of *volonté de tous*[43] given the plurality of particular interests, only a legal order can create citizenship. For example, non-nationals may become citizens, despite their initial status being a synonym for people with whom one allegedly has nothing in common. Carl Schmitt's notorious claim that 'the specific political distinction [...] is that between friend and enemy'[44] does not apply to Kelsen's concept of the political. In Kelsen's democracy, there is no obligatory public norm for each citizen to comply with, there are no essential commonalities or 'friendly qualities' – and, therefore, there is no fundamental opposition to 'the other' (i.e. the enemy, stranger, the non-friend).

But since there are no absolute values and no political truths, the endeavour for considerateness, balance and co-operation is necessary in order to arrive at discussions and compromises under the conditions of democracy. Therefore, all citizens are willing to be respectful and co-operate with each other for rational reasons. The *democratic will*, formed according to the principle of majority, is thus not a dictate, but the result of a dialectics of contrasting and competing interests. The fact of pluralism – i.e. the heterogeneity of the population, the disagreements between citizens that have no thick values in common – entails that democracy has to be established by discussions, the exchange of arguments, deliberations and, one hopes, compromises.[45]

However, this means that actual democracy is not only a method or a political technique of problem-solving. It also presupposes a sufficiently large number of citizens who support the democratic structures by acting according to values and the democratic ethos, 'Because this type of government guarantees internal peace, it is preferred by [and one could add: is reliant on] the peace-loving, nonaggressive type of character.'[46] Furthermore, 'If democracy is a just form of government, it is so because it means freedom, and freedom means tolerance.'[47]

The idea of democratic justice with freedom, peace and tolerance, as its supreme political values, presupposes an idea of a *democratic type of personality*. On the one hand, and following the modern conception of associational membership, I do not have to be interested in my fellow citizens at all – it only suffices to be willing to co-operate in some respects. But, on the other hand, for Kelsen, this willingness is not the mere result of rational insight, but a question of personality. A democratic personality will be willing to co-operate, because she carried out the *Metamorphose der Freiheit*, and has acquired a stable socio-psychological identity, 'From a psychological point of view the synthesis of freedom and equality, the essential characteristic of democracy, means that the individual, the ego, wants freedom not only for himself but also for the others, for the *tu*.'[48] This reminds us – although Kelsen makes no corresponding reference – of the ancient notion of virtuous character. Kelsen even mentions 'feelings' and 'dispositions' (and 'friendship'!) that make up the democratic identity:

> The personality whose desire for freedom is modified by his feeling of equality recognizes himself in the other. He represents the altruistic type, for he does not experience the other as his enemy but is inclined to see in his fellow-man his friend. He is the sympathizing, peace-loving kind of man whose tendency toward aggression is diverted from its original direction against others to himself and thus is manifested in the tendency toward self-criticism and increased disposition of a feeling of guilt and a strong consciousness of responsibility.[49]

Modern, disenchanted democracies can and have to flourish without absolute values, shared ideals, collective conceptions of the good or civic friendship. This is the consequence of refuting absolutism in philosophy or politics. Another consequence is the intimate connection between – perhaps even the dependency of – the prosperity and vitality of democracies and a majority of democratically minded and democratically deliberating and negotiating citizens. The question of how to honour the claim of the *tu* is not a question of philosophical justification or scientific explanation, but of individual voluntary consent to democratic values:

> The ideal of freedom – as any social ideal – is from the point of view of political science only a relative ideal. But it may be from the point of view of emotional evaluation the highest, the supreme, ideal of an individual, a value which the individual prefers to any other value conflicting with the former.[50]

For Kelsen, this affirmative attitude is the *Gefühlston* (emotional tone) above the everyday noise of arguing and compromising that guarantees the stability and vitality of democracy within pluralism.

Notes

1 M. Weber, *Science as a Vocation*, London: Unwin Hyman, 1989, pp. 3–31, '[The intellectual rationalization through science means] the knowledge or the belief that, *if one only wanted to*, one *could* find out at any time; that there are in principle no *mysterious, incalculable powers* at work, but rather that one could in principle master everything through *calculation*. But that means the disenchantment of the world', p. 13.
2 See J. Rawls, *A Theory of Justice*, Cambridge, MA: Harvard University Press, 1971, part I; J. Rawls, *Political Liberalism*, New York: Columbia University Press, 1993, lecture IV.
3 Rawls, *Political Liberalism*, ibid., p. xxx.
4 Ibid., p. xvi.
5 Ibid., p. xviii.
6 J. Rawls, 'The Idea of an Overlapping Consensus', in S. Freeman (ed.), *John Rawls: Collected Papers*, Cambridge, MA: Harvard University Press, 2001, p. 426.
7 For an overview, see M. Van Gelderen and Q. Skinner (eds), *Republicanism*, Cambridge: Cambridge University Press, 2002; D. Casassas and J. De Wispelaere, *Republicanism*, New York: Continuum, 2012; D. Bell, *Communitarianism and Its Critics*, Oxford: Clarendon Press, 1993; H. Tam, *Communitarianism: A New Agenda for Politics and Citizenship*, Basingstoke: Macmillan, 1998; A. Etzioni (ed), *The Essential Communitarian Reader*, Lanham: Rowman & Littlefield, 1998.
8 For such normative foundations of liberalism, see N. Rosenblum (ed), *Liberalism and the Moral Life*, Cambridge, MA: Harvard University Press, 1989; St. Macedo, *Liberal Virtues: Citizenship, Virtue, and Community in Liberal Constitutionalism*, Oxford: Oxford University Press, 1990; W. Galston, *Liberal Purposes: Goods, Virtues, and Diversity in the Liberal State*, Cambridge: Cambridge University Press, 1991; P. Berkowitz, *Virtues and the Making of Modern Liberalism*, Princeton: Princeton University Press, 1999.
9 See J. Keane (ed), *Civil Society and the State*, London: Verso, 1988; J. L. Cohen and A. Arato, *Civil Society and Political Theory*, Cambridge, MA: MIT Press, 1992; J. Keane, *Civil Society: Old Images, New Visions*, Stanford: Stanford University Press, 1998; C. Elliott (ed), *Civil Society and Democracy*, Oxford: Oxford University Press, 2006.
10 See M. Friedman, 'Dislocating the Community', *Ethics* (1989), 99, 275–90; J. Schall, 'Friendship and Political Theory', *Review of Metaphysics* (1996), 50, 121–41; D. Brink, 'Eudaimonism, Love, and Friendship, and Political Community', *Social Philosophy and Policy* (1999), 16, 252–89; J. L. Jenkins, 'The Advantages of Civic Friendship', *Journal of Philosophical Research* (1999), 24, 459–71; D. Kahane, 'Diversity, Solidarity and Civic Friendship', *The Journal of Political Philosophy* (1999), 7, 267–86; G. Zanetti, *Political Friendship and the Good Life: Two Liberal Arguments against Perfectionism*, The Hague: Kluwer, 2002; J. Grunebaum, *Friendship: Liberty, Equality, and Utility*, Albany: State University of New York Press, 2003; E. Velásquez, *Love and Friendship: Rethinking Politics and Affection in Modern Times*, Lanham: Lexington Books, 2003; and S. Schwarzenbach, *On Civic Friendship: Including Women in the State*, New York: Columbia University Press, 2009.
11 Rawls, *Political Liberalism*, op. cit., p. xviii.
12 For detailed illustrations of these concepts, see my *Politische Philosophie. Eine Einführung*, Hamburg: Junius, 2013, ch. 2.
13 Aristotle, *Politics*, in J. Barnes (ed), *The Complete Works of Aristotle*, vol. 2, Princeton: Princeton University Press, 1984, p. 1253a.
14 Aristotle, *Nicomachean Ethics*, in Barnes (ed), *The Complete Works of Aristotle*, vol. 2, ibid., book VIII. p. 1159b.
15 Ibid., book VIII, pp. 1160b–61b.
16 Ibid., book VIII, p. 1155a. For Aristotle's concept of friendship, see M. Pakaluk, *The Nicomachean Ethics: Books VIII and IX*, Oxford: Oxford University Press, 1998.

17 T. Hobbes, *Leviathan*, R. Tuck (ed), Cambridge: Cambridge University Press, 1991, p. 87, 'And therefore if any two men desire the same thing, which nevertheless they cannot both enjoy, they become enemies; and in the way to their End, endeavour to destroy, or subdue one another.'
18 For a critical evaluation of ethical and political concepts of friendship, see my 'Freundschaft', in P. Kolmer and A. Wildfeuer (eds), *Neues Handbuch philosophischer Grundbegriffe*, Freiburg: Karl Alber, 2011, pp. 833–41.
19 H. Kelsen, 'Foundations of Democracy', *Ethics* (1955), 66, 1–101, p. 16.
20 See H. Kelsen, 'Platonic Justice', in H. Kelsen, *What is Justice? Justice, Law, and Politics in the Mirror of Science: Collected Essays*, Berkeley: University of California Press, 1960, pp. 82–109.
21 H. Kelsen, 'The Idea of Natural Law', in O. Weinberger (ed), *Hans Kelsen. Essays in Legal and Moral Philosophy*, Dordrecht/Boston: Reidel, 1973, pp. 27–60, pp. 28/29, 'By a "natural" order we mean one which does not rest on a human and therefore inadequate will, an order which is not created "arbitrarily", but comes about "on its own", so to speak, from a basic fact somehow *objectively* given, and thus existing independently of man's subjective willing, though it can somehow be grasped and recognised by him; from a basic principle not originally produced by human understanding or will, yet capable of being reproduced thereby.'
22 For this extraordinary interpretation, see H. Kelsen, 'Aristotle's Doctrine of Justice', in Kelsen, *What is Justice?*, op. cit., pp. 110–36; and H. Kelsen, 'The Philosophy of Aristotle and the Hellenic-Macedonian Policy', *The International Journal of Ethics* (1937), 48, 1–64, p. 43, 'The political ideal of a virtue remote from all active share in political life, corresponds to monarchy alone. . . . God himself justifies the ideal of a nonpolitical life. Only here, where ethics and metaphysics meet in politics, do their central ideas, the pre-eminence of theoretical over practical virtue and the self-regarding Godhead resting in himself, show their real, i.e., their political, significance.'
23 For his critique of absolute justice as an irrational and empty ideal, see Kelsen, 'What is Justice?', in Kelsen, *What is Justice?*, op. cit., pp. 1–24.
24 Kelsen, 'Foundations of Democracy', op. cit., 33.
25 Ibid., 21; and J. J. Rousseau, *The Social Contract*, 1762, book I, ch. 6, in J. J. Rousseau, *The Social Contract and Other Later Political Writings*, V. Gourevitch (trans and ed), Cambridge: Cambridge University Press, 1997, p. 49ff. For more on Rousseau's fundamental problem, see my 'Bürgerschaft und Freundschaft. Über eine mögliche Lösung des *problème fondamental*', *Jahrbuch für Recht und Ethik* (2012), 20, 119–37.
26 H. Kelsen, 'God and the State', in O. Weinberger (ed), *Hans Kelsen. Essays in Legal and Moral Philosophy*, Dordrecht: Reidel, 1973, pp. 61–82, p. 81.
27 H. Kelsen, *Staatsform und Weltanschauung*, Tübingen: Mohr Siebeck, 1933, p. 23; H. Kelsen, 'State-Form and World-Outlook', in Weinberger (ed), *Hans Kelsen. Essays in Legal and Moral Philosophy*, ibid., pp. 95–113, p. 108, 'The political theory of this type of person can be summed up in the words: "*l'état, c'est nous*".'
28 H. Kelsen, *Der soziologische und der juristische Staatsbegriff. Kritische Untersuchung des Verhältnisses von Staat und Recht*, Aalen: Scientia, 1981, p. 208.
29 Kelsen, 'Foundations of Democracy', op. cit., 21.
30 For Kelsen 'it is nature itself which in the quest of freedom rebels against society', ibid., 18.
31 Ibid.
32 Ibid., 19.
33 Kelsen, 'What is Justice?' op. cit., 4.
34 Ibid., 21f.
35 Ibid., 4.
36 H. Kelsen, 'Foundations of Democracy', op. cit., 16.

37 Ibid., 17. For a critical account of these relativistic principles, see J. Njarup, 'Kelsen's Theory of Law and Philosophy of Justice', in R. Tur and W. Twining (eds), *Essays on Kelsen*, Oxford: Clarendon Press, 1986, pp. 272–303; for a defence, see Ph. Pettit, 'Kelsen on Justice: A Charitable Reading', in ibid., pp. 305–18.
38 Kelsen, 'What is Justice?', op. cit., 22.
39 Kelsen, 'Foundations of Democracy', op. cit., 15. For him, this analogy is a structural and historical matter of fact.
40 Ibid., 28.
41 Ibid., 38f.
42 H. Kelsen, *General Theory of Law and State*, Cambridge, MA: Harvard University Press, 1945, p. 241. H. Kelsen, 'On the Essence and Value of Democracy', in A. Jacobson and B. Schlink (eds), *Weimar. A Jurisprudence of Crisis*, London: University of California Press, 2000, pp. 84–109, pp. 89/90, 'Democracy, according to its idea, is a form of state or society in which the will of the community, or, speaking non-metaphorically, the social order, is created by those subject to it: by the *people*. Democracy is the identity of the leader and the led, of the subject and object of rule; it means the rule of the people over the people. But what is this "people"? [. . .] Split by national, religious and economic conflicts, that unity is – according to sociological findings – more a bundle of groups than a coherent mass of one and the same aggregate state. Only in a *normative* sense one can speak of a unity. For the unity of the people as a concord of thought, feeling, and desire, as a solidarity of interests, is an ethical-political *postulate*.'
43 Ibid, p. 93, 'After all, the ideal of a collective interest *above* and beyond group interests and thus "supra-partisan" of a solidarity of interests of all members of the community irrespective of religion, nation, class, etc., is a metaphysical, or even better, a metapolitical illusion.'
44 C. Schmitt, *The Concept of the Political*, Chicago: University of Chicago Press, 2007, p. 26.
45 Kelsen, 'State-Form and World-Outlook', op. cit., 102, '[T]he entire parliamentary process, with its techniques of dialectics and contradiction, plea and contraplea, argument and counterargument, aims at achieving *compromise*. Therein lies the true significance of the majority principle in actual democracies [. . .] [B]y dividing the totality of those subject to norms into essentially only two groups, majority and minority, it creates the *possibility* of compromise in forming the collective will, after having prepared this final integration through the *pressure* to compromise, because compromise alone allows formation of a majority as well as of a minority. Compromise means deferring that which divides those who are to be united, in favor of that which unites them.'
46 Kelsen, 'Foundations of Democracy', op. cit., 28.
47 Kelsen, 'What is Justice?', op. cit., 23.
48 Kelsen, 'Foundations of Democracy', op. cit., 25.
49 Ibid., 26. See also Kelsen, 'State-Form and World-Outlook', op. cit., 100, 'It is the type of personality whose basic experience is the *Tat twam asi*, the man who, when he looks across at another, hears a voice within him saying: That is you. This kind of personality recognises himself again in the other, experiences the other a priori, not as something essentially alien, not as an enemy, but as an equal and therefore a friend.'
50 Kelsen, 'Foundations of Democracy', opt. cit., 4.

Part II

Hans Kelsen, Max Weber and the State

Chapter 3

Max Weber's conception of the State: the State as Anstalt and as *validated conception* with special reference to Kelsen's critique of Weber[1]

Hubert Treiber[2]

Für Ulrike

> The sociologist who makes the state the object of his attention must first of all realise: I do not see it in *my* world of social realities, and cannot conceive it as a unity with the concepts available to me [. . .].[3]

Introduction

In seeking to answer the question of what Max Weber understood by the term 'State', it is advisable to treat his 'Basic Sociological Concepts' as a key source.[4] One reason for this is that this text comes from the final period of his working life.[5] Another is that the lecture course that he gave during the summer semester of 1920 under the title '*Allgemeine Staatslehre und Politik (Staatssoxiologie)*' 'draws heavily on the related paragraphs from *Wirtschaft und Gesellschaft*, his major contribution to the *Grundriß der Sozialökonomik*, which Weber had shortly beforehand sent to the press.'[6] Kelsen's critique of Weber can be found in paragraph 27 of his text *Der Soziologische und der Juristische Staatsbegriff. Kritische Untersuchungen des Verhältnisses von Staat und Recht*.[7] The discussion of Max Weber's conception of the State presented here has a particular point, because it is only by precise presentation of Weber's conceptual definitions and elaborations that many of Kelsen's misunderstandings, or misinterpretations, can be dealt with. It will also become apparent that there are not only differences between Kelsen and Weber, but also points at which they converge.

Paragraph 17 of *Economy and Society*, part 1, states, 'A political *institutional organisation enterprise (Anstaltsbetrieb)* will be called a *State* to the extent that its administrative staff can successfully exercise a monopoly of legitimate physical force in the execution of its orders.'[8] The most important aspects of Weber's concept of the State can be opened up through this definition; above all it prompts a thorough discussion of the (logical) conceptual architecture developed in the 'Basic Sociological Concepts' which culminates in this passage. It will become evident that Weber makes use of established legal concepts such as *Verband* or *Anstalt*, and in this regard fulfils his announcement in the 1913 essay that sociology 'has to make use of precise legal expressions' and lend them a different meaning.[9] Thus Weber himself stated that some of his key definitions relate to legal concepts. The question, therefore, becomes the degree to which sociological terminology not only adopted the shells of legal concepts, but in assuming legalistic expressions also took on their related substantive meanings.

At the same time, it will also become evident that 'the isolated individual and his action is the prime unit'[10] of this conceptual architecture, articulating the intent of an interpretative sociology to be 'a science that seeks interpretative understanding of social action, and *hence* causal explanation of the course and effects of such action.'[11] Weber conceives one of sociology's tasks to be the treatment of a collective concept such as 'the State' 'as a complex arising from the specific interaction of men',[12] 'reducible to "action that can be understood", and that means exclusively: the action of participating individual persons [. . .].'[13] This raises the interesting question of how Weber himself approached this difficult task, given Thoma's view, citing Kelsen, that 'the sociologist, by penetrating to the level of individual behaviour and its motives as the sole reality of the social, dissolves the State and to some extent denies its existence.'[14] As will be demonstrated, the concept of validity (*Geltung*), a concept heavily overshadowed by neo-Kantianism, plays a not unimportant role in resolving this problem.

The State as 'Anstalt' (der Staat als 'Anstalt' – a structure of social formation along institutional lines ('anstaltsmäßige Vergesellschaftung'))

'Social relationship' as a fundamental category

As already noted, for Weber, interpretative sociology is 'a science which seeks interpretative understanding of the meaning of typical processes of social action (typical here meaning typically alike), and so providing causal explanation of the course taken and their effects.'[15] 'Of the course taken' refers primarily to the capacity of the actor to define a given situation, something of which an observer of this situation must also be capable.[16] 'And their effects' refers to both intended and unintended consequences of a concrete action, 'requiring above all the analysis of the consequences of the action of many actors and their knitting together into structures that either constrain but also facilitate further action.'[17]

Social action is, in turn, the intended meaning of an actor or actors 'related to the behaviour of others, and conduct so oriented.'[18] The orientation of behaviour which is referred to here depends on the predictability of behaviour, which, in turn, 'to a great extent depends on the possibility of being able to calculate behavioural regularities, hence that in a given situation a specific behaviour is uniformly repeated.'[19] This is made possible by the capacity to typify, and so presupposes a work of abstraction based upon 'the equivalence of behavioural processes in equivalent situations.'[20] Hence 'similarities, regularities and continuities in outlook (*Einstellung*) and action'[21] on the part of the actor can arise, which is particularly the case with action that is 'determined by interests', or which is 'purposively rational'.[22]

Within the conceptual architecture of the 'Basic Sociological Concepts' the definition of 'social relationship' (§ 3) has a special valency; defined as it is in terms of several actors reciprocally taking account of each other and so mutually orienting themselves. This is, first, because 'the quite central and dominating concept in the Basic Sociological Concepts is not ("mere") "social action" with its processes and effects, but rather "social relationship" (which does of course include "social action" as an attribute)'.[23] And, second, because that 'social construct', 'the State', in order 'to avoid an "essentialist" view', is connected to the existence of a social relationship.[24] In this respect 'social relationship' goes beyond action and social action, since now 'orientations and ultimately actions, plans for action, are co-ordinated',[25] through which structures of action (such as organization (*Verband*), State) can be formed.[26] The co-ordination of action can either just happen (through practice and custom), or be achieved through the 'rules' which are intended to be binding (convention, law). Weber also writes of 'maxims'[27] in this context. This refers, on the one hand, to § 4 of the 'Basic Sociological Concepts' involving practice (*Brauch*), custom (*Sitte*) and action 'conditioned by interests', as well as § 6 dealing with convention and law.[28] Behind these last two regularities in behaviour there is hidden a 'rule' (*Regel*) intended to be binding, whose observation, according to Weber, is conditioned by the validation of a conception of a norm, '[. . .] the reason for this is not the "ideal validity" of a norm, but rather the empirical conception on the part of the actor that the norm "should be valid" for his behaviour.'[29] If the actors orient themselves to a 'conception (*Vorstellung*) of the existence of a legitimate order',[30] the valid order undergoes an 'inner acceptance', increasing its stability.[31] Weber calls the 'substantive meaning of a social relationship'[32] an order (*Ordnung*) if 'maxims' can be formulated to which actors orient themselves. If this actual orientation results because the maxims are perceived to be 'binding or exemplary' (*verbindlich oder vorbildlich*), then this order is *valid*. If this occurs alongside other motives which can be taken into consideration then the chance that actors really will orient themselves to this order is considerably increased. Weber makes these statements more explicit by going on to talk of 'the prestige of commitment (*Verbindlichkeit*) and exemplary character (*Vorbildlichkeit*)' and equates this with 'legitimacy'; and so the border between the validity of an order and the validity of a legitimate order is not especially clear cut.[33] By present day standards, the validity of a legitimate order means no more than an orientation to a legal order that has been legally established but is certainly open to modification, the legality of this legal order being accepted.[34] This 'belief in legality' is also supported by general cultural values, from:

> generally accepted belief(s) that the conditions of everyday life [. . .] are for the greater part rational in nature, i.e., that rational knowledge, creation and control are accessible human artefacts [and also from the] assurance [. . .]

that they function rationally in the sense of conforming to known rules, and not irrationally like the powers that the savage seeks to influence with his magic; that one can in principle at least 'count on' them, 'calculate' their behaviour, and that one can orient one's action to unambiguous expectations formed thereby.[35]

The actual behavioural regularities emerging there from (such as custom and practice), like the valid order (convention, law) but also valid legitimate orders[36] – all of these are, for Weber, actual conditions of social action or social relations,[37] given that he recognized the 'parallel validity of differing and mutually contradictory orders' within any possible social composite (*Gesellschaftsintegrat*).[38] These conditions are taught to a child during socialization, for example;[39] nonetheless, they determine action 'at quite different levels of consciousness.'[40] Weber is indeed convinced that 'the chance of legal coercion [. . .] has a very minor' impact upon conformity to norms.[41] On the one hand, the 'rules of co-ordination' ('orders') presented are internalized, suppressing their coercive character, while, on the other hand, external coercion remains very real for many; as when the actor is confronted with the requirements of 'role norms' and discovers in this way that demands are being made of him that apply to others in similar positions (so that there is a clear moment of de-individualization).

However, before we pursue Weber's conceptual architecture relating to *Verband*, *Anstalt* and *Staat* any further, we need to consider in greater detail his concept of validation (*Geltungsbegriff*).

On Weber's concept of validation[42]

If one puts together the various statements on validation that we can find in the 'Basic Sociological Categories',[43] the Essay on Categories,[44] the Critique of Stammler[45] and also the fragment 'The Economy and Social Orders',[46] then it becomes plain that Weber is not entirely consistent. As a rule, he does not simply establish the fact of observed behavioural regularities, but, instead, places emphasis upon the way that in the *heads* of the actors (involved in a social relation) there exists an empirically ascertainable *idea* (*Vorstellung*) of the binding nature of an established (legal) order,[47] whereby the chance of an *actual orientation* to this order arises. If this is, in fact, the case then there is also an increased chance that this order will be respected. Insofar as the substantive meaning of social relations can be expressed in 'maxims',[48] then Weber talks in terms of 'orders' (*Ordnungen*), as has already been noted. If the actors in question perceive this order as 'binding or exemplary', then this order is *valid*. If, on the other hand, the existing idea of such a binding and exemplary order in the heads of the actors is supplemented by the additional value of prestige – and the relevant text in § 5 of the 'Basic Sociological Categories' can certainly be read this way – then this additive[49] lends the order the quality of a (valid) legitimate order. What is nonetheless decisive for Weber is that the fact of 'validation' is decided by 'the fact of an "orientation" of an actor to an order and not through its "observance"'.⁵⁰ As will be shown below, this distinction underpins a very consequential difference with respect to Kelsen.

The use of the term 'exemplary' (*vorbildlich*) seems to come from Rickert, who understood this to be an evaluative concept (*Wertbegriff*), 'the concept of something good to which a value was attached.'⁵¹ The path upon which Weber set out, making the 'idea of a norm' into the 'actual determining basis of real [regular] human action',⁵² brings to mind similar thoughts in Windelband first sketched in 1882, according to Fritz Loos,⁵³ in his text on 'norms and natural laws' which can be found in his *Präludien*.⁵⁴ The outlines of similar thoughts can be detected in Windelband's *Habilitationsschrift, On the Certainty of Knowledge*⁵⁵ (1873), in the context of the normative theory of truth that he sketches there. There, Windelband states that 'the logical law [. . .] like the ethical law, is a maxim, where in the latter one acts correctly, in the former case, where one should think correctly, without the involvement of any compulsion of the sort normal for natural laws, where one has to really act correctly, or really think correctly.'⁵⁶ In his essay 'Norms and Natural Laws' Windelband elaborates upon this, 'that logical and ethical norms can become determinants of ideational connections and decision-making in the purposively-active, voluntaristically thinking and consciously striving individual.'⁵⁷ Further, Windelband also speaks in the context of the 'consciousness of an obligation', or of the 'idea of an obligation' which has a lasting impact upon the logical and ethical norms that function as 'determinants', increasing the degree to which they are observed:

> For the idea of such a norm brings with it a feeling that the real process, whether of thinking or wanting (*Wollen*), should be formed in its image. Quite obviously there is associated with the emergent consciousness of a norm a form of psychological compulsion that it be observed. [. . .] Whoever recognises a norm as such is convinced that he, like everyone else, should act in conformity with it. Since the norm involves a sense of the obvious (*Evidenz*), once anyone has clearly and vitally made this norm conscious it necessarily becomes applicable (*geltend*) to them; and so every logical and ethical rule [in individual consciousness] becomes a determinant of thinking or striving.⁵⁸

This reminds one of Hellpach's 'feeling of commitment',⁵⁹ but also of Weber's procedure in lending the concept of validity a sense of value orientation.⁶⁰

The influence of Windelband on the conception of Weber's use of 'validity' is apparent when we examine more closely the associated meanings with which Weber endowed his concept. Windelband lent the concept a meaning which runs back to his teacher Hermann Lotze. His concept of validity rested upon an unusual interpretation of the Platonic idea, which interpretation was subsequently adopted by prominent representatives of the south-western school of neo-Kantianism (Windelband and Rickert). We need then to consider Lotze, because, for Weber, the idea of the binding nature of an order for an actor is, on the one hand, a definitive reason that the order *should* be valid, while, on the other hand, it opens up the possibility of empirical validation, that is, a connection to reality. The following statement of Lotze can be paralleled in Weber:

> *Ideas*, to the extent we have and hold them, lend *reality* to the meaning of an event, they occur within us [. . .]; however its substantive content, insofar as we can consider it separately from the envisaged activity directed to this content, no longer happens, is not at all as things are, but remains *valid*.[61]

This is also a reason that for Weber *only* 'the fact of an action "being oriented" to an order' decides on its validity.[62]

We cannot here pursue a detailed genealogy of the concept of validity in the work of the most important representatives of German neo-Kantianism.[63] Instead, we will limit our discussion to Windelband, and in particular, how he dealt with the concept within the framework of his doctrine of judgment (*Urteilslehre*).[64] Windelband begins by distinguishing a ruling (*Urteil*) from the act of judgment (*Beurteilung*), not least because he seeks to make the process of passing judgment the object of philosophy, rendering it an evaluative science (*Wertwissenschaft*). While rulings relate to particular objects, the judgment aims at evaluations (*wertende Stellungnahmen*), in which not only cognitive aspects play a role.[65] Judgments are also ideational in character (*vorstellungsmäßigen Charakter*), since they dissect ideas or make connections between ideas. Windelband calls the general norm that guides the connection of ideas in a judgment a 'rule' (*Regel*) in the context of a wilful interpretation of Kant.[66] He regards those ideas to be 'true' that can be connected with each other with the aid of such a generally valid rule. According to Windelband, this is related to his discussion of general validity – in the domains of logic, ethics and aesthetics – and in no way involves an 'actual recognition', but rather an 'ought to be recognised'.[67] In this respect Sommerhäuser is quite right, 'What is valid is what ought to be recognised; it is not always realised as such, but always a stipulation. What is valid turns out to be what ought to be.'[68] Even when Weber uses another concept of rule[69] he still gives great emphasis in the concept of validity to this 'oughtness'.[70] If one considers that 'given maxims' are treated as 'binding or exemplary',[71] hence introducing a value rational component ('feeling obliged'), then this once again originates with Windelband and his doctrine of judgment. Windelband assumes that 'in the "ruling" there is, alongside the idea, also a form of value definition (*Wertbestimmung*) as a material moment.'[72] This is true both of negative and positive rulings (*affirmative Urteile*). Whoever subjectively considers a 'rule' to be 'binding or exemplary' is not only making an affirmative judgment, but rather attaches to this an evaluation (*wertende Stellungnahme*). Weber's concept of validity constantly involves an idea of commitment (*Verbindlichkeitsvorstellung*), whose 'oughtness' is reinforced by the value orientedness of the actor, and this is clearly expressed in affirmative judgment.

Particular 'social relations': *Verband, Anstalt, Staat*

Verband[73]

For Weber, an organization (*Verband*) is a 'social relationship which is externally closed or limited' in which 'the observance of its order is guaranteed by the behaviour of particular persons charged specifically with its implementation: by the behaviour of a managing head and, quite probably, of an administrative staff.'[74] Consequently, an organization has members, it may also have one or perhaps several orders (*Ordnungen*);[75] the observance of, or compliance with, some of those orders (not all) is in the hands of an administrative staff. This, in turn, entails that there could exist orders which are not controlled by an administrative staff. The existence of such an administrative staff is a characteristic which is easy to ascertain, and, when present, the existence of an organization is established. The presence of an organization therefore depends 'on the existence of the chance that the action of certain persons occurs and is directed to the execution of the organisation's orders [. . .]. In the absence of a staff or an individual performing action in the manner defined there is in our terminology just a "social relationship" and no "organisation" (*Verband*).'[76]

Weber distinguishes in this way an organization (*Verband*) from an association (*Verein*) and an *Anstalt*, both of which are characterized by rational statutory orders, but where membership of an association is a voluntary matter, while that of an *Anstalt* is compulsory. Since Weber characterizes the State as an enterprise formed as an *Anstalt*,[77] we need to address ourselves to this concept. This is also because the sociological concept of an *Anstalt*,[78] marked out by the imposition of a statutory order, is also the endpoint of a development that Weber summarized in his *Sociology of Law* in one sentence, 'From the charismatic revelation of new commandments there leads, via the imperium, the most direct route to the development of law formed through fixed and imposed statute.'[79] Since this developmental line is in § 2 of the *Sociology of Law*, also identified as a process of legal rationalization, the definition of the State presented in § 17 of the 'Basic Sociological Concepts' is directly related to Weber's theme of rationalization. The concept of an *Anstalt* is also subject to the methodological pronouncement[80] that precise legal concepts should be employed in the process of constructing sociological concepts, concepts which are, however, then given a different meaning.[81] Since Weber, even if with a degree of distortion, treats the development of the English State from a sociological perspective in terms of the *Anstalt* model, then we can treat this as initial support for the claim that 'Weber was convinced that he had found in the form of the *Anstalt* the decisive criterion of State formation.'[82]

The origin of the sociological conception of **Anstalt**

The model for Weber's sociological concept of *Anstalt* is the legal concept that he briefly introduces in § 2 of the *Sociology of Law*,[83] and about which he says that 'from the purely legal point of view, it was modern theory that first made this complete.'[84] He alludes here to the theory of the State as an *Anstalt*, whose development during the second half of the nineteenth century ran more or less chronologically in parallel with that of the conception of the State as a legal person from Gerber to Laband. Along the way, there was a great deal of argument, and the *Anstalt* conception of the State was more or less completed by Otto Mayer in debate with Laband. Of course, there is more agreement than disagreement between Mayer and Laband. This applies, for instance, to the view that the State's existence precedes that of the law, as well as to the position (disputed by Kelsen) that follows from this, that the State limits itself, not least given the view that is of especial interest here, that the State represents 'with regard to its citizens an entirely autonomous apparatus.'[85]

There are clear affinities between Otto Mayer's characterization of an *Anstalt* – which it might be noted appeared in a *Festschrift* for Paul Laband – and Max Weber's sociological concept of an *Anstalt*, 'The term *Anstalt* really means no more than an enterprise that is intended to persist.'[86] The following passage from Mayer highlights just how close this was to Weber's sociological concept of the *Anstalt*:

> So that he might rule the land the Duke made suitable arrangements, putting material and personnel in systematic (*planmäßig*) order. That is an *Anstalt*. The people, the population, is the object of the work that they perform; quite possibly privileged members of this mass who made up the citizenry were able to suggest some small alterations to the running of this *Anstalt*; but that does not change anything. [. . .] And so the state is of course one great *Anstalt*! State power means the guidance of this *Anstalt*. For that you need both people and territory, for without these the great historical purpose of the *Anstalt* is inconceivable.[87]

These terms 'persistence', 'enterprise', 'territory' and also 'conduct of the *Anstalt* according to heteronymous acts of authority' – an aspect that has an 'ecclesiastical origin', as we shall soon see – enter either directly or indirectly into Weber's sociological concept of the *Anstalt*.[88]

Not only was Weber aware of the contemporary debate over the legal conception of an *Anstalt*, he also noted that materially this 'was of ecclesiastical origin', developed out of Canon Law.[89] The relevant source here is Otto von Gierke's *Genossenschaftsrecht*, especially volumes two and three of this multi-volume monument. Of especial importance is Gierke's 'Comprehensive Theory of Canon Law' (Landau), a critical conception requiring particular evidential support since it played a central part in his argument that there is 'continuity from the Germanic conception of law right up to the present.' This theory was used in support of the idea that:

> canonistic corporate doctrine had an intrinsically different foundation to that of the Germanic conception of the corporation (*Körperschaft*), or *Genossenschaft*,

for apart from anything else the foundation of the former concept derived from Christian universalism and not from the spirit of the Germanic peoples (*germanischer Volksgeist*).⁹⁰

The 'Comprehensive Theory of Canon Law' thus acquires a particular importance because Gierke's conception of a Germanic *Genossenschaft* could only be filled out in opposition to his theory of the Canonistic *Anstalt*. Moreover, this theoretical element is embedded within an all-encompassing developmental-historical perspective which starts out from the basic assumption that '*Herrschaft* and *Genossenschaft* originally represented mutually supportive and specifically Germanic legal structures.'⁹¹ This underlying assumption formed the starting point of a developmental process that ran from the Germanic tribes to the foundation of the German Empire in 1871, in which the two dichotomous principles found an accommodation in the reconciliation of the monarchical claim to rule and the civil insistence on independent self-administration. According to Gierke, this development unfolded in the tensions existing between the *Genossenschaft(sverband)* and the *Herrschaft(sverband)*, between *Körperschaft* and *Anstalt*, or in other words between (older) Germanic Law and Romano-Canonical Law. Canon Law here played a particularly decisive role:

> Canonistic doctrine transformed the concept of corporation into a concept of *Anstalt*, such that the legal personality of all the subjects defined by Canon Law, from the universal Church to the benefice of a cleric, was no longer founded on volition, but instead upon a heteronymous act of authority, in the case of the *ecclesia universalis*, on divine benefaction (*göttliche Stiftung*).⁹²

Gierke considered the Canonical concept of the *Anstalt* to be 'the model for the concept of temporal authority' (*Obrigkeitsbegriff*) so that, according to Landau, Gierke 'here partially anticipated Max Weber'.⁹³ Naturally, Landau does at the same time make clear that 'the medieval Canon Law sources lend little support'⁹⁴ to Gierke's view that 'the legal person in Canon Law was transpersonal', which his concept of *Anstalt* sought to capture in legal terms.

Anstalt *and* Staat

The sociological definition of an *Anstalt* that can be found in § 15 of the 'Basic Sociological Categories' – 'an *Anstalt* is an organisation (*Verband*) whose statutes can within a given domain be (relatively) successfully imposed upon all whose action has specified particular characteristics' – has features taken from the legal concept of an *Anstalt*. This is especially clear in the way that the *Anstalt*, as a form of sociation constituted through action, is characterized by rational statutory (legal) orders imposed upon those subordinated to the direction of the *Anstalt* (compulsory participants);⁹⁵ that is, they are subject to a heteronymous act of authority.⁹⁶ The use of the term 'imposition'⁹⁷ implies the compulsion also involved in rulership, but it is only in the definition of an *Anstalt* in the 1913 'Essay on Categories' that this idea of force and compulsion is stated explicitly by reference to an 'apparatus of compulsion'.[98] There, the use of *Oktroyierung* means that a particular group of persons (executive directors, administrative staff) proclaim a rational statutory order to which 'institutional inmates' (*Anstaltsgenossen*) orient themselves (through consent or '*Einverständnis*'). In practice, *Oktroyierung* presupposes power,[99] just as 'any compulsory power' is subject to the influence of the prevailing form of rule (*Herrschaft*),[100] which besides other motives of compliance also makes use of physical and psychic compulsion. It can above all count upon compliance (obedience) if those who do the obeying 'also subjectively regard the relationship of rule as "obligatory" for them' – what is called in the terminology of the 1913 'Essay on Categories' 'legitimacy-compliance' (*Legitimitäts-Einverständnis*).[101] In this respect, an *Anstalt* possessing powers of compulsion is also an 'organisation of rule' (*Herrschaftsverband*).[102] The characteristic of a (purposively) rational statutory order (or orders) also represents the termination of a process of development underlying Weber's rationalization principle. The conceptual distinctions that we encounter in the 1913 Essay (communal, compliant and societal action, or the action of organization and *Anstalt*),[103] like the conceptual architecture of the 'Basic Sociological Categories', represent a framework of logical relationships. But Weber also wished to make the point that the sociological basic concepts he used not only related to each other logically, but also according to a developmental history 'expressive of the degree to which its inherent social potential for rationalisation had been realised.'[104]

The administrative staff is also expressly referred to in the definition of the State with which this essay began. In a modern State, this is synonymous with the 'modern' (rational) bureaucracy, which Weber presents in the form of an ideal construct[105] in his 'structural-typological terminology' (Zingerle). It should be noted that this thought construct (*gedankliche Gebilde*) serves particular cognitive ends, and, hence, assumes the function of a cognitive instrument. Weber seeks in this manner to respond to a question thrown up in the 'Preface' (*Vorbemerkung*): why it is only in the Occident that cultural phenomena (such as rational bureaucracy, rational State, modern capitalism and so forth) first appeared, proceeding then, following the then plausible assumption, to advance ultimately to 'world domination'.[106] In the material part of the *Sociology of Religion* and of *Rulership*, Weber also makes use of this structural-typological terminology, which is bound up with a particular problem to which Zingerle has drawn attention, as has also Hermes:

> [. . .] On the one hand, in his methodological writings [as also in the 'Basic Sociological Concepts'] Weber elaborates his principles in terms of a theory of action, for this purpose reducing institutional moments to action-oriented analysis [. . .]; on the other hand, he nonetheless employs in his substantive studies structural-typological terminology which cannot be directly 'retranslated' in action-theoretical terms.[107]

We still lack a structural-typological 'retranslation' of the ideal-typical construct of the modern bureaucracy, but it would be possible to develop one if the joint action of those in bureaucracies, ordered hierarchically and subject to a division of labour, were broken down into role norms.[108]

It is plain that it is in the conception of an *Anstalt* that the *initial* outlines emerge of what Weber would mean by *Staat* and *Staatlichkeit* (so long as one does not omit Weber's rider: 'The *Anstalt* can in particular be a territorial organisation (*Gebietsverband*)'):[109]

> The concept of *Anstalt* developed in Continental Canon and common Roman Law clearly contains [major] components, which for an understanding of the rational State as a legal organisation requires a sociological theory of organisations oriented to the phenomena of rationalisation. (Compulsory membership, rational statutory orders, bureaucratic institutional organs with statutorily-regulated competences.)[110]

By explicitly identifying the requirement for an administrative staff in § 17, Weber refers to the definitions of an organization (*Verband*) and of the State.[111] This emphasizes that the members of the administrative staff are distinguished from the organizational leadership (the governors) by a particular inner disposition, and in so doing makes a link to basic assumptions of the sociology of rule (*Herrschaftssoziologie*).[112] This becomes quite plain if Weber's treatment of the *Sociology of Rule* is treated as a response to Hume's question (Popitz): why are the many governed by the few? According to Weber, the rule of the few over the many is based upon their superior organizational ability (which is expressed by the creation and use of an administrative staff) as well as in the ability to arouse and sustain a belief in the 'justness' (legitimacy) of their rule.

But if the sociological concept of *Anstalt* and its various features claims that it provides substantive meaning to a legal conceptual source now freed of its temporal context, we should recall that the proximity of the legal concept of *Anstalt*, originating in the nineteenth century to the Prussian-German constitutional monarchy is quite obvious. We can go back to Otto Mayer's characterization of the '*Anstalt "Staat"*' above:

> The monarch is 'the leader of this great *Anstalt*' and popular representation can only 'suggest some small alterations' in the conduct of the enterprise, without this having any lasting or fundamental impact upon the system. But it is precisely this *Anstalt* apparatus dominated by a monarch which in Laband's system equates the legal personality of the State with the monarchical possessor of State power. The manner in which, in Wilhelminian Germany, the State was identified with the bureaucracy is rendered particularly concrete in Mayer's description of the State as an *Anstalt*.[113]

As we have shown, in respect of 'imposition' and 'direction from above', Weber's sociological concept adopts important features of the legal concept of an *Anstalt*, recapitulating the everyday 'reality' of Prussian constitutional monarchy; and so

Weber's sociological concept of *Anstalt* has a striking proximity to a present 'reality',[114] so that the State appears to become incorporated in the monarchical and bureaucratic apparatus (the '*Anstalt* "state"').

An *Anstalt* equipped with compulsory powers is still a 'ruling organisation' (*Herrschaftsverband*),[115] characterized by the fact that its commands are complied with, not least because those who obey desire the same end as those who command.[116] Here, there is a striking similarity with the 'doctrine that begins with Gerber' that treats the State as a legal person, equipped with 'the power and will of the ruler, the state power to which its citizens are subordinate.'[117] According to Schönberger, 'the idea that command and compliance constituted the real central characteristic of public law (*Staatsrecht*)' could only then develop 'because the state was considered to be a bureaucratic apparatus separate from and external to its citizens',[118] something which did correspond with the actual state of affairs, but which on the other hand was certainly also an idea favoured by the legal concept of the *Anstalt* (in Otto Mayer). Hence, we cannot simply dismiss Hermes' assumption that the:

> centralised character of organisation and rule as constituted in politico-legal theory had a considerable influence on the structure of meaning in the parallel terminology of sociology. And precisely because Weber also imported from jurisprudence, along with the legal concept, the criteria of relevance for the constitutions of sociological objects.[119]

Here, only Laband will be called as a 'crown witness' for the way in which politico-legal theory presumed the centrality of rule, and also because of his importance to Weber; to this end we can draw upon some especially striking passages from his *Staatsrecht des Deutschen Reiches* (1876):

> Since von Gerber in his *Grundzügen* made the leading principle of *Staatsrecht* the idea that the peculiar substantive will of the state personality be considered to be 'ruling', and the power to rule over the state be called state power (*Staatsgewalt*), there have been any number of politico-legal texts which talked of rulership and the rights of the state to rule, it was not thought necessary to examine more closely what state rule meant.[120]

Laband himself proceeds to set about dealing with this alleged deficiency, 'Rule is the right to command free persons (and associations of the same) to perform actions, to desist from actions, to make services (*Leistungen*), and to compel their compliance therewith.'[121] Then stating, a few pages later, that 'to rulership there also belongs the authority to compel adherence to commands through the application of physical force.'[122] And if Laband, taking account of the multiplicity and constantly changing aims (tasks) that State power considered, and considers, itself called upon to perform, then believes it an impossibility to assemble all of these in one legal concept,[123] and so notes the one 'unchangeable and established' fact, that 'the state has the right to command free persons with coercive power',[124] this could have served as a model for Weber. In support of this we can cite Weber's dictum that, 'it is not possible to define a political organisation – not even the "state" – by listing the aims of its organisational action', together with the conclusion which was derived from this, that the consequence was that here only the means specific to the State – force – could be considered.[125] Accordingly, for Weber, a 'political *Anstaltsbetrieb*' will be called a State 'if, and to the extent that, its administrative staff can lay claim to a monopoly of legitimate physical force in the execution of its orders.'[126] Hence the 'monopoly of legitimate physical force' is the demarcation criterion between State and *Anstalt*, in other words, between a political organization (*politischer Verband*) and the State.[127]

With this criterion of demarcation, Weber once more emphasizes that the modern State involves the means to 'found the rule of man by man upon force',[128] it is a ruling organization (*Herrschaftsverband*) which those who are subordinated to its rule, to the extent that they accept the use of force, regard as legitimate.[129] Hermes has noted that Weber traced the monopoly of force and the capacity to enact statutes back to military charisma.[130] If both the monopoly of force and the capacity to enact statutes are available, the political organization becomes a State, capable of securing its orders through the use of legitimate force. This lends emphasis, on the one hand, to the way in which force creates order, but, on the other hand, any order which comes about and is guaranteed by force also has need of a limitation to the use of force.[131] The problem that arises here, the limitation of institutionalized force, was something of which Weber was also conscious, noting that '[. . .] there is "legitimate" force [. . .] only to the extent that the state order permits or prescribes it.'[132] To this extent, for Weber, the modern State is always a State based on the rule of law (*Rechtsstaat*).[133]

Weber's sociological 'concept of law' presumes that a (statutory) order is guaranteed externally by force, assisted by a staff capable of coercion.[134] According to Weber, rule (*Herrschaft*) consists of the 'factual existence of a power of command' plus actual compliance with such commands.[135] Since rule generally seeks legitimacy,[136] and rule based exclusively upon force (coercion) is very considerably less stable than rule that is inwardly accepted by those ruled, rule and law are categorically connected through legitimacy.[137] If the concept of rulership is not exhausted by the idea that a command be followed, but also requires that the ruled 'make the substance of the command, for its own sake, a maxim for their action',[138] accept it therefore as a 'valid norm', then this signals the general inner acceptance of the relationship of rule ('low-level legitimacy'). The use of this concept of maxim indicates, in addition, that the concepts with which we are here dealing (law, rule) are adapted to an empirical and sociological perspective, as is the concept of the 'idea of a norm' (*Normvorstellung*) and the sociological conception of validation in the 'Essay on Stammler',[139] and, also, in the textual fragment 'The Economy and its Orders'.[140] As Kelsen states,[141] for Weber, 'organisation' (*Verband*) and 'law' do not map seamlessly on to each other, they are, instead, 'mediated by the concept of rule'.[142] As has already been demonstrated, commands which make evident the exercise of rule can also be understood as 'maxims' in the sense of rules of action (*Handlungsregeln*) that are both binding and subjective,[143] rules that are, for Weber, 'factual determinants of real human action'[144] and so to this extent prove themselves to be 'valid norms'. These are legal norms if the chance of their validation is 'guaranteed' by the expectation that a sanctioning instance will intervene,[145] something upon which one can count if members are guided by the idea that the 'obligation' imposed upon them to act (secondary normativity)[146] is to be treated as binding. Hermes sums this up as follows, 'A political organisation (*politischer Verband*) is not only the empirical domain of validation of commands which are "taken" to be normative [i.e. rule/*Herrschaft*], but simultaneously the empirical domain in which compulsorily guaranteed norms [i.e. law] have effect.'[147] If one accepts this view, then it is possible to agree with Weber that 'an "organisation" (*Verband*) is the "bearer" (*Träger*) of, the support and medium for, the law.'[148] This should be understood as meaning that the rulership (*Herrschaft*) and law are not exclusively bound up with the modern State, but appeared long before as a historically demonstrable phenomenon – for instance in the form of 'numerous "legal communities" whose autonomies cross-cut with each other, among which political organisation – to the extent that it could at all be treated as such a unity – was only one such body.'[149] The concepts that Weber develops are intended to capture this particularity, including the fact that not all ordered organizations are legal in nature. The following two sections will examine the degree to which there are, even here, differences with Kelsen in respect of epistemological premises.

The State as validating idea (*der Staat als Geltungsvorstellung*)

So far, we have talked about the conceptual architecture of the 'Basic Sociological Concepts', finishing with the definition of the State in § 17. Weber thinks that there are very specific difficulties with the categories that he there introduces:

> It is a peculiarity not only of language, but also of our thinking, that the categories which deal with action present it as an enduring being, as a 'personified' form that is tangible or leads its own life. This is true, and especially true, for sociology. Concepts such as 'the state' [. . .] and others amount for sociology, quite generally, to categories for particular modes of mutual human action, and so it becomes the task of sociology to reduce such modes to 'intelligible' action, and that means without exception: to the action of the individual persons involved.[150]

Two lengthy passages – one in the 'Essay on Objectivity',[151] the other in the elaborations to the 'Basic Sociological Concepts'[152] – seem, at first glance, to provide an insight into what Weber understood by State in terms of this reduction of collective forms to the specific mutual action of persons. However, once we examine the passage from the 'Essay on Objectivity' more closely it becomes plain that this cannot here be of any assistance: Weber briefly discusses the enormous difficulties involved in constructing the State as an ideal type which takes account of the sometimes clear, sometimes diffuse syntheses of the ideas which contemporaries associate with the State, given the massively complex interconnection of diverse actions together with factual and legally ordered relationships, all of which are held together by 'belief in valid norms and relations of rule, or in norms and relations that are supposed to be valid.'[153] Weber also draws attention to the inherently 'hybrid' property of ideal types, 'They seek to be, or implicitly are, regular ideal types not only in the *logical* sense but also in a *practical* sense – they are exemplary types.'[154] And so we can only resort to the passage from *Economy and Society*, which can therefore be quoted at length:

> The interpretation of action has to acknowledge a fundamental and important fact: that the conceptions associated with a collective construct – whether drawn from everyday thought or derived from some specialized discipline, such as the law – have a meaning in the minds (heads) of real people (not just judges and officials, but also the wider 'public') as something which in part exists, and in part should exist, to which their action is *oriented*, and as such have a quite powerful, often dominating influence, for the manner in which the action of real people is performed. Above all, as conceptions of something that should become valid (*gelten soll*), or not. (A modern 'state' consists to a not inconsiderable extent of this form – as a complex of the specific interaction of people – because specific men and women orient their action in regard to their *conception* that the state exists in this form, or *should* exist in this form; that in other words, legally-oriented regulations of this kind *have validity* [. . .].)[155]

Weber turns here to what he had written about the sociological perspective in the 'Essay on Stammler' and the 'Essay on Categories':[156] if particular ideas or conceptions form in the heads of people ('as something which in part exists, and in part should exist'), there is the chance that they will orient themselves to these ideas, and so these ideas are to this extent 'valid'; there is the chance that they will act in accordance with these ideas (their chance of realization); and so, in sum, their action is causally determined in this way. The task of the sociological perspective is to establish not only whether there really are such ideas of validation in respect of the State, but also how widespread such ideas are.[157] Of course, there are problems with the investigation of ideas of validation. As regards the 'empirical validation' of legal norms whose guarantee is always external, this external perspective (observation) relates initially only to more or less regularly performed action to which one cannot without further qualification impute 'obligatoriness',[158] since the normative aspect of this as a conception of validity is something that the actor has hidden in his head. The outer view has to be complemented by the corresponding view from within, the meaning associated with the action displayed. According to Weber, this occurs by causal imputation (*kausale Zurechnung*), which is based upon experience and judgments of objective possibility. This calls for 'interpretative understanding', as is shown by the concept of validation itself, since it is, of course, aimed at the chance of orientation to an actually given norm or conception of obligation. In this regard, the concept of validation is jointly determined by a 'quite particular element internal to action' (*Handlungssinnenelement*), such that action 'in respect of this (causal) feature can only be inferred, not observed.'[159] This 'inference' or 'interpretation' is a construction in thought related to probable actions which excludes 'unreal causal contexts and connections' 'in order to penetrate to the real.'[160] Weber says of this, 'We practise a "dogmatics" of "meaning".'[161] To this extent, we can agree with Möller when he points out that Kelsen:

> did not accept epistemologically that the facts with which sociology deals are themselves constructions. Kelsen's distinction between causality as a category oriented to facts and imputation as a legal concept was not,[162] unlike Weber, carried on to the point at which the world of objects as conceived by the social sciences could be interpreted as one of constructs of social processes creative of meaning.[163]

When Weber states explicitly that 'legally-oriented regulations of this kind *have validity*', this demonstrates very particularly both proximity to, and disagreement with, Kelsen. Proximity, since both have the legal order in mind and both recognize the dualism of is and ought.[164] Disagreement, to the extent that, for Weber, this legal order (or the 'maxims' that can be imputed to it) is an idea present in the heads of real people as normatively valid and hence their action is possibly also influenced by it; while, for Kelsen, the State is identical to the legal order.[165] For Dreier:

> the identity of state and law follows quite necessarily from the epistemological premises: while it is a strict 'methodological demand' of the legalistic perspective that it presents everything in terms of the law, the state cannot appear to jurisprudence as a spatial and temporal phenomenon, as a causal structure; it is only a normativity, more: it is simply a normative order, to be understood as the 'perfect form of positive law'.[166]

The consequence of this is that Kelsen's theory of the State treats all State forms as the same thing, since, for him, 'every state is a state based upon the rule of law (*Rechtsstaat*).'[167] While, at first glance, this is a possibly alienating, if nonetheless consistent, perspective,[168] it is directed against the hypostatization of the State in terms of an organism, a view that Kelsen shared with Weber,[169] and also against Jellinek's two-sided theory[170] and the associated doctrine of the self-restraint of the State (the legal taming of Leviathan imposed by Leviathan itself).[171] Kelsen argues that Jellinek violates the 'requisites of normative argument' because his doctrine of self-restraint combines both a systematic and a historical approach and draws 'a legal conclusion from a historical observation.'[172] Weber proceeds differently, however, since he gives historical observation particular attention from two connected aspects. The first is that 'the struggle between (political or hierocratic) lords and those ranks with particular powers (nobles, priests, cities etc.) for the appropriation or expropriation of powers (*Herrengwalten*)' is quite evident. The second adopts a historico-developmental approach marked by a quite specific conception of history, characterized by a 'consciousness of contingency' that 'is expressed methodologically in ideal-typical concepts and developmental constructions, and which can conceptualize historical processes only as hypothetical causal progressions (objective possibilities) by applying rules derived from long experience to specific sections of reality.'[173] The development that this reveals serves as proof of the probability of the improbable: the formation and development of the modern State,[174] in which historical development, whose temporary 'endpoint' is the *Anstaltsstaat* with its imposed statutory order,[175] is at the same time marked out in § 2 of the *Sociology of Law* as a process of legal rationalization, directly connecting Weber's conceptualization of the State in terms of *Anstalt* to his axiom of rationalization.

If one takes a relatively early text of Kelsen – his essay 'Zur Soziologie des Rechts' which was published in 1912 in the *Archiv für Sozialwissenschaft und Sozialpolitik* – the distinction dealt with above is not apparent:

> A sociology of law will not be developed by investigating some particular social human behaviour in abstraction from all norms, but by taking the legal norms themselves as existential facts (*Seinstatsachen*), that is, by investigating the causes and effects of complex conceptions inhabiting the consciousness of men (*Vorstellungskomplexe*). From this standpoint – in my view, the only possible one for legal sociology – only that human behaviour which relates to the legal order, their law-governed life and their legal reality, will be investigated; that is, behaviour motivated by consciousness of legal norms. A psychological investigation of this kind – its scientific method and practical conduct is yet to be determined – would very probably reveal that only a very small part of those human actions that relate to the law can be causally traced back to the legal order as a motive, and that very many actions that externally seem to be related to the law find their motivation exclusively in the consciousness of morality and custom.[176]

In later publications, Kelsen does make criticisms of Weber, that he 'did not consider the cause of *sollensgemäß* being [. . .], or [. . .] action conforming to law [. . .], to be what ought to be, or [. . .] the law, or the norm in its quite specific sense (*Eigensinn*)', but instead 'thinking, feeling, wanting, the existential fact of the psychical experience of the norm.'[177] Kelsen thought that Weber had wandered into 'a psycho-physical parallel world that represented not law, but mere facts of existence (*Seinstatsachen*): human ideas, evaluations, the setting of aims, actions.'[178] Weber did not dispute this, but said quite plainly, 'When what is normatively valid becomes the object of empirical investigation it loses, as an object, the character of a norm: it is treated as something that "exists", not as something that is "valid"'.[179] Generally, Weber's application of the sociological perspective to the law could draw upon the success with which he had employed it in his *Protestant Ethic*.[180] There, the concept of validity is related to the existence of 'binding' ideas of religious belief in the heads of Puritans, the chance thereby arising that Puritans do in fact orient themselves to these beliefs, these beliefs thus having had historical effects.[181] If one wishes to ascertain the 'power of such ideas to guide conduct' we need to explore their meaningful foundation, which involves the construction of a '"dogmatics" for "meaning"' ('"*Dogmatik*" des "*Sinns*"'),[182] hence work of analysis and interpretation (as is the usual practice for lawyers). Weber would have, here, readily admitted that interpretative sociology necessarily becomes involved 'with other cognitive systems (systems of thought) which from the standpoint of sociology are quite various',[183] and he had in fact acted on this, examining the 'normative core of Calvinist theology, including their doctrine of predestination and of personal proof', as also 'the need for practical pastoral care' and the consequent 'reinterpretation' of radical belief in predestination with its implications for the guidance of conduct.[184] This does not, however, mean that as a sociologist of religion his interpretative activity was exclusively limited to the Calvinistic theological system of meaning, or that he completely entered into the system of meaning possessed by a faithful Calvinist. Whoever, as a sociologist of religion, practices a '"dogmatics" for "meaning"' does not necessarily have to succumb to the influence of the Calvinists, but can nonetheless posit theological value judgments.[185]

There is, of course, a fundamental difference in the way in which Weber and Kelsen use their respective concepts of validity.[186] In Kelsen, the concept of validity belonged to the realm of what should be (*Sollen*) and indicates the normative character of a legal norm, although it does in its effects have a 'twin sister' in the realm of being (*Sein*) – although under particular conditions. Since, for Kelsen, the basis for a norm's validity can be ultimately only another, higher norm, there comes into play ('an assumption treated in part as a hypothesis, in part as a fiction')[187] a founding norm (*Grundnorm*), a consequence of the strict observation of dualism of *Sein* and *Sollen*. Of course, not any and every normative order can lay claim to legal validity, but only those that evince a specific quotient of applicability and adherence, 'As he states, their norms are not valid *because* of this, they are valid only *if* this has effect: "Effectivity is the condition of validity, but is not the same thing as validity" (Kelsen)'.[188] As we know, Weber associated the empirical concept of validity *solely* with 'orientation', and not adherence (*Befolgen*). Hence, he is able to deal with cases of the open infringement or evasion of an order in terms of a gradualistic concept of validity, 'Even where this averagely understood meaning [of an order] is "evaded" or "infringed" it is likely that this validity will still to some extent remain *effective* as a binding norm.'[189] Weber here deploys a gradualist concept of validity:[190] that is, within a particular social composite (*Gesellschaftsintegrat*) an order is regarded by an overwhelming part of its members as binding or obligatory. The empirical, if also gradual, validity of the order exerts predictable pressure upon a deviant, so that he '*must* conceal his violation of the order.'[191] While Kelsen has in view the normal case which presumes adherence ('effectivity is the condition of validity [. . .]'), in the light of Weber's concept of validity this only follows if in a 'marginal case' there is a conscious avoidance or infringement of an order with a predictable effect. Hence the 'gradual validity' of a (legal) order is the condition of a predictable effect upon a deviant who behaves in a purely 'purposively-rational manner' when concealing his action 'through orientation to the "validity" of criminal law.'[192]

In Stegmüller's book, *Hauptströmungen der Gegenwartsphilosophie*, there is a little-noticed passage[193] in which he cautiously draws a parallel between Gilbert Ryle[194] and Max Weber, where a 'correct' reading of Ryle's concept of disposition[195] contributes to a better understanding of the matters discussed here. Stegmüller argues that Ryle seeks to 'do away with an obsolete idea in the philosophy of consciousness: the myth of the "ghost in the machine"', whereas Weber wishes to 'destroy the myth of the superghost in the supermachine.' He continues:

> The supermachine is called 'the state' and the superghost has names such as 'people' and 'nation'. Weber traces all of these entities, including their characteristic features such as validating legal norms, valid economic system, customs and usages to the dispositional behaviour of individual persons. The expression 'chance', which he lights upon with great linguistic instinct, [. . .] expresses two things: firstly, that this is a matter of dispositional features; and secondly, that these features are such as to permit only probabilistic predictions, hence predictions about putative behaviour.[196]

In contrast to the contemporary position, Ryle does not see any particular properties in dispositions,[197] even if the use of concepts of disposition for explanatory purposes in ordinary language leads one to ascribe or deny particular capacities or properties to a particular 'bearer' (a person or a thing). Instead, Ryle treats dispositional statements as 'inference-tickets' (*Schlussfahrkarten*) which permit us to draw conclusions when faced with particular 'circumstances'.[198] Ryle provides vivid examples of this: the (dispositional) statement 'this lump of sugar is soluble' leads to the conclusion 'that it would dissolve, if submerged anywhere, at any time and in any parcel of water'; or the statement, 'this sleeper knows French' permits the conclusion to be drawn 'that if he is ever addressed in French [. . .] he responds pertinently in French.'[199] For Ryle:

> Dispositional statements about particular things and persons are [. . .] like law statements in the fact that we use them in a partly similar way. They apply to, or they are satisfied by, the actions, reactions and states of the object; they are inference-tickets, which license us to predict, retrodict, explain and modify these actions, reactions and states.[200]

Jansen thus considers Ryle's treatment of dispositional statements to be 'condensed ways of speaking about hypothetical events in particular types of situation' which allow the conclusion to be drawn that 'if a situation belongs to such a type of situation a corresponding event will occur.'[201]

If one reads the following example from Stegmüller in the light of this understanding of dispositional statements, then light is shed upon Weber's unusual 'conception of the state', a conception which found dramatic confirmation in the bloodless 1989 revolution in the German Democratic Republic (GDR):

> That in state X a particular form of 'perfect dictatorship' will still be there tomorrow, whereas in state Y there will tomorrow be a 'well functioning' democracy of a particular kind – this only means that the members of two groups of persons will tomorrow retain their disposition generally to accept particular forms of conduct. A coup of the most bloodless kind would occur if, for instance, members of X all behaved tomorrow as if they were members of Y.[202]

If we consider matters more closely there is another significant affinity between Ryle and Weber. If Ryle sees in dispositional claims inference-tickets which '[license] its possessors to move from asserting factual statements to asserting other factual statements', or 'to provide explanations of given facts',[203] then this has a certain connection with Weber's objective judgments of possibility. These rest, of course, on a 'general consideration of the individual case' (v. Kries)[204] in which nomological knowledge in the form of rules based upon experience are introduced – it is no coincidence that Ryle compares dispositional statements with statements of law. This is, therefore, a matter of judgments regarding the probability of the course of events, in which there is a resort to existing experiential knowledge. Weber uses an 'inference-ticket' himself when he states:

> That a 'friendship' or a 'state' exists, or did exist, means exclusively and only that: we (the observers) judge that there is or has been a probability that on the basis of certain kinds of known subjective attitude of certain individuals there will result in the *average sense* a certain specific type of action.[205]

Or more emphatically:

> For sociology the state is no more than the chance that particular kinds of specific actions occur, as the action of particular individual people. No more than that [. . .]. What is 'subjective' here: is that the action is oriented to definite conceptions (*Vorstellungen*). And 'objective': that we – the observer – make a judgment of whether the chance exists that an action oriented to these ideas will follow. If this chance no longer exists, so then the 'state' no longer exists.[206]

Final remarks

If one compares the following quotation from Kelsen with those just made from Weber, there does, at first glance, seem to be a striking agreement between them:

> In Gorky's drama 'The Lower Depths' the pilgrim replies to the actor's question of whether there was a God by saying: if you believe in Him then there is a God. That applies literally to the state, to the real existence of the state – the thinking, feeling and wanting of a particular content, of a particular ideology: if one believes in it, i.e., if the conception of the order described by 'state' becomes a motivation of action, then the state 'exists' as a reality, the state becomes reality.[207]

And as Kelsen writes elsewhere, 'if this ideology loses its motivating force, then state "power" no longer exists [. . .]'.[208]

Closer examination, however, leads nonetheless straight into the problematic of validity and effectivity, of normativity and facticity and once again renders evident the quite fundamental difference between the sociological and the juridical conception of the State, between Weber and Kelsen. It becomes apparent that the devil is already in the detail, the conceptual uncertainties that we can there observe are no more than indicators of the problematics we have just mentioned. We can gain access to these through the question: how can the condition of effectivity, as well as the correspondence of normativity and facticity, be harmonized with the basic principle of Kelsen's legal doctrine, the dualism of is and ought?

First, we should recall that, for Kelsen:

> the origin of being in conformity with the ought (*des sollensgemäßen Seins*) [. . .] is not that which ought to be (*das Sollen*) [. . .] but thinking, feeling and wanting, the existential facts of the psychical experience of the norm. [. . .]. To this psychical experience, especially to that of 'wanting' this norm, is related the conception of *realisation*, more, the transfer from the mere inwardness of wanting into the externality of action, of moral or lawful action. In action conforming to the norm *wanting* is '*realised*', for it is just this wanting which is the motivation, the origin of the action as an *effect*.[209]

For Weyma Lübbe, there are a number of things wrong with this, 'psychic experience' is certainly no 'experience of the norm' but rather an 'experience of a want or a wish', while it is not a particular norm that is wished for, but a particular action. Corresponding to the distinction made by Kelsen, the State belongs, as an 'ideal order', as a normative order (or as a 'system of compulsory norms'),[210] to the level of the ought (*Sollensebene*), whereas the 'real psychic acts of will by men' belong to the level of being (*Seinsebene*).[211] As a normative order, the State is, for Kelsen, 'cognitive substance' (*geistiger Inhalt*), but this lives on 'ultimately only in psychical acts, but this fact has no consequence for theoretical knowledge. For such knowledge the substance remains something that is thought.'²¹² Kelsen illustrates this by referring to the Pythagorean principle according to which one could say that it could not exist 'if there was no-one to think it.' Besides that, however, Kelsen argued that this principle was not valid by virtue of the thinking, but by virtue of some ultimate axioms.²¹³ He considered that the legal order conceived as a State, as 'a uniquely normative category (*Sollenskategorie*)',²¹⁴ likewise forcibly raised the question of the basis of its validity, that of the origin and basic norm (or founding hypothesis) which secured the unity and particular nature of a legal system.²¹⁵

Even if Kelsen does not admit that 'any kind of reality apparent to pre-scientific understanding can influence the constitution of a science',²¹⁶ he is certainly aware that ordinary, commonplace and everyday theories (*Alltagstheorien*), as well as conventional political theory (*Staatslehre*), identify the State with 'power' or 'force':

> It is not coercion as the substance of the norm – as it seems from the point of view of a lawyer concerned with the validity of legal statutes – but rather the actual psychic coercion inhering in the effectiveness of particular conceptions of norm (*Normvorstellungen*), a motivational rule that determines the actual behaviour of men and women, hence a real power that one thinks of when one characterises the state as a coercive *Anstalt*.²¹⁷

This perspective 'allows cognitive substance to be replaced by the psychic process attributed to it', in which 'the misleading equivocation of our language, failing to distinguish sufficiently precisely between thinking and the thought, wanting and what is wanted' plays a part.²¹⁸ Kelsen here seeks support in the conceptual distinction between State order and State ideology. Insofar as people fail to recognize that decrees and commands emanate not from a State power, but from a valid legal order, they are victims of an ideology which, as an 'ideal order',²¹⁹ is experienced by them as a motive, and which, as such, becomes effective. One can agree with Lübbe's pithy solution to this, 'The "state order" (*Staatsordnung*) is *valid*, "state ideology" is *experienced* as a motive, and the putative "power of the state" is the effective "work of ideology"'.²²⁰

The (conceptual) distinction between the validity of the state order and the effective work of State ideology is owed to the unbridgeable gap between *Sollen* and *Sein*.²²¹ Nonetheless, Kelsen posits 'a certain relationship between the validity and the effective work of state ideology', although following this with a characteristic remark in brackets, 'insofar as this word [State ideology] can be used for the two different objects.'²²² It is not only this conceptual uncertainty (inexactness) that indicates the problem of the 'correspondence of normativity and facticity' implicit in legal validity.²²³ Kelsen had also seen this problem, and he maintained that 'pure' legal science must have to be certain that, 'despite the basic difference between *effect* and *validity*, only an order that was as a rule *effective* should be treated as *valid*.'²²⁴ This is of importance in that a 'pure' legal science is also concerned to have an impact upon 'a political community whose law it recognised' by using this law to guide or stabilize the community.[225] On the part of those who applied the law, and those to whom the law applied, this also presupposes a degree of acceptance, or willingness to conform,[226] which in Kelsen leads to a gradualist concept of effectivity.[227] The dilemma highlighted here has two aspects. The first is that the pure theory of law 'is helpless when faced with the phenomenon of revolution, or more exactly, when faced with the problem of repairing the gaps torn by revolution in the chain of legal statutes and applications leading back to the basic norm (*Grundnorm*).'[228] And if we push this to its logical conclusion, then the pure theory of law also cannot overlook the 'facticity of existing law', and must moreover presuppose 'a minimum of social stability',[229] so that the question of whether Kelsen's theory of the State 'represents an ideology legitimating the status quo' seems in no respect improper.[230] Second, the dilemma noted above is expressed by the fact that the legal perspective 'cannot explain, without exceeding its methodological boundaries, why a legally constructed legal order has empirical validity, and corresponds to what in fact exists.'[231]

Given his basic dualism of *Sein* and *Sollen*, Kelsen cannot see that 'the *Sein* perspective can register "that which has value", if only in a purely subjective sense.'[232] Weber had already foreseen this and taken note. For Weber, the legal order is an order of men and women acting in a meaningful way,[233] men and women who help to validate this order so long as they *orient* themselves to the *idea* that it is obligatory. This is not a matter 'of the "proper" motivation corresponding to a legal norm, but to a factually effective motivation.'[234] It is thus a matter of the effectiveness of a legal order, which Weber treats as 'a complex of maxims in the heads of particular empirical people [. . .], which maxims causally influence their concrete action and so indirectly that of others',[235] so that the substance of a legal order is incorporated in an entirely concrete manner. In this instance of empirical validation, Weber treats the correspondence of normativity and facticity in a much more elegant fashion without having to surrender the dualism of *Sein* and *Sollen*. He does see the existence of a threat to the State if 'the human action from which the state is constituted'[236] through orientation to the legal order is 'no longer sufficiently motivated' by the legal order.[237] But Stegmüller's apt example of the GDR shows that the evident probability of a State collapsing, that 'particular forms of meaningfully oriented social action'[238] simply no longer 'take place', can happen without direct orientation to the legal order (something that Weber's conceptual apparatus allows us to understand).[239] The example of the peaceful revolution in the GDR lends substance to Schluchter's conception of the 'marginal case', 'that a "state" that from the sociological point of view no longer exists be nonetheless legally recognised.'[240] Hence we need add nothing to Schluchter's conclusion that 'Kelsen's legal theory of the state needs to be extended sociologically.'[241]

Notes

1 The usually accepted translation of *Anstalt* as 'institution' is misleading. The model that Weber had in mind for his sociological concept of *Anstalt* was the legal concept as

it stood towards the end of the nineteenth century. This legal concept was characterized by a number of features, some of which Weber adopted. For details of this, see the third section. Given this particular problem, I have opted to leave the term *Anstalt* untranslated.

2 Stefan Breuer (Hamburg), Christoph Schönberger (Konstanz) and Gerhard Wagner (Frankfurt) read the first draft of this chapter and made helpful comments on it; while I was able to discuss some aspects of the present chapter with Horst Dreier (Würzburg) during a long forest walk. I would like to express my gratitude to all four. I would like to express my thanks to Keith Tribe for his translation.

3 R. Thoma, 'Der Begriff der modernen Demokratie in seinem Verhältnis zum Staatsbegriff. Prolegomena zu einer Analyse des demokratischen Staates der Gegenwart', in H. Dreier (ed), *Rechtsstaat-Demokratie-Grundrechte. Ausgewählte Abhandlungen aus fünf Jahrzehnten*, Tübingen: Mohr Siebeck, 2008, pp. 76–119, p. 109; first published in 1923. Here, Thoma, whose essay originally appeared in the Max Weber memorial volume, sums up a central axiom of Kelsen.

4 Since current English translations of Weber's 'methodological' writings and *Economy and Society* are in many respects problematic, while the publishing strategy of the *Gesamtausgabe* is to supersede the idea that there is a finished text known as *Economy and Society*, reference to these writings are to the standard German versions, to the *Gesamtausgabe* where available. Note that 'Basic Sociological Concepts' is Chapter 1 of *Economy and Society*, specific reference to this below being made as WuG since Part One of *Economy and Society* has yet to appear in the *Gesamtausgabe*. Abbreviations: ES = *Economy and Society: An Outline of Interpretive Sociology*, 2 vols, G. Roth, and C. Wittich (eds), Berkeley, Los Angeles, London: University of California Press, 1978; GSG = Georg Simmel Gesamtausgabe; HKW = Hans Kelsen Werke; MWG = Max Weber Gesamtausgabe; WL = Max Weber, *Gesammelte Aufsätze zur Wissenschaftslehre*, J. Winckelmann (ed), 7th edn, Tübingen: J.C.B. Mohr (Paul Siebeck), 1988; WuG: *Wirtschaft und Gesellschaft. Grundriss der verstehenden Soziologie*, 2 vols, J. Winckelmann (ed), 5th edn, Tübingen: J.C.B. Mohr (Paul Siebeck), 1976.

5 The extent to which Weber developed his 'Basic Sociological Categories' 'by reworking his 1913 Essay on Categories' has been vigorously debated by W. Schluchter and S. Hermes in particular. Disagreeing with Schluchter, Hermes argues, on the basis of textual and historical study of the two main texts, 'that the changes of the latter are for the most part terminological, rather than substantive' (cf. S. Hermes, *Soziales Handeln und Struktur der Herrschaft. Max Webers verstehende historische Soziologie am Beispiel des Patrimonialismus*, Berlin: Duncker und Humblot, 2003, p. 48). Hermes does, in fact, maintain that there were 'substantive shifts and additions'. S. Breuer, in his introduction to *Herrschaft in der Soziologie Max Webers*, Wiesbaden: Harrassowitz, 2011, demonstrates that there are a number of major changes between the 1913 Essay and the first chapter of *Economy and Society*. In later publications, Hermes claims that the conceptual definitions in the essay on categories, first published in the journal *Logos* in the course of 1913, are something of a 'late invention'. Further contributions related to this issue are: W. Schluchter, 'Vorbemerkung: Der Kategorienaufsatz als Schlüssel', in his *Individualismus, Verantwortungsethik und Vielfalt*, Weilerswist: Velbrück Wissenschaft, 2000, Appendix, pp. 179–89, containing further contributions to this discussion; W. Schluchter, 'Zur Entstehung von Max Webers Hauptbeitrag zum Handbuch der politischen Oekonomie, später: Grundriss der Sozialökonomik', in his *Handlung, Ordnung und Kultur. Studien zu einem Forschungsprogramm im Anschluss an Max Weber*, Tübingen: Mohr Siebeck, 2005, pp. 229–38; Max Weber, *Wirtschaft und Gesellschaft. Entstehungsgeschichte und Dokumente*, introduced and edited by W. Schluchter, Tübingen: J.C.B. Mohr (Paul Siebeck), 2009 (MWG I/24); S. Hermes, 'Das Recht einer "Soziologischen Rechtslehre". Zum Rechtsbegriff in Max Webers Soziologie

des Rechts', *Rechtstheorie* (2004), 35, 195–231, esp. 200ff.; S. Hermes, 'Vom Aufbau der sozialen Welt. Zur Genese, Genealogie und Kategorienlehre von Max Webers Soziologie des Rechts', *Rechtstheorie* (2007), 38, 419–49.

6 G. Hübinger, 'Einleitung', in G. Hübinger with A. Terweg (eds), *Allgemeine Staatslehre und Politik (Staatssoziologie). Unvollendet. Mit- und Nachschriften 1920*, Tübingen: J.C.B. Mohr (Paul Siebeck), 2009, pp. 1–41 (2) (MWG III/7). Cf. G. Hübinger 'Die "Staatssoziologie" Max Webers', in F.-J. Peine and H. A. Wolff (eds), *Nachdenken über Eigentum. FS für Alexander v. Brünneck*, Baden-Baden: Nomos, 2011, pp. 443–52.

7 H. Kelsen, *Der Soziologische und der Juristische Staatsbegriff. Kritische Untersuchungen des Verhältnisses von Staat und Recht*, 2nd edn, Tübingen: J.C.B. Mohr (Paul Siebeck), 1928.

8 ES, 54; WuG, 29.

9 WL, 440. Cf. W. Gephart, 'Juristische Ursprünge in der Begriffswelt Max Webers', *Rechtshistorisches Journal* (1990), 9, 343–62.

10 WL, 439.

11 ES, 4; WuG, § 1; cf. W. Schluchter, 'Handlungs- und Strukturtheorie nach Max Weber', *Berliner Journal für Soziologie* (2000), 10, 125–36, p. 130.

12 WuG, 7.

13 WL, 439. Weber wrote to Hermann Kantorowicz on 29 December 1913 about the 1913 Essay, '"Interpretative sociology" – unintelligible? To *you*? "For if they do these things in a green tree" [St. Luke 23.31] – how poorly I must have formulated this! // It is an effort to *get rid of everything* "organicist", Stammlerish, supraempirical, "valid" (= *normatively* valid), and instead conceive the "sociology of the state" as a sociology of purely empirical typified *human action* – this is in my opinion the sole way forward – while the individual *categories* themselves are a matter of convenience', M. Weber, *Briefe 1913–1914*, M. R. Lepsius and W. J. Mommsen, with B. Rudhard, and M. Schön (eds), Tübingen: J.C.B. Mohr (Paul Siebeck), 2003, p. 442f. (MWG II/8).

14 Thoma, 'Der Begriff der modernen Demokratie in seinem Verhältnis zum Staatsbegriff', op. cit., p. 109.

15 This is a translation of G. Wagner's suggested more easily grasped rephrasing of the passage from WuG, § 1, (ES, 4), quoted above.

16 One reference here can stand for several others: Schluchter, 'Handlungs- und Strukturtheorie nach Max Weber', op. cit., 130. See also R. Greshoff, '"Soziales Handeln" und "Ordnung" als operative und strukturelle Komponenten sozialer Beziehungen', in K. Lichtblau (ed), *Max Webers 'Grundbegriffe'. Kategorien der kultur- und sozialwissenschaftlichen Forschung*, Wiesbaden: VS-Verlag, 2006, pp. 257–91, p. 258ff.

17 Schluchter, ibid., 130.

18 ES, 4; WuG, § 1.

19 H. Popitz, *Die normative Konstruktion von Gesellschaft*, Tübingen: J.C.B. Mohr (Paul Siebeck), 1980, p. 4.

20 Ibid., p. 5. See also H. Popitz, *Der Begriff der sozialen Rolle als Element der soziologischen Theorie*, Tübingen: J.C.B. Mohr (Paul Siebeck), 1967, p. 32ff. Still worth reading on typification: G. Simmel, 'Exkurs über das Problem: Wie ist Gesellschaft möglich?', in his *Soziologie. Untersuchungen über die Formen der Vergesellschaftung*, O. Rammstedt (ed), Frankfurt am Main: Suhrkamp, 1992, pp. 42–61, p. 47ff., GSG vol. 11.

21 ES, 30, no. 3; WuG, 15, no. 3.

22 Ibid.

23 Greshoff, '"Soziales Handeln" und "Ordnung" als operative und strukturelle Komponenten sozialer Beziehungen', op. cit., p. 261.

24 ES, 27, § 3, no. 2; WuG, 13, § 3, no. 2.

25 W. Schluchter, 'Replik', in A. Bienfait, and G. Wagner (eds), *Verantwortliches Handeln in gesellschaftlichen Ordnungen. Beiträge zu Wolfgang Schluchters 'Religion und Lebensführung'*, Frankfurt am Main: Suhrkamp, 1998, pp. 320–65, p. 335.

26 Schluchter, 'Handlungs- und Strukturtheorie nach Max Weber', op. cit., p. 131. Of course, Weber does not use the term 'structures of action'.
27 Strictly speaking, 'maxims' are 'not equivalent to "norms"' (Kelsen, *Der Soziologische und der Juristische Staatsbegriff*, op. cit., p. 161), but are 'conception(s) (*Vorstellungen*) of the "norm" which operate as the real impulse for the actor' (WL, 329), something which is lent emphasis by the use of the expression 'norm-maxim' (WL, 334), W. Lübbe talks of 'rules of action' (*Handlungsregeln*) in *Legitimität kraft Legalität. Sinnverstehen und Institutionenanalyse bei Max Weber und seinen Kritikern*, Tübingen: J.C.B. Mohr (Paul Siebeck), 1991, p. 44.
28 ES, 34; WuG, 18: convention and law are behavioural requirements that are intended to be binding, i.e. deviation from them results in the application of a sanction. In the case of a convention anyone can do this, while if the law is involved this has to be done by a coercive staff created for the purpose.
29 WL 330f. For this reason we find in respect of custom, 'Custom would not in this sense be something "validating": no one can "require" its observance, that one conform to it' (ES, 29, no. 2; WuG, 15, no. 2).
30 ES, 31; WuG, § 5.
31 There are inconsistencies in §§ 5–7 (ES, 31–38) in the presentation of what is in itself a consistent conception.
32 See on this 'substantive meaning', ES, 28, nos 5, 6; WuG, 14, nos 5, 6.
33 ES, 31, nos 1, 2; WuG, 16, nos 1, 2. This is because in § 5 there is an express reference to the 'existence of a *legitimate* order'. Cf. Lübbe, *Legitimität kraft Legalität*, op. cit., p. 43ff.
34 ES, 36ff.; WuG, § 7. Also M. Weber, *Wirtschaft und Gesellschaft. Die Wirtschaft und die gesellschaftlichen Ordnungen und Mächte. Nachlaß. Teilband I: Gemeinschaften*, W. J. Mommsen, with M. Meyer (eds), Tübingen: J.C.B. Mohr (Paul Siebeck), 2001, p. 207f. (MWG I/22-1; ES, 903f.).
35 WL, 473f.
36 That is, the order is as such treated (considered) to be binding by the actors.
37 ES, 311ff.; WuG, 181.
38 ES, 32, no. 3; WuG, 16, § 5, no. 3; WL, 445.
39 WL, 330.
40 WL, 330, 339. See also WL, 473, 'The empirical "validity" of a "rational" order centres upon the acceptance of an adaptation to the accustomed [practice], it is absorbed, taught, constantly repeated [custom]. Considered with regard to its subjective structure, behaviour can even take the form of a more or less regular mass action without connection to any meaning.'
41 ES, 324f.; WuG, 190.
42 Cf. H. Treiber, 'Im "Schatten" des Neukantianismus: Norm und Geltung bei Max Weber', in J. Brand and D. Strempel (eds), *Soziologie des Rechts. Festschrift für Erhard Blankenburg zum 60. Geburtstag*, Baden-Baden: Nomos, 1998, pp. 245–54 (esp. pp. 246–49).
43 ES, 31ff.; WuG, 16f.
44 WL, 323, 329, 330f., 334.
45 WL, 445f., 456–57, 459f., 468.
46 ES, 311ff., 326; WuG, 181f., 191.
47 Weber calls 'an empirical legal order' the '"empirical existence" of the law as a maxim-generating "knowledge" shared by actual men and women' (WL, 350). Accordingly, for Weber a legal order consists of 'a complex of maxims in the heads of particular empirical people [. . .], which maxims causally influence their concrete action and so indirectly that of others' (WL, 348).
48 ES, 28; WuG, 14, no. 6.

49 M. Weber, *Wirtschaft und Gesellschaft. Die Wirtschaft und die gesellschaftlichen Ordnungen und Mächte. Nachlaß. Teilband 4: Herrschaft*, E. Hanke with T. Kroll (eds), Tübingen: J.C.B. Mohr (Paul Siebeck), 2005, p. 138 (MWG I/22-4).
50 ES, 312f.; WuG, 182. Cf. N. Bobbio, 'Max Weber und Hans Kelsen', in M. Rehbinder and K.-P. Tieck (eds), *Max Weber als Rechtssoziologe*, Berlin: Duncker & Humblot, 1987, pp. 109–26, p. 118.
51 *Die Grenzen naturwissenschaftlicher Begriffsbildung. Eine logische Einleitung in die historischen Wissenschaften*, 3rd and 4th edns, Tübingen: J.C.B. Mohr (Paul Siebeck), 1921, p. 247f., (original publication 1896).
52 ES, 312; WuG, 181; WL, 331., 348, 374f., 440.
53 F. Loos, *Zur Wert- und Rechtslehre Max Webers*, Tübingen: J.C.B. Mohr (Paul Siebeck), 1970, p. 98f.
54 W. Windelband, *Präludien. Aufsätze und Reden zur Philosophie und ihrer Geschichte*, 7th and 8th edns, Tübingen: J.C.B. Mohr (Paul Siebeck), 1921, vol. 2, pp. 59–98, esp. pp. 64f., 84–86 (although this is in relation to logical and aesthetic rules (norms)).
55 W. Windelband, *Ueber die Gewissheit der Erkenntniss. Eine psychologisch-erkenntisstheoretische Studie*, Berlin: Henschel, 1873. Reprinted Saarbrücken: VDM Verlag Müller, 2006.
56 Ibid., p. 64.
57 Windelband, *Präludien*, op. cit., vol. 2, pp. 85f., 95.
58 Ibid., vol. 2, p. 85f.
59 ES, 322; WuG, 189; also WuG, 188f.
60 ES, 31; WuG, 16, § 5, no. 1; WL, 442, 446.
61 H. Lotze, *Logik. Drei Bücher vom Denken, vom Untersuchen und vom Erkennen*, G. Misch (ed), 2nd edn, Leipzig: Meiner, 1928, p. 512 (original publication 1874); emphasis added.
62 ES, 312f.; WuG, 182.
63 See H. Sommerhäuser, *Emil Lask in der Auseinandersetzung mit Heinrich Rickert*, Berlin: Ernst-Reuter-Gesellschaft, 1965; H. Schnädelbach, *Philosophie in Deutschland 1831–1933*, Frankfurt am Main: Suhrkamp, 1983, pp. 19–66.
64 W. Windelband, 'Was ist Philosophie? (Über Begriff und Geschichte der Philosophie)', in his *Präludien*, op. cit., vol. 1, pp. 1–54, p. 29ff.
65 Schnädelbach, *Philosophie in Deutschland 1831–1933*, op. cit., p. 220.
66 Windelband, *Präludien*, op. cit., vol. 1, p. 134ff.
67 W. Windelband, 'Kritische oder genetische Methode?', in his *Präludien*, op. cit., vol. 2, pp. 99–135, p. 122.
68 Sommerhäuser, *Emil Lask in der Auseinandersetzung mit Heinrich Rickert*, op. cit., p. 34.
69 WL, 322ff.
70 WL, 330f.
71 ES; 31; WuG, 16, § 5, nos. 1, 2; WL, 446.
72 W. Windelband, 'Beiträge zur Lehre vom negativen Urteil', in *Strassburger Abhandlungen zur Philosophie: Eduard Zeller zu seinem siebenzigsten Geburtstag*, Freiburg, Tübingen: Mohr, 1884, pp. 165–95, p. 176.
73 For the sake of clarity in the resulting definitions, *Verband* is here translated simply as 'organization'.
74 ES, 48; WuG, §12.
75 ES, 324f.; WuG, 190.
76 ES, 49; WuG, 26, no. 2.
77 ES, 54; WuG, § 17; S. Hermes, 'Der Staat als "Anstalt". Max Webers soziologische Begriffsbildung im Kontext der Rechts- und Staatswissenschaften', in K. Lichtblau (ed), *Max Webers 'Grundbegriffe'. Kategorien der kultur- und sozialwissenschaftlichen Forschung*, Wiesbaden: VS Verlag, 2006, pp. 184–216.
78 ES, 52; WuG, § 15.
79 ES, 765; WuG, 449; now as M. Weber, *Wirtschaft und Gesellschaft. Die Wirtschaft und*

die gesellschaftlichen Ordnungen und Mächte. Nachlaß, Teilband 3: Recht, W. Gephart and S. Hermes (eds), Tübingen: J.C.B. Mohr (Paul Siebeck), 2010, p. 454 (MWG I/22-3); see in particular Hermes, Soziales Handeln und Struktur der Herrschaft, op. cit., pp. 110, 149f. On the concept of statute, see Hermes, ibid., p. 110f., note 370.
80 WL, 440; Gephart, 'Juristische Ursprünge in der Begriffswelt Max Webers', op. cit.
81 The 'proximity' of the sociological perspective to legal concepts also arises because 'this perspective proceeds from the fact that "factual" powers of command tend to believe that they significantly supplement a normative "order" created "by legal means", and so of necessity operate with a legal conceptual apparatus' (ES, 948; WuG, 545; MWG I/22-4, 138).
82 S. Hermes, 'Staatsbildung durch Rechtsbildung – Überlegungen zu Max Webers soziologischer Verbandstheorie', in A. Anter and S. Breuer (eds), *Max Webers Staatssoziologie. Positionen und Perspektiven*, Baden-Baden: Nomos, 2007, pp. 81–101, p. 87.
83 ES, 707f.; WuG, 425; MWG I/22-3, 383f., 195.
84 ES, 714; WuG, 429; MWG I/22-3, 397.
85 C. Schönberger, *Das Parlament im Anstaltsstaat. Zur Theorie parlamentarischer Repräsentation in der Staatsrechtslehre des Kaiserreichs (1871–1918)*, Frankfurt am Main: Vittorio Klostermann, 1997, p. 314. On the 'theory of the state' developed from Gerber to Laband see here pp. 21–120; on Otto Mayer's conception of an *Anstalt*, see pp. 311–18. See also H. Speer, *Herrschaft und Legitimität. Zeitgebundene Aspekte in Max Webers Herrschaftssoziologie*, Berlin: Duncker & Humblot, 1978, p. 37ff.
86 O. Mayer, 'Die juristische Person und ihre Verwertbarkeit im Öffentlichen Recht', in *Staatsrechtliche Abhandlungen. Festgabe für Paul Laband zum fünfzigsten Jahrestage der Doktor-Promotion*, Tübingen: J.C.B. Mohr (Paul Siebeck), 1908, vol. 1, pp. 1–94, p. 40.
87 Mayer, ibid., p. 55; see also Hermes, 'Der Staat als "Anstalt"', op. cit., pp. 197ff., 206ff., and Schönberger, *Das Parlament im Anstaltsstaat*, op. cit., p. 315.
88 ES, 52, 54; WuG, § 15, § 17.
89 ES, 714; WuG, 429; MWG I/22-3, 397.
90 P. Landau, 'Otto Gierke und das kanonische Recht', in J. Rückert and D. Willoweit (eds), *Die Deutsche Rechtsgeschichte in der NS-Zeit, ihre Vorgeschichte und ihre Nachwirkungen*, Tübingen: J.C.B. Mohr (Paul Siebeck), 1995, pp. 77–94, p. 82.
91 Ibid., p. 80.
92 Ibid., p. 85. See also Schönberger, *Das Parlament im Anstaltsstaat*, op. cit., p. 343, 'The characteristic feature of the *Anstalt* is that it does not involve the legal subjectivity (*Rechtssubjektivität*) of a self-organising totality of members as in a corporation (*Körperschaft*), but instead involves the binding together of persons through a will that comes "from above and without". [...] The model for this is the Canonical concept of the *Anstalt*. The Church and all its subordinate elements thus primarily takes the form not of a community of believers, but of the expression of a transcendental divine will that shapes it from on high'.
93 Landau, 'Otto Gierke und das kanonische Recht', op. cit., p. 87.
94 Ibid., pp. 91, 92ff.
95 Compulsory participants also because it is the occupation of a particular territory (birthplace, presence etc.) that determines the subordination to action taken by the *Anstalt*, unlike the situation for members of an association or a corporation (ES, 50f., WuG, 27, § 13; ES, 52, WuG, 28, § 15, no. 2; WL, 466).
96 In this regard the concept of the State, or of an *Anstalt*, is as presented in the 'Basic Sociological Concepts' 'blind to party'; even if sufficient scope is given to the sociology of political parties in *Politics as a Vocation*. See H. Tyrell, 'Physische Gewalt, gewaltsamer Konflikt und "der Staat" – Überlegungen zu neuerer Literatur', *Berliner Journal für Soziologie* (1999), 9, 269–288 (283f.).
97 Oktroyierung, – ES, 51, WuG, 27, § 13, no. 1, 'An imposed order in the sense used

here is *any* order not established on the basis of a free personal agreement by all participants.' Majority decision, therefore, also involves something which is imposed.
98 WL, 466.
99 WL, 469.
100 WL, 470.
101 WL, 470.
102 ES, 52; WuG, 29.
103 Terms in brackets: *Gemeinschafts-, Einverständnis- und Gesellschaftshandeln bzw. Verbands- und Anstaltshandeln.*
104 K. Lichtblau, '"Vergemeinschaftung" and "Vergesellschaftung" in Max Weber: A reconstruction of his linguistic usage', *History of European Ideas* (2011), 37, 454–65, p. 460.
105 ES, 217ff., WuG, 124ff.; ES, 956ff., WuG, 551ff., MWG I/22-4, 157ff.
106 M. Weber, *Gesammelte Aufsätze zur Religionssoziologie*, 6th edn, Tübingen: J.C.B. Mohr (Paul Siebeck), 1972, p. 1.
107 A. Zingerle, 'Max Webers Analyse des chinesischen Präbendalismus. Zu einigen Problemen der Verständigung zwischen Soziologie und Sinologie', in W. Schluchter (ed), *Max Webers Studie über Konfuzianismus und Taoismus. Interpretation und Kritik*, Frankfurt am Main: Suhrkamp, 1983, pp. 174–201, p. 195. See also Hermes, *Soziales Handeln und Struktur der Herrschaft*, op. cit., p. 233ff.
108 Popitz, *Der Begriff der sozialen Rolle als Element der soziologischen Theorie*, op. cit., pp. 7, 8ff.
109 ES, 28; WuG, 28, § 15, No. 2, final sentence. In § 17 of the 'Basic Sociological Concepts' ('political organisation') Weber introduces the characteristic of a territory, which of course excludes those political forms that favour the personality principle. See Hermes, *Soziales Handeln und Struktur der Herrschaft*, op. cit., p. 90. 'Territory' is with respect to the 'state' a supplementary category which can be added to the concept of the *Anstalt*, but not necessarily (cf. the Church), while it is *conditio sine qua non* for the concept of the State. Hence my qualification that it is the '*initial*' outlines' of what Weber means by a *Staat* and *Staatlichkeit* that emerge from the conception of an *Anstalt*.
110 Hermes, 'Vom Aufbau der sozialen Welt', op. cit., p. 95; here 'major' has been substituted for 'all' (see also the preceding footnote). For considering the definition of the State in § 17 of the 'Basic Sociological Concepts', to which we are about to turn, we would need to add 'persistence' or 'continuity' to the features of an *Anstaltsbetrieb*, since they too are borrowed from the legal concept of an *Anstalt*.
111 ES, 55; WuG 29, no. 2.
112 ES, 953; MWG I/22-4, 147.
113 Schönberger, *Das Parlament im Anstaltsstaat*, op. cit., p. 315.
114 Certainly Weber overlooked the consensual elements to which G. Lehmbruch has drawn attention in respect of the German Reich: G. Lehmbruch, *Parteienwettbewerb im Bundesstaat: Regelsysteme und Spannungslagen im politischen System der Bundesrepublik Deutschland*, 3rd revised and expanded edn, Wiesbaden: Westdeutscher Verlag, 2000.
115 ES, 54; WuG, 29.
116 ES, 946; WuG, 545; MWG I/22-4, 163f.
117 Schönberger, *Das Parlament im Anstaltsstaat*, op. cit., p. 52; see also Hermes, 'Der Staat als "Anstalt"', op. cit., p. 208ff.
118 Schönberger, ibid., p. 53.
119 Hermes, 'Der Staat als "Anstalt"', op. cit., p. 212. This critique does not, however, coincide with Kelsen's argument, according to which 'Weber's sociology of the state reveals itself to be a legal doctrine' (Kelsen, *Der Soziologische und der Juristische Staatsbegriff*, op. cit., pp. 156ff., 169). See on this, Lübbe, *Legitimität kraft Legalität*, op. cit., pp. 29ff., 31 and her note 2, 'Kelsen's formulation comes from his ontological dualism, which compels him to hypostasise action "in itself" or "the facticity of action" in terms of a

natural scientific terminology which treats them as "muscular contractions", rather than as events that have a "sense" which belongs to the world of "validity"'.
120 P. Laband, *Das Staatsrecht des Deutschen Reiches*, 5th revised edn in four volumes, Tübingen: J.C.B. Mohr (Paul Siebeck), 1911, vol. 1, p. 66.
121 Ibid., vol. 1, p. 68.
122 Ibid., p. 71.
123 Ibid.
124 Ibid., p. 72.
125 ES, 55; WuG, 30, no. 2.
126 § 17 'Basic Sociological Concepts'. For a sceptical view concerning the possibility of implementing this monopoly on a global basis, see T. v. Trotha, 'Ordnungsformen der Gewalt oder Aussichten auf das Ende des staatlichen Gewaltmonopols', in B. Nedelmann (ed), *Politische Institutionen im Wandel*, Sonderheft 35 of the *Kölner Zeitschrift für Soziologie und Sozialpsychologie*, Opladen: Westdeutscher Verlag, 1995, pp. 129–66.
127 C. Colliot-Thélène, 'Das Monopol der legitimen Gewalt', in Anter and Breuer (eds), op. cit., pp. 39–55.
128 M. Weber, *Wissenschaft als Beruf (1917/1919) – Politik als Beruf (1919)*, W. J. Mommsen and W. Schluchter, with B. Morgenbrod (eds), Tübingen: J.C.B. Mohr (Paul Siebeck), 1992, pp. 159f., 166f. (MWG I/17).
129 MWG I/17, 160.
130 Hermes, *Soziales Handeln und Struktur der Herrschaft*, op. cit., p. 148ff.; ES, 1134f., 1141ff., WuG, 670f., 676f.; ES, 771f., WuG, 453; MWG I/22-4, 470ff., 514f.
131 H. Popitz, *Phänomene der Macht*, 2nd edn, Tübingen: J.C.B. Mohr (Paul Siebeck), 1992, p. 61ff. 'Every potential order is subject to this vicious circle in dealing with force: social order is a necessary condition for the restraint of force – while force is a necessary condition for the maintenance of social order', p. 62.
132 ES, 56; WuG, 30, no. 3.
133 ES, 908; WuG, 519; MWG I/22-1, 214, 'In this way the political community monopolises the legitimate use of force for its coercive apparatus and gradually transforms it into an institution for the protection of rights.'
134 ES, 34; WuG, 17.
135 ES, 948; WuG, 545; MWG I/22-4, 138f.
136 ES, 953; WuG, 549f., MWG I/22-4, 147f.
137 Hermes, *Soziales Handeln und Struktur der Herrschaft*, op. cit., p. 147. See on this, Weber, 'For the exercise and threat of such coercion there is therefore in a fully developed political community a system of casuistic order to which a specific "legitimacy" tends to be ascribed: this is the "legal order", whose normal and sole source is today the political community, since it has in actuality usually usurped the monopoly of providing the observance of this order with a physical compulsion' (ES, 904; WuG, 516; MWG I/22-1, 208).
138 ES, 946; WuG, 544.; MWG I/22-4, 135.
139 WL, 331ff.
140 ES, 311ff.; WuG, 181ff.; MWG I/22-3, 191ff. See also Hermes, *Soziales Handeln und Struktur der Herrschaft*, op. cit., p. 142.
141 Kelsen, *Der Soziologische und der Juristische Staatsbegriff*, op. cit., pp. 164f., 167.
142 On this and the following, see Hermes, 'Das Recht einer "Soziologischen Rechtslehre"', op. cit., p. 229.
143 WL, 446, 470.
144 ES, 312; WuG, 181; MWG I/22-3, 193; WL, 331.
145 ES, 312; WuG, 182; MWG I/22-3, 195.
146 T. Geiger, *Vorstudien zu einer Soziologie des Rechts*, Neuwied, Berlin: Luchterhand, 1964, p. 218f.

147 Hermes, 'Das Recht einer "Soziologischen Rechtslehre"', op. cit., p. 229. Even if Hermes' suggestion is convincing, see statement in note 73, Weber's definition of *Verband* (group, association) is essentially simpler and more elegant. Weber speaks of a *Verband* when the distinguishing feature of a 'leader' is present. If, in addition to the principal characteristic of the 'leader', the further feature of an 'administrative staff' is sometimes present, as an additional characteristic, this merely means that the order (*Ordnung*) of the *Verband*, is a legal order (*Rechtsordnung*).
148 ES, 324; WuG, 190; MWG I/22-3, 221.
149 ES, 697; WuG, 418; MWG I/22-4, 364f. See in addition, Hermes, *Soziales Handeln und Struktur der Herrschaft*, op. cit., p. 144.
150 WL, 439; a similar formulation can be found in ES, 13f.; WuG, 6f.
151 WL, 200f. See also Hübinger, MWG III/7, 8f.
152 ES, 14; WuG, 7.
153 WL, 200.
154 WL, 199.
155 ES, 14; WuG, 7, no. 9.
156 WL, 329f.; WL, 440.
157 WL, 440.
158 W. Lübbe 'Der Normgeltungsbegriff als probabilistischer Begriff. Zur Logik des soziologischen Normbegriffs', *Zeitschrift für philosophische Forschung* (1990), 44, 583–601, p. 589.
159 Lübbe, *Legitimität kraft Legalität*, op. cit., p. 46.
160 WL, 287.
161 WL, 333f., 443f.; see, further, M. Weber, 'Diskussionsrede zu dem Vortrag von H. Kantorowicz, "Rechtswissenschaft und Soziologie"', in his *Gesammelte Aufsätze zur Soziologie und Sozialpolitik*, 2nd edn, Tübingen: J.C.B. Mohr (Paul Siebeck), 1988, pp. 476–83, p. 481ff.
162 In German: *Kausalität als faktenorientierte Kategorie vs. Zurechnung als Rechtsbegriff.*
163 C. Möllers, *Staat als Argument*, München: Beck, 2000, p. 43. See especially Loos, *Zur Wert- und Rechtslehre Max Webers*, op. cit., p. 100, note 55, who reminds us that '"law" and "state" as objects of empirical sociology [...] are always real actors in a real subjectively intended sense', something that Kelsen overlooked (*Der Soziologische und der Juristische Staatsbegriff*, op. cit., p. 156ff.). 'The ideal-typical "substantive meaning" of a legal order served only as a cognitive instrument; hence the task was not the construction of an ideal meaning (which is what Kelsen supposed, 1928, 159, 162) but the investigation of actual conceptions of meaning. [...] Legal sociology could not therefore be reduced to jurisprudence, a position to which Kelsen is impelled by a tendency to an ultimately naturalistic concept of empirical science (see Kelsen 1928, 8ff., 120) for which "meaning" is a foreign body (see Kelsen 1928, 58, 169).' Among other things, Kelsen overlooks the important reference in Weber's essay on Roscher and Knies (WL, 69) in which he writes, comparing the behaviour of Frederick II in 1756 to an avalanche, that '"interpretability" here adds to "calculability", compared to natural processes that are not open to "interpretation".' On this problematic, see also Lübbe, *Legitimität kraft Legalität*, op. cit., p. 26ff. The concept of imputation (*Zurechnung*) is, however, much more complex than it appears in the passage from Möller cited above, and not only because of the different meanings implied by its use in different phases of Kelsen's writing, see the contributions on this by J. Renzikowski, 'Der Begriff der "Zurechnung" in der Reinen Rechtslehre Hans Kelsens', in R. Alexy, L. H. Meyer, S. L. Paulson and G. Sprenger (eds), *Neukantianismus und Rechtsphilosophie*, Baden-Baden: Nomos, 2002, pp. 253–82, and C. Heidemann, 'Der Begriff der Zurechnung bei Hans Kelsen', in S. L. Paulson and M. Stolleis (eds), *Hans Kelsen. Staatsrechtslehrer und Rechtstheoretiker des 20. Jahrhunderts*, Tübingen: Mohr Siebeck, 2005, pp. 17–34.

164 On Kelsen see, for example, his arguments in the first chapter of his *Hauptprobleme der Staatsrechtslehre, entwickelt aus der Lehre vom Rechtssatze*, Tübingen: J.C.B. Mohr, 1911, HKW 2, Erster Halbband, pp. 80–116, esp. p. 86; and H. Kelsen, 'Über Grenzen zwischen juristischer und soziologischer Methode. Vortrag gehalten in der Soziologischen Gesellschaft zu Wien' (1911), in HKW, 3, 22–55, esp. 27f., each of them makes explicit reference to G. Simmels, *Einleitung in die Moralwissenschaft. Eine Kritik der ethischen Grundbegriffe* (1892), K. Ch. Köhnke (ed), Frankfurt am Main: Suhrkamp, 1989, vol. 1, Ch. 1, 'Das Sollen', pp. 15–91, esp. p. 18ff. (GSG, 3). H. Kelsen, 'Die Rechtswissenschaft als Norm- oder Kulturwissenschaft. Eine methodenkritische Untersuchung', *Schmollers Jahrbuch für Gesetzgebung, Verwaltung und Volkswirtschaft im Deutschen Reich* (1916), 40, 95–153, 95ff. See also HKW, 3, 551–605, 553ff. On Weber, see the Stammler essay in WL, 291ff.

165 H. Dreier, *Rechtslehre, Staatssoziologie und Demokratietheorie bei Hans Kelsen*, Baden-Baden: Nomos, 1986, p. 208ff.; Möllers, *Staat als Argument*, op. cit., p. 40ff. cf. H. Kelsen, 'Autobiographie' (1947), *Geschichte der Germanistik. Mitteilungen*, Ch. König, and M. Lepper (eds), Göttingen: Wallstein, 2006, Doppelheft 29/30, pp. 70–81, p. 75, 'The critical question in respect of the nature of the state seemed to be this: that which constituted unity within the diversity of the individuals making up this community. And for this question I could find no answer that might have a scientific basis other than this: that a specific legal order constitutes this unity; and that all efforts to found this unity meta-juristically, that is, sociologically, are to be considered failures. The argument, that the state by nature is a – relatively centralised – legal order, that therefore the dualism of state and law is a fiction that is based upon an animistic hypostatisation of personification, with the aid of which one seeks to represent the legal unity of the state – this has become an important element of my legal teaching. It may well be that I came to this view not least because the state to which I am closest and which from personal experience I knew best, the Austrian state, was quite plainly only a legal unity. Held up against the Austrian state, a state which is composed of so many groups who differ by race, language, religion and history, all theories which seek to base the unity of the state on some kind of socio-psychological or of socio-biological connection between the people who legally belong to this state are quite obviously fictional.' See on this also HKW 1, 29–91, as well as the section 'Habsburgischer Hintergrund und "Liberalismus" von Kelsens staatsrechtlichem Entwurf', in C. Schönberger, 'Hans Kelsens "Hauptprobleme der Staatsrechtslehre". Der Übergang vom Staat als Substanz zum Staat als Funktion (Einleitung)', in M. Jestaedt (ed), *H. Kelsen, Werke. Band 2: Veröffentlichte Schriften 1911*, Erster Halbband, Tübingen: Mohr Siebeck, 2008, pp. 23–35, p. 30ff. (HKW 2).

166 Dreier, *Rechtslehre, Staatssoziologie und Demokratietheorie bei Hans Kelsen*, op. cit., p. 209.

167 Ibid., p. 211. Kelsen, *Der Soziologische und der Juristische Staatsbegriff*, op. cit., p. 90, 'In the state of primitivism the legal order originally transfers its material coercive force to those to be protected by the law but whose interests had suffered injury. The injured person functions here as the "organ" of coercive order (blood feud).'

168 See also H. Dreier, 'Hans Kelsens Wissenschaftsprogramm', in H. Schulze-Fielitz (ed), *Staatsrechtslehre als Wissenschaft, Die Verwaltung*, Beiheft 7, Berlin: Duncker & Humblot, 2007, pp. 81–114, 94.

169 ES, 13f.; WuG, 6f.

170 G. Jellinek, *Allgemeine Staatslehre*, reprint of the 3rd edn of 1913, Berlin: Julius Springer, 1922 (original publication 1900), esp. Ch. 2. For an example of the representative literature, see S. Breuer, *Georg Jellinek und Max Weber. Von der sozialen zur soziologischen Staatslehre*, Baden-Baden: Nomos, 1999; C. Schönberger 'Ein Liberaler zwischen Staatswille und Volkswille: Georg Jellinek und die Krise des staatsrechtlichen Positivismus um die Jahrhundertwende', in S. L. Paulson and M. Schulte (eds),

Georg Jellinek – *Beiträge zu Leben und Werk*, Tübingen: Mohr Siebeck, 2000, pp. 3–32. In his *System der subjektiven Rechte*, Freiburg: J.C.B. Mohr, 1892/1905, p. 14f., Jellinek had already associated himself with the then customary distinction between the human and the natural sciences and, considering the dual nature of the State, clarified the nature of the two modes of cognition by contrasting on the one hand a physiological and a psychological approach representing natural scientific, theoretical knowledge, to an aesthetic approach on the other. Both approaches dealt with one and the same object, which was a symphony, whose 'reality' was in the first case 'fluctuations on air pressure' and the 'sensations of sound that they created', in the second enjoyment and aesthetic feelings. He also made it clear that the two modes of knowledge could neither be substitutes for each other, nor did they stand in contradiction. If the example of the symphony is a reference to H. v. Helmholtz (*Die Lehre von den Tonempfindungen als physiologische Grundlage für die Theorie der Musik*, 3rd edn, Brunswick: Vieweg & Sohn, 1870, p. 369ff.), the conclusion that he draws also involves a reference to the first 'neo-Kantian', F. A. Lange (*Geschichte des Materialismus und Kritik seiner Bedeutung in der Gegenwart*. Zweites Buch, *Geschichte des Materialismus seit Kant*, 3rd edn, Iserlohn: J. Baedeker, 1877, p. 538ff.), who he cited in his *Habilitationsschrift* (*Die sozialethische Bedeutung von Recht, Unrecht und Strafe*, reprint of the 1878 Vienna edn, Hildesheim: Georg Olms, 1967, p. 9). On Helmholtz and Lange, see K. Ch. Köhnke, *Entstehung und Aufstieg des Neukantianismus. Die deutsche Universitätsphilosophie zwischen Idealismus und Positivismus*, Frankfurt am Main: Suhrkamp, 1986, pp. 151ff., 233ff. The works by Jellinek there cited are notably epistemological, showing that he was well acquainted with the basic views of the Southwest German neo-Kantians, in addition to which he was a close friend of Windelband during his time in Leipzig. On Lange and the dualism of the 'two worlds', the 'world that is' and the 'world of values', see B. Jacobsen, *Max Weber und Friedrich Albert Lange. Rezeption und Innovation*, Wiesbaden: Deutscher Universitäts Verlag, 1999, pp. 9ff., 104ff. Jens Kersten, *Georg Jellinek und die klassische Staatslehre*, Tübingen: Mohr Siebeck, 2003, p. 147ff., rightly draws attention to the fact that 'Jellinek does not take as his starting point the cognitive interest of the subject, which posits an object to be known'. On Jellinek's doctrine of types in contrast to Weber's ideal-type, ibid., p. 102ff.

171 Kelsen, *Der Soziologische und der Juristische Staatsbegriff*, op. cit., p. 132ff.; Dreier, *Rechtslehre, Staatssoziologie und Demokratietheorie bei Hans Kelsen*, op. cit., p. 212f.; Möllers, *Staat als Argument*, op. cit., p. 38f. According to Kelsen (ibid., p. 133), the theory of self-restraint (*Selbstverpflichtungstheorie*) sought to 'make the unintelligible intelligible – how the power opposed to law would be made law, how a state which was assumed to be beyond law, metalegal, alien to law, even the foe of law, could be transformed into law.'
172 Möllers, ibid., p. 39.
173 Hermes, *Soziales Handeln und Struktur der Herrschaft*, op. cit., p. 135.
174 Ibid., p. 138.
175 ES, 765; WuG, 449; MWG I/22-3, 454, 'From the charismatic revelation of new commandments there leads, via the imperium, the most direct route to the development of law formed through fixed and imposed statute.'
176 H. Kelsen, 'Zur Soziologie des Rechtes. Eine kritische Betrachtung', in S. L. Paulson (ed), *Hans Kelsen und die Rechtssoziologie. Auseinandersetzungen mit Hermann U. Kantorowicz, Eugen Ehrlich und Max Weber*, Aalen: Scientia Verlag, 1992, pp. 601–14, p. 613f.; original publication in *Archiv für Sozialwissenschaft und Sozialpolitik* (1912), 34, 601–14; see also HKW, 3, 77–92. On this last aspect, see WL, 473; from this reference it can be inferred that Weber shared Kelsen's perspective.
177 Kelsen, *Der Soziologische und der Juristische Staatsbegriff*, op. cit., p. 80.
178 Hermes, 'Das Recht einer "Soziologischen Rechtslehre"', op. cit., 215.
179 WL, 531.

180 H. Treiber, 'Vom Nutzen und Nachteil juristischer Dogmatik', *Rechtshistorisches Journal* (1997), 16, 411–52 (esp. 416ff).
181 M. R. Lepsius, 'Eigenart und Potenzial des Weber-Paradigmas', in G. Albert, A. Bienfait, S. Sigmund and C. Wendt (eds), *Das Weber-Paradigma. Studien zur Weiterentwicklung von Max Webers Forschungsprogramm*, Tübingen: Mohr Siebeck, 2003, pp. 32–41, esp. p. 35ff.
182 WL, 333f.
183 Kelsen, *Der Soziologische und der Juristische Staatsbegriff*, op. cit., p. 157.
184 Lepsius, 'Eigenart und Potenzial des Weber-Paradigmas', op. cit., p. 35f. Lübbe has however reminded us that this is not a matter of 'deducing "immanent meaning" from "cognitive systems", but rather of the given meaningful bases of action ("systems of meaning for action").' See Lübbe, *Legitimität kraft Legalität*, op. cit., p. 28f.
185 Weber succumbed to this danger, see Treiber, 'Vom Nutzen und Nachteil juristischer Dogmatik', op. cit., 424f. See also F. W. Graf, 'Die "kompetentesten" Gesprächspartner? Implizite theologische Werturteile in Max Webers "Protestantischer Ethik"', in V. Krech, and H. Tyrell (eds), *Religionssoziologie um 1900*, Würzburg: Ergon, 1995, pp. 209–48.
186 Weber, 'Diskussionsrede zu dem Vortrag von H. Kantorowicz "Rechtswissenschaft und Soziologie"', op. cit., p. 478: 'The "validity" of a legal statute in the sociological sense is a matter of empirical probability involving facts, while validity in the legal sense is a logical imperative, and those are two quite different things [. . .].'
187 H. Dreier, 'Hans Kelsen (1881–1973), "Jurist des Jahrhunderts"?', in H. Heinrichs, H. Franzki, K. Schmalz and M. Stolleis (eds), *Deutsche Juristen Jüdischer Herkunft*, München: Beck, 1993, pp. 705–32, p. 719.
188 Dreier, ibid., p. 724; See also Dreier, *Rechtslehre, Staatssoziologie und Demokratietheorie bei Hans Kelsen*, op. cit., pp. 121–29.
189 ES, 32; WuG 16, no. 3.
190 Just as Geiger (*Vorstudien zu einer Soziologie des Rechts*, op. cit., p. 71f.) employed a gradualistic concept of obligation, Weber draws upon a gradualist concept of validity (see also ES, 32; WuG, 17). Kelsen (*Der Soziologische und der Juristische Staatsbegriff*, op. cit., p. 93) likewise has a gradualist concept of effectiveness.
191 ES, 32; WuG, 16, no. 3.
192 ES, 32; WuG, 16, no. 3.
193 W. Stegmüller, *Hauptströmungen der Gegenwartsphilosophie. Eine kritische Einführung*, 8th edn, Stuttgart: Kröner, 1987, vol. 2, p. 83f. I have Gerhard Wagner (Frankfurt) to thank for drawing Stegmüller's book to my attention.
194 G. Ryle, *The Concept of Mind*, London, New York: Routledge, 2009.
195 'Correct' reading in Ryle's sense.
196 Stegmüller, *Hauptströmungen der Gegenwartsphilosophie*, op. cit., p. 83f.
197 Ryle, *The Concept of Mind*, op. cit., p. 100ff. See also L. Jansen, 'Dispositionen und ihre Realität', in Ch. Halbig and Ch. Suhm (eds), *Was ist wirklich? Neuere Beiträge zu Realismusdebatten in der Philosophie*, Frankfurt am Main: ontos verlag, 2004, pp. 117–37, p. 121f.
198 Ryle, ibid., p. 105.
199 Ibid., p. 107.
200 Ibid., p. 108.
201 Jansen, 'Dispositionen und ihre Realität', op. cit., p. 121.
202 Stegmüller, *Hauptströmungen der Gegenwartsphilosophie*, op. cit., p. 84. A 'state' may in this way cease to 'exist' sociologically, although the administrative staff (in the form of a modern bureaucracy) can indeed continue to 'exist' as a result of 'a practised ability to adapt oneself' on the part of both officials and the ruled within the existing administrative order, but also as a result of the 'objective indispensability of the once-existent

203 apparatus, in conncection with its peculiarly, "impersonal" character' (ES, 988; WuG, 570; MWG I/22-4, 209).
203 Ryle, *The Concept of Mind*, op. cit., p. 105.
204 On this problematic, see H. Treiber, 'Wie wirkt Recht? Methodische Aspekte bei der Erforschung von Wirkungszusammenhängen', in G. Wagner (ed) *Kraft Gesetz. Beiträge zur rechtssoziologischen Effektivitätsforschung*, Wiesbaden: VS Verlag, 2010, pp. 119-44, esp. pp. 133–42.
205 ES, 28; WuG 14, § 3, no. 4.
206 Letter from Max Weber of 9 March 1920 to R. Liefmann, cited in W. J. Mommsen, 'Diskussion über "Max Weber und die Machtpolitik"', in O. Stammer (ed), *Max Weber und die Soziologie heute. Verhandlungen des 15. Deutschen Soziologentages*, Tübingen: J.C.B. Mohr (Paul Siebeck), 1965, pp. 130–38, p. 137, note 12, now available in NWG ii/10–2, pp. 946f.
207 Kelsen, *Der Soziologische und der Juristische Staatsbegriff*, op. cit., p. 90, note 1.
208 Ibid., p. 89. See on this also, Dreier, *Rechtslehre, Staatssoziologie und Demokratietheorie bei Hans Kelsen*, op. cit., p. 210: the State for Kelsen 'volatises into a thought object which, like religion, evaporates if one loses one's belief in it.' See also Dreier, 'Hans Kelsens Wissenschaftsprogramm', op. cit., p. 94.
209 Kelsen, ibid., p. 80.
210 Ibid., p. 91.
211 On this and the following, see W. Schluchter, *Entscheidung für den Rechtsstaat. Hermann Heller und die staatstheoretische Diskussion in der Weimarer Republik*, Köln, Berlin: Kiepenheuer & Witsch, 1968, and the essay included there, 'Der Staat als Recht in der "Reinen Rechtslehre" von Hans Kelsen', pp. 26–52, p. 34. See Kelsen, ibid., p. 75f.
212 Schluchter, ibid., p. 34. It would certainly be very misguided if one sought to imply that, for Kelsen, the substance of a given legal order was not influenced by political and/or social disputes. See Dreier, 'Hans Kelsens Wissenschaftsprogramm', op. cit., p. 83.
213 Kelsen, *Der Soziologische und der Juristische Staatsbegriff*, op. cit., p. 93.
214 Dreier, 'Hans Kelsen (1881–1973), "Jurist des Jahrhunderts"?', op. cit., p. 719.
215 Kelsen, *Der Soziologische und der Juristische Staatsbegriff*, op. cit., p. 93ff. For a recent philosophical account of the basic norm (*Grundnorm*), see S. L. Paulson, 'Zwei radikale Objektivierungsprogramme in der Rechtslehre Hans Kelsens', in Paulson and Stolleis (eds), op. cit., pp. 191–220. Loos (*Zur Wert- und Rechtslehre Max Webers*, op. cit., p. 110) sees in the 'recognition of the hypothetical *validation* of law for the purpose of analysis with the aid of an interpretative schema which is either logically compelling or conventional (hence for its part only hypothetically valid)', as does Weber in *Science as a Vocation* (MWG I/17, 95), a parallel to Kelsen's basic norm (*Grundnorm*), or founding hypothesis. On the function of the basic norm, see the parable that M. T. Fögen borrows from Luhmann concerning the 'Handing back of the twelfth camel' in *Das Lied vom Gesetz*, München: Carl Friedrich von Siemens Stiftung, 2007, p. 104. On Luhmann, see his 'Die Rückgabe des zwölften Kamels. Zum Sinn einer soziologischen Analyse des Rechts' (1985), in G. Teubner (ed), *Die Rückgabe des zwölften Kamels. Niklas Luhmann in der Diskussion über Gerechtigkeit*, Stuttgart: Lucius & Lucius, 2000, pp. 3–60 (*Zeitschrift für Rechtssoziologie* (2000), 21, 1, 3–60).
216 Schluchter, *Entscheidung für den Rechtsstaat*, op. cit., p. 27.
217 H. Kelsen, *Allgemeine Staatslehre*, Berlin: Julius Springer, 1925, p. 17; Kelsen, *Der Soziologische und der Juristische Staatsbegriff*, op. cit., p. 91.
218 Kelsen, ibid., p. 92.
219 Ibid., p. 92.
220 Lübbe, *Legitimität kraft Legalität*, op. cit., p. 54, on the distinction made by Kelsen (*Der Soziologische und der Juristische Staatsbegriff*, op. cit., p. 91ff.).

221 A few pages earlier Kelsen (ibid., p. 78) explains that 'every connection to "realisation" is excluded from "*Sollen*"', so that 'the normative perspective is treated as something entirely different from the teleological or technical perspective, i.e. any perspective directed to the relation of means and ends.' But there is a possible cognitive connection (*Gedankenbrücke*) established here between *Sollen* and *Sein* when he writes that 'what one states as that which ought to transpire is regarded as in some way not yet complete.' Such a completion, he states, would be as follows, '*Das Sollen* of the law realises itself in the *Sein*, in the actual, as something belonging to the world of natural reality, in the causally determined behaviour of men and women, in behaviour which conforms to law, is legally appropriate, proper in the legal sense' (Kelsen, ibid.).
222 Kelsen, ibid., p. 93.
223 Schluchter, *Entscheidung für den Rechtsstaat*, op. cit., p. 42.
224 H. Kelsen, *Das Problem der Souveränität und die Theorie des Völkerrechts. Beitrag zu einer Reinen Rechtslehre*, reprint of the 2nd edn of 1928, Aalen: Scientia, 1960, p. 96; also Schluchter, ibid., p. 42f. See also Kelsen, *Der Soziologische und der Juristische Staatsbegriff*, op. cit., p. 93.
225 Schluchter, ibid., p. 43.
226 Ibid., p. 43; Dreier, *Rechtslehre, Staatssoziologie und Demokratietheorie bei Hans Kelsen*, op. cit., p. 127.
227 Kelsen, *Der Soziologische und der Juristische Staatsbegriff*, op. cit., p. 93.
228 Dreier, *Rechtslehre, Staatssoziologie und Demokratietheorie bei Hans Kelsen*, op. cit., p. 127; Kelsen, ibid., p. 96ff.; Kelsen, *Das Problem der Souveränität und die Theorie des Völkerrechts*, op. cit., p. 96.
229 Dreier, ibid., 128f.; Schluchter, *Entscheidung für den Rechtsstaat*, op. cit., p. 43.
230 Schluchter, ibid., p. 43.
231 Ibid., p. 49; Lübbe, *Legitimität kraft Legalität*, op. cit., p. 53ff., regarding Kelsen's concept of legal validity. In respect of the impossibility of 'exceeding methodological boundaries', the following italicized formulations are telling, 'In this determination normativity and facticity link up in a quite particular manner parallel to validity and effect. What should here become evident is the fact that the ideal system of state and legal order, as specifically normative lawfulness, is, *in some fashion* a fragment of real life, a part of the causal regularity of ongoing human behaviour; and that *there has to be a degree of agreement* between the substance of the "legal" system (or the "state" system) and that of the relevant part of the "natural" system' (Kelsen, *Der Soziologische und der Juristische Staatsbegriff*, op. cit., p. 96). This agreement can on the one hand 'not exceed a certain maximum', while on the other it cannot fall below 'a certain minimum' (ibid.).
232 Schluchter, *Entscheidung für den Rechtsstaat*, op. cit., p. 48. Kelsen could have gained initial access to this insight from reading Simmel's *Soziologie* (op. cit., pp. 42–61), since he does cite this work repeatedly. Or more precisely, by reading Simmel's digression, 'Wie ist Gesellschaft möglich?', which Popitz (*Der Begriff der sozialen Rolle als Element der soziologischen Theorie*, op. cit., p. 32ff.) reformulated as the epistemological question, 'What cognitive processes are to be presupposed, as conditions of possibility, for men to see, understand, feel themselves to be part of society, as parts of a social whole?' This question draws upon Kant, as did Kelsen too. On the pros and cons of Kelsen's use of Kant, see Dreier, *Rechtslehre, Staatssoziologie und Demokratietheorie bei Hans Kelsen*, op. cit., pp. 56–90; also, more recently, Paulson and Stolleis (eds), *Hans Kelsen*, op. cit., pp. 191–220.
233 See the discussion of this in Lübbe, *Legitimität kraft Legalität*, op. cit., p. 29ff.
234 Schluchter, *Entscheidung für den Rechtsstaat*, op. cit., p. 50.
235 WL, 348.
236 ES, 14; WuG, 7.

237 Schluchter, *Entscheidung für den Rechtsstaat*, op. cit., p. 49.
238 ES, 27; WuG, 13, no. 2.
239 See the definition of the concept of order (ES, 31; WuG, 16 § 5, no. 2), but also the distinction of (observed) behavioural regularities in the non-obligatory (custom and practice) as well as the obligatory (convention and law): ES, 29f., WuG, 14f., § 4; ES, 33f., WuG, 17, § 6; ES, 319ff., WuG, 187ff. (MWG I/22-3, 210ff.).
240 Schluchter, *Entscheidung für den Rechtsstaat*, op. cit., p. 49.
241 Ibid.

Chapter 4

Kelsen reading Weber: Is a sociological concept of the State possible?

Catherine Colliot-Thélène[1]

In 1922, Kelsen published a book entitled *Der soziologische und der juristische Staatsbegriff* (*The Sociological and Juristic Concept of State*), in which he returned to and expanded on analyses that he had developed over the previous decade.[2] In the brief foreword that he penned for the second edition in 1928, he justified his decision not to make any modifications to the original text by asserting that his thesis was, in his view, still unassailable; he summed up this thesis in these terms:

> The State is a specifically *normative* unit and not a structure that can be apprehended via causal laws, whatever they may be, [. . .] as an order, it is the *legal* order, as a supra-individual will, it is the *personification* of this legal order, and [. . .] the usual *dualism* of the State and law constitutes an unacceptable doubling of the object of legal-normative knowledge.[3]

This is a clear – and radical – thesis. Kelsen does not stop at asserting the autonomy of a legal apprehension of the State compared to other possible approaches to this 'object', a view that most sociologists would probably agree with, and that Max Weber (whom we will speak about in this chapter) would most certainly have agreed with. He goes further by asserting that the legal interpretation of the State is the sole admissible one, insofar as the State is nothing other than the legal order, i.e. a normative order, and inasmuch as the intelligibility of a normative order can lie only in the logic of norms, which is, in essence, different from the logic of causal explanation. His demonstration of this thesis naturally entails an uncompromising confrontation with sociology. Thus, sociologists hold a premier place among the authors that Kelsen mentions during this demonstration, notably Max Weber, not only because he belonged to the cultural and academic milieu that Kelsen trained in (unlike Spencer and Durkheim, to whom Kelsen still dedicates a few pages), but also, and especially, because he was a jurist by training, and therefore gave particular emphasis to the different angles of approach in legal theory and sociology with regard to the State and law.

The following pages will focus solely on Kelsen's critique, as laid out in the 1922 book, of Weber's definition of the State.[4] This critique, as we shall see, ultimately comes down to challenging the possibility not only of a sociology of the State, but also of a sociology of law, or even, generally speaking, the very possibility of sociology as a science. If we consider all of Kelsen's works, we note that his relationship with Weber was a complex one. However, while his judgment of Weber in the text studied here may have been temporary, a careful reading of this text highlights a point of friction between the project of a pure theory of law (Kelsen's attempt at such a theory is undoubtedly the most uncompromising) and the sociological approach to legal phenomena. Such a reading also casts light on what was to remain the fundamental difficulty of Kelsen's endeavour throughout his works. He attempted to resolve this difficulty with the notion of the Basic Norm[5] (which he redefined on several occasions). At the same time, this reading highlights a particularity of sociological concepts of collectives: their relative indeterminacy. Apart from the distinction between State and law, which Kelsen presents (in order to dispute it) as the central issue of his critical work, he, in fact, questions the conditions for the intelligibility of institutional collectives.

The third chapter of Kelsen's book aims to give 'critical proof of the identity of the State and law',[6] i.e. to demonstrate, based on the very texts of the authors that he studies one after the other, that it is impossible to produce a concept of the State that would be different from the legal concept. In this section, as elsewhere, Kelsen gives varying degrees of attention to the authors mentioned. Jurist Georg Jellinek is given a very long reading, while Kant gets just three pages. Kelsen apparently takes Weber seriously; he dedicates nearly 15 pages to him, showing at first glance detailed knowledge of his texts, which are quoted extensively. Nevertheless, the interpretation of these texts is devastating. Indeed, Weber is called on to give evidence against himself, to admit – based on his own words – that it is impossible to establish a specifically sociological definition of the State. To demonstrate this, Kelsen proposes a very detailed, even pedantic, commentary of the beginning of the first part of *Wirtschaft und Gesellschaft*,[7] i.e. Chapter 1, 'Basic Sociological Terms', from paragraph 1, which defines interpretive sociology, up to the last paragraph (17), which defines the 'political organisation' and the 'State' as a particular form of such an organization. However, Kelsen entirely ignored the beginning of Part 2 of this classic version of *Wirtschaft und Gesellschaft*, namely, the chapter entitled 'The Economy and Social Norms'. Paragraph 1 of this chapter, 'Legal Order and Economic Order', contains basic indications regarding the main notions that, according to Weber, are involved in differentiating between sociology and legal theory. We shall return to this point later on.

Kelsen's analysis thus begins with a comment on Weber's definition of interpretive sociology. Here, he puts forth what will prove to be a cornerstone of his argument: sociology by its very method is condemned to heteronomy. Indeed, the criterion that Weber uses to determine the object of interpretive sociology does not designate a specific object, but, instead, forces him to borrow basic concepts from other disciplines. The second part of this analysis focuses more specifically on the ideal type of the State, i.e. (according to Kelsen) its 'essence'. In this context, Kelsen addresses the difference (which Weber views as fundamental) between normative validity and the facticity of law. He endeavours to demonstrate that this difference cannot justify a difference between a sociological and legal interpretation of law and the State, insofar as the 'validity' of a normative order can only be understood in a normative sense. In a third section, Kelsen reviews the various types of social relationships that Weber distinguishes and defines in paragraphs 10 to 17 of 'Basic Sociological Terms': open and closed social relationships; organization (*Verband*); administrative and regulative order; enterprise (*Betrieb*); compulsory institution (*Anstalt*); domination (*Herrschaft*); political organization; and, lastly, the State, with the famous definition of the monopoly of the legitimate use of physical force, which is the culminating point of the entire chapter.[8] Kelsen cites each of these definitions, adding comments of varying lengths depending on the case, and repeatedly asserting that each one applies to law. Law, 'while this is not directly said, must indeed be considered a "closed" social relationship'; it 'must be classified as an organisation'; it is necessarily an 'administrative order', and 'the legal organisation is an administrative organisation'; law 'must necessarily be valid as an enterprise', it is a compulsory institution (*Anstalt*), it is a *Herrschaft*, and lastly, it is a political organization. While Kelsen explicitly disputes the pertinence of only a few of the distinctions drawn by Weber (notably the distinction between administrative and regulative orders), he presents them in such a way as to deny their overall usefulness. Solely preoccupied in showing that each of the concepts cited is applicable to law, he ignores or wastes little time looking at the specific contrasts that, each time, warrant Weber's conceptual precision: between an open and closed social relationship, between an organization (*Verband*) and a compulsory institution (*Anstalt*), between domination and power, and between a political and hierocratic organization. This third section of his argument[9] has, in fact, just one objective: to show that, following Weber's own definitions, 'law is ultimately identical to the State', or, at the very least, 'the State is a legal order'.[10] Hence, what interpretive sociology can say about the essence of the State includes 'not a word more than what the normative theory of law teaches'.[11]

To assess the accuracy of this critical reconstruction of Weber's concept of the State, we must go back to the starting point, i.e. the interpretation of the object of interpretive sociology. Giving a relatively faithful reproduction of paragraph 1 of 'Basic Sociological Terms', Kelsen writes that the aim of this sociology is to 'interpret comprehensively (*deutend verstehen*) social action, i.e., an action that, according to its meaning, is related to the behaviour of other individuals, and thereby to explain this action causally in its occurrence and its effects'.[12] The reference to the meaning of action, which must be the meaning that this action has for the actor himself (Kelsen refers to this as its 'immanent' meaning), is enough to prove sociology's heteronomy, according to Kelsen. A sociologist cannot boast a specific principle of interpretation because he must, instead, borrow this principle from actors, who direct their action according to 'systems of knowledge', which can be, for instance, the laws of physics for a physicist carrying out an experiment, the rules of trade for a merchant, etc. Weber, as we know, immediately makes a further distinction that is important methodologically, concerning the conditions for determining the meaning of an action: this can be the meaning actually targeted by the actor, or, instead, the 'theoretically conceived *pure type* of subjective meaning attributed to the hypothetical actor or actors in a given type of action', and this type is generally that of an instrumentally rational (*zweckrational*) action.[13] Kelsen uses this distinction to shift the ideal type (i.e. the conceptual construction) to the side of the ideal. Using the example of the State – which is his sole object of interest – he notes that, also in this case, the ideal type can only be a 'conceptual construction of an action that is rigorously instrumentally rational'.[14] Of course, Weber would have agreed with this, but Kelsen suggests at the same time – and here he strays from Weber – that this construction can be nothing other than the legal theory of the State. The difference that Weber concedes to exist between the meaning actually targeted by actors and the meaning reconstructed as an ideal type would, according to Kelsen, necessarily set an unequivocal ideal type that must act as the principle of interpretation, and this principle, unique for each concept, must correspond to an ideal. We can understand the actual behaviour of men, 'at least when working with the ideal type, only insofar as it corresponds to the conceived *ideal* purposive system (*Zwecksystem*)'.[15]

As detailed as Kelsen's reading of Weber's text appears to be, it includes a certain number of omissions. With regard to sub-paragraph 1 of 'Methodological Foundations',[16] which explains the meaning of the terms used to characterize the subject of interpretive sociology, Kelsen only distinguishes between the meaning actually targeted by actors and the meaning conceived theoretically. However, Weber adds a remark actually intended to prevent confusion between the ideal type and the ideal. According to Weber:

> In no case does [this theoretically conceived meaning] refer to an objectively 'correct' meaning or one which is 'true' in some metaphysical sense. It is this which distinguishes the empirical sciences of action, such as sociology and history, from the dogmatic disciplines in that area, such as jurisprudence, logic, ethics, and aesthetics, which seek to ascertain the 'true' and 'valid' meanings associated with the objects of their investigation.[17]

This precision is important, as we can see, and the fact that Kelsen ignores it cannot be attributed to simple negligence. Indeed, his entire demonstration is based on the assumption that the immanent meaning of an action can only be a 'logical connection',[18] unique for each entity considered, and, therefore, identical to the 'correct' meaning that the dogmatic sciences, in each case, must determine. This voluntary negligence is very likely the reason why Kelsen did not take into account the very beginning of the second part of *Wirtschaft und Gesellschaft*, where, in order to determine the general relationship between law and economics, Weber expounds further on the difference between the viewpoints of the dogmatic and empirical sciences.

The misunderstanding regarding what is meant by the 'meaning' of the action, which begins with the confusion between the ideal type and the ideal, continues – or even grows deeper – in the rest of Kelsen's commentary. Kelsen cites a passage in which Weber basically notes that, for a sociologist, a social relationship consists 'exclusively' of the probability of an action that is determined by its meaning. This remark, despite the circularity of its formulation, is clearly aimed at excluding substantialist interpretations of collective concepts, with Weber giving the examples of 'social organizations' such as a 'State, church, association, or marriage'.[19] In simpler terms, this means that social structures have no other reality, from a sociologist's standpoint, than that which is given to them by the human practices that bring them into existence. These practices must form the basis for understanding the structures and their evolution, and not *vice versa*. It is not certain that Weber always followed this methodology,[20] but it is entirely consistent with the definition of the object of interpretive sociology, which – contrary to what Kelsen wishes to believe – cannot be reduced to understanding the action, but which seeks to understand it *in order to explain its occurrence and its effects*. Objective institutions, such as the State, the Church, marriage, etc. are among these 'effects'. In some way, they are the coagulation of practices to which they owe their existence and, possibly, their transformations. Kelsen's interpretation of this passage is biased as he pretends to believe that it deals with the specific difference between each of the collective entities cited, or even their essence. Yet, Weber certainly does not intend to determine the essence of the State or of any other collective entity. Generally speaking, Weber's sociology is an historical one, and his sociological definition of the State based on its monopoly on the legitimate use of violence (which Kelsen dissects at the end of his critique) is a thesis that he borrows from *legal historians* not from legal dogmatism: the modern State is the result of a process whereby a centralized power monopolizes the guarantee of law, the corollary of the abolition or subordination of the pluralist communities of law of earlier societies.[21] This appropriation of a historical thesis for a categorization system intended for sociology is not without problems. Notably, it means that we can only actually speak of the State, in a strict sense, when referring to the modern Western forms of political associations. However, it also implies that, from the standpoint of a sociologist or an historian, the actual existence of the State (i.e. the reality of this monopoly) is what matters, not its ideal essence.

However, Kelsen refuses to recognize the relevance of the distinction between existence and essence. In his view, if we apply only the principles of interpretive sociology, the State's existence coincides with its validity (*Geltung*), just as is the case for the Pythagorean theorem. We can readily agree that the validity of the Pythagorean theorem does not derive from the fact that some people at a certain point in time thought of it and thought of it correctly. According to Kelsen, the same holds true for the existence – in other words, the validity – of the State, which cannot derive from the actual actions of individuals, whoever they might be.[22] Citing a passage in which Weber states that a State 'ceases to exist in a sociologically-relevant sense whenever there is no probability that certain kinds of meaningfully-oriented social action will take place', Kelsen decries an 'inadmissible conceptual shift'.[23] According to Kelsen, Weber surreptitiously identifies the

State with actions reduced down to their 'corporeal-mechanical' reality, entirely forgetting what gives them meaning. Apart from the fact that assimilating existence to validity is particularly stretched,[24] we can wonder whether the conceptual shift is Kelsen's rather than Weber's. For, while Weber, in this passage and everywhere else, speaks of actions only to refer to behaviour organized by meaning, therefore not reducing them to their physical reality, Kelsen only retains the meaning of action, which amounts to annihilating it as action *per se*. Furthermore, in Weber's view, the inexistence of a State is a borderline case. He seeks to emphasize that, for a sociologist and historian, the existence of a State is not based solely on the existence of a legal order that demands respect and obedience from a defined circle of individuals; its existence depends on the reality of this respect and obedience:

> Thus for sociological purposes there does not exist, as there does for the law, a rigid alternative between the validity and lack of validity of a given order. On the contrary, there is a gradual transition between the two extremes.[25]

To this, Kelsen retorts that 'for the State, which is the object of legal theory', there is indeed the alternative that Weber denies.[26] However, is this not to acknowledge, in fact, in agreement with Weber,[27] the difference between two concepts of the State: that of legal theory and that of sociology? And, apart from begging the question, what justification is there for refusing to allow a sociologist to ask different questions regarding the State than those asked by a legal theoretician?

As would be expected, Kelsen's critique culminates in an interpretation of the validity (*Geltung*) of a normative order. Weber highlighted that the validity of an order of this sort, from the standpoint of interpretive sociology, cannot be inferred merely from the regularity of social behaviour.[28] Custom or self-interest may produce such uniformity. However, he notes, a civil servant that arrives at the office on time every morning, while partly motivated by custom and self-interest, is generally also motivated by the conviction that this punctuality is a 'duty' implied by acknowledging the validity of civil service rules. Kelsen sees this comment as the expression of the basic idea, 'powerfully repressed by the constant reference to the factual occurrence of the action',[29] that the meaning of what we call a valid order is duty, i.e. the imperative norm (*Sollnorm*). Starting from the interpretation – which we have already noted is disputable – that the object of interpretive sociology is the meaning of action, Kelsen believes that he can assert that the question of the reality of this action must generally be a secondary matter for this sociology. Therefore, since the meaning of action, in the case of a legitimate order, lies in the actor's acknowledgement of the validity of the norm, Kelsen concludes that, for normative orders (i.e. law and the State), interpretive sociology has no concepts at its disposal other than those used by legal theory. Insofar as these orders are central objects for this sociology, it must 'be a legal theory, or at least, see through the eyes of a jurist, in order simply to see anything.'[30] A sociology of law or the State, separate from legal theory, would be impossible. And, suggesting that the study of normative orders is probably the essential object of interpretive sociology, Kelsen goes so far as to doubt the very possibility of this sociology being a science.[31]

The meaning that should be given to the 'validity' of a normative order is clearly at the centre of the divergence between the Pure Theory of Law and Weberian sociology. However, the positions defended by Kelsen and Weber are not symmetrical. Weber never disputed the legitimacy of a purely legal interpretation of the law (or of the State, insofar as it is a legal order), even though he obviously could not know the particularly exacting form that Kelsen would give such an interpretation. Kelsen emphasizes on several occasions that the object of a science is determined by its method, and thus there cannot be different approaches, i.e. different methods, for a single object. Yet, Weber is entirely in agreement with him on this point. Indeed, Weber noted, with regard to the 'economic order', that the problems raised by legal theory (which he calls 'legal dogmatics') and sociology are totally different, to such an extent that 'their [objects] cannot come directly into contact with one another.' Furthermore:

> the ideal 'legal order' of legal theory has nothing directly to do with the world of real economic conduct, since both exist on different levels. One exists in the realm of the 'ought' while the other deals with the world of the 'is'.[32]

Weber and Kelsen both spoke the Neo-Kantian language, and with this language, they shared a very particular ontology, whereby 'is' (*Sein*) and 'ought' (*Sollen*) are two independent worlds, referring to cognitive patterns that must also be entirely different. For both men, however, the question of the relationship between these two worlds could not be avoided. Such a relationship is indirect, obviously, because any direct relationship was excluded by hypothesis. This question underlies the entirety of Kelsen's work, and is even present in *Der soziologische und der juristische Staatsbegriff*, via the recurring reference to the opposition between normativity and facticity. However, he 'represses' it (to use the term that he applies to Weber), here and elsewhere – perhaps here more than elsewhere – by asserting that the validity of an order can only be understood in a normative sense.[33] Weber gave a completely different answer to this question, by conceding that the difference between *is* and *ought* must have an impact on 'validity' itself, and while the term validity is always applied to a norm or a normative order, it can also be understood in two ways: normatively *and* empirically. This is, notably, what he says in the passage that follows:

> If it is nevertheless said that the economic and the legal order are intimately related to one another, the latter is understood, not in the legal, but in the sociological sense, i.e. as being *empirically* valid. In this context, 'legal order' thus assumes a totally different meaning. It refers not to a set of norms of logically demonstrable correctness, but rather to a complex of actual determinants [*Bestimmungsgründe*] of human conduct.[34]

Conversely, for Kelsen, the validity of a normative order is unequivocal. When an individual acts out of duty, within the framework of a given normative order, the meaning of his action must coincide, according to Kelsen, with the meaning that this order holds for a jurist or legal theoretician. What Kelsen is unable or unwilling to understand is the difference between the *belief* in the validity of a normative order (e.g. a law, rule, legal system or institutionalized power)[35] and the logician's interpretation of this validity; or, in other words, the difference between the practical relationship that an actor subject to a norm has with that norm, and the theoretical relationship that a scholar has with the same norm. All individuals acting 'out of respect for the law' (or who knowingly break the law, which is another way of acknowledging its 'validity') are not subsequently jurists, much less legal theoreticians. The 'duty' that the actor subscribes to is a motivation (i.e. a 'factual' reason) for the action, and in this respect, interpretive sociology takes into account this duty in order to explain the structure of the action and its effects. It is worth noting that, after first basing his argument on Weber's definition of the object of interpretive sociology in order to assert its inevitable heteronomy, Kelsen feels the need to rectify this definition. He writes that it is untrue that:

> as is asserted in the definition of the concept of 'sociology', interpretive understanding is identical to its causal explanation [. . .] There is a single principle of interpretation, whereas the motivations – and thus the causes – whereby men behave in compliance with an order can be very different, and these remain completely unknown to this interpretive method; they are, basically, indifferent [to it].[36]

This apparently insignificant remark (in a footnote) reveals how Kelsen has to twist interpretive sociology around to make it contradict itself. It is no accident, as we can see here, that Kelsen failed to cite the passage in which Weber indicates the difference between the 'empirical sciences of action' and 'dogmatic disciplines'. In fact, Kelsen does not want to concede that, in law (or the State as a legal entity), an action's immanent meaning may differ from the 'correct' meaning given by a scholar interpreting this norm. As a result, for all questions related to these two objects, seeking a causal explanation (i.e. looking for motivations) has simply no legitimacy. In an essay from 1913 ('Some Categories of Interpretive Sociology'[37]), Weber notes that sociology cannot avoid using legal expressions, precisely insofar as such terms are based on 'a syllogistic interpretation of norms', in order to look at real action. However, the sociologist, given the object of his research, must also 'slip his own meaning underneath [*unterschieben*]' these expressions – a meaning that is 'radically different from the legal meaning.'[38] This is undoubtedly a difficult process, which is why Weber returned to this issue so often. However, to declare that it is impossible, as Kelsen does, amounts to declaring that sociology of the State, or even of the law, is impossible.

To a reader of Weber, Kelsen is intellectually dishonest in omitting texts in which Weber refers explicitly to the difference in the cognitive objects of the 'dogmatic' disciplines and the empirical sciences of action. The central and predominant critical focus of Kelsen's book is a sociology that is intended as a social psychology, and therefore a sociology that claims to reduce social facts to their psychological aspects. Weber did, indeed, pay attention to the psychology of his time.[39] However, he concluded that psychology, with its variants, was of no aid in defining the purpose of 'interpretive sociology'. By placing action at the centre of its object, Weber clearly signals that the representations and emotions of actors were of interest only insofar as they shape these actors' actions. To Weber, these actions – and these alone – underlie the existence of social phenomena, regardless of the extent to which they are institutionalized. Such a principle enables him to avoid both diluting sociology in individual psychology, and (what might be considered erring in the other direction) the reification of collectives. When Kelsen attacks the concepts of 'collective consciousness' (*Gesamtbewußtsein*), 'ethnic soul' (*Volksseele*), or even 'objectivated spirit' (*objektiver Geist*),[40] when he denounces hypotheses that easily tend towards mythology, when he stigmatizes organismic conceptions of the social,[41] a reader of Weber easily follows his arguments. However, this reader can nevertheless not join Kelsen in concluding that the *objectiveness* of social structures, and of the State in particular, can only be sought in the ideal system of norms.[42]

What would have been Weber's answer to Kelsen? He probably would have written a scathing article, similar to the one he wrote about Stammler.[43] However, he probably would not have added any new arguments to those which he had already put forth on several occasions. Yet, the fact that he felt a need to return to this matter so often is an indication of a difficulty that he was fully aware of, and which Kelsen's critique highlights. Here, we must return to a previously cited formula, whereby Kelsen pinpoints this difficulty: when dealing with law and the State, the sociologist must 'see through the eyes of a jurist, in order simply to see anything.'[44] By acknowledging that a sociologist cannot avoid using some terms borrowed from the lexicon of jurists, Weber is partly in agreement. But only partly so. For, although a sociologist (or an historian) cannot ignore the legal dimension of the State, and cannot simply determine the State as a relationship of domination or constraint, he cannot reduce the State to this dimension either. While Kelsen argues (at least in this text) that there is no concept of the State other than its legal concept, Weber notes that this concept does not meet the specific conceptual requirements for sociological intelligibility. Concepts must be adapted to their cognitive objectives. Yet, while a legal theoretician can keep facticity at a distance, this is not the case for an empirical science of action, be it sociology or history. Between the jurist's stance, aimed at explaining the coherence of a normative system, and that of the sociologist or historian, investigating the effects of such systems on the real behaviour of actors, the difference is so blatant that Kelsen himself could not fail to notice it. And he most certainly pushed his argument to the extreme in this 1922 text given his need at that time to justify the autonomy of the pure theory of law. Indeed, a year later, in the introduction to the second edition of *Hauptprobleme der Staatsrechtslehre* (1923), he claimed to follow Hermann

Cohen's theory of experience, 'according to which the orientation of knowledge determines the object of knowledge', such that 'the State, insofar as it is the object of legal knowledge, cannot be anything other than law, because legal knowledge or understanding cannot mean anything other than understanding something as law'.[45] By formulating his epistemological position in these terms, Kelsen leaves open the possibility of more than one concept of the State.

Nevertheless, his critique is interesting in that it emphasizes the relative indeterminacy that characterizes sociological concepts of collectives, compared to legal concepts. The legal concept of the United States, cited as an example by Weber in his speech at the first Congress of the German Sociological Association, 'has, compared to the sociological concept of the United States, the enormous superiority of a *logically* clear validity in its principle'.[46] This is why, he added, sociological concepts and, more generally, collective concepts from disciplines other than legal theory, must be oriented towards legal concepts.[47] What does this 'orientation' consist of, and how far does it extend? What remains of the legal concept of law or the State in the terminology used by a sociologist, when terms are borrowed from a jurist, while another meaning is 'slid underneath'? We must admit that Weber was rather vague on this point. However, the answer must certainly be sought in the process of building the ideal type. As the latter is deliberately artificial, several ideal types can correspond to a single referent. Deciding on the essence of the State will not resolve the equivocal meaning of the term in its ordinary usages. The sociologist, if he wishes to work scientifically, must build his concepts according to the specific questions that he asks; these questions may vary depending on the context. And we can assume that, depending on the context, the sociologist will have to give more or less emphasis to a strictly legal understanding of the State. On a methodological level, the confusion that Kelsen produces, from the very start of his commentary, between the ideal type and the (legal) ideal, is indeed at the root of the misunderstanding that takes several forms in the 15 pages of his critique of Weber. And we should be glad that these pages were not Kelsen's final word on Max Weber or on sociology.

Notes

1 Translated from the French by Christopher Mobley.
2 H. Kelsen, *Der soziologische und der juristiche Staatsbegriff*, Tübingen: Mohr/Siebeck, 1922 was published in a second edition, without modifications, in 1928. The present article cites the latter edition (republished by Scientia Verlag Aalen, 1981), using the abbreviation *SJS* (our own translation from German to English). Previous texts dealing with the same theme were collected, along with texts from some of the authors Kelsen critiques (H. Kantorowicz, E. Ehrlich and M. Weber), in S. Paulson (ed), *Hans Kelsen und die Rechtssoziologie*, Amsterdam: Scientia, 1992.
3 *SJS*, ibid., p. v.
4 This scope implies two restrictions: compared to the rest of *SJS*, and compared to some of Kelsen's other texts, where he generally expresses a more measured, or even laudatory, view of Weberian sociology. For a more general comparison of Weber and Kelsen, see (in French) N. Bobbio, 'Max Weber et Hans Kelsen', in *Essais de théorie du*

droit, Paris/Brussels: Bruylant/LGDJ, 1998, pp. 255–70; and A. Carrino, 'Max Weber et Hans Kelsen', in C. M. Herrera (ed), *Le droit, la politique. Autour de Max Weber, Hans Kelsen, Carl Schmitt*, Paris: L'Harmattan, 1995, pp. 185–203.

5 The interpretation of the 'Basic Norm' is widely discussed in commentary on Kelsen's work. Obviously, this cannot be dealt with in the present chapter, nor can we summarize the numerous studies dedicated to this issue. For a recent analysis and a unique and stimulating proposal, see J.-F. Kervégan, 'À propos de l'ontologie des normes: le "paradoxe de Kelsen" a-t-il une solution institutionnelle?' ('About the ontology of norms: is there an institutional solution for the "Kelsen paradox"?') (unpublished; to be published in English).

6 *SJS*, op. cit., p. 114.

7 Kelsen refers to the 1921 edition of Weber's *Wirtschaft und Gesellschaft*. In this chapter, we refer to the second edition of the first complete English translation, based on the fourth German edition of *Wirtschaft und Gesellschaft*: *Economy and Society*, G. Roth and C. Wittich (eds), 2nd edn, Berkeley: University of California Press, 1978. For the purposes of this chapter, it was not absolutely necessary to refer to the corresponding volumes of *Max Weber-Gesamtausgabe*, Tübingen: Mohr/Siebeck, which is now considered the reference, but which spreads the manuscripts later assembled and published under the title *Wirtschaft und Gesellschaft* across several volumes, according to when they were written.

8 Paragraph 17 also looks at the difference between a political and hierocratic organization, which Kelsen does not mention.

9 Here, we sum up the last section, which we shall not return to later on, as Kelsen only draws conclusions from the demonstration laid out in the first two sections.

10 *SJS*, op. cit., p. 168.

11 Ibid., p. 170.

12 Ibid., p. 157.

13 Weber, *Economy and Society I*, op. cit., p. 4.

14 *SJS*, op. cit., p. 158.

15 Ibid. 'Ideal' is emphasized by Kelsen.

16 Weber, *Economy and Society I*, op. cit., p. 4.

17 Ibid.

18 *SJS*, op. cit., p. 158.

19 See Weber, *Economy and Society I*, op. cit., p. 27.

20 For a balanced discussion of this point, see, for instance, S. Breuer, *'Herrschaft' in der Soziologie Max Webers*, Wiesbaden: Harrassowitz Verlag, 2011, pp. 21–24.

21 See A. Anter, *Max Webers Theorie des modernen Staats*, Berlin: Duncker & Humblot, 1996; and C. Colliot-Thélène, 'La fin du monopole de la violence légitime?', in M. Coutu and G. Rocher (eds), *La légitimité de l'Etat et du droit*, Laval: Presses Universitaires de Laval, 1995, pp. 23–46.

22 Kelsen borrows the example of the Pythagorean theorem from Georg Simmel, whom he discusses and critiques earlier in the text (p. 43).

23 *SJS*, op. cit., p. 159.

24 It is worth noting that Kelsen can only refer to the 'existence' of the Pythagorean theorem using quotation marks.

25 Weber, *Economy and Society I*, op. cit., p. 32.

26 *SJS*, op. cit., p. 160, note.

27 See Weber, *Economy and Society I*, op. cit., p. 28, 'For the purposes of legal reasoning it is essential to be able to decide whether a rule of law does or does not carry legal authority, hence whether a legal relationship does or does not "exist". This type of question is not, however, relevant to sociological problems.'

28 All these analyses are in paragraph 5 of 'Basic Sociological Terms': 'Legitimate Order', pp. 31–33.

29 *SJS*, op. cit., p. 161.
30 Ibid., p. 163.
31 See ibid., 'The essence of sociology – at least "interpretive" sociology – must lie in this unique duality of object and perspective. Hence it is problematic as a science.'
32 Weber, *Economy and Society I*, op. cit., p. 312.
33 See *SJS*, op. cit., p. 162, 'If the order as meaningful content is identical to the norm, then the "validity" of *this* order is identical to the *Sollen*.'
34 Weber, *Economy and Society I*, op. cit., p. 312. See also Weber's speech at the first Congress of the German Sociological Association, regarding H. Kantorowicz's lecture, 'The sociological validity of a legal proposition is an empirical example of the relative probability of facts, [while] legal validity is a logical norm, and these are two totally different things' (M. Weber, *Gesammelte Aufsätze zur Soziologie und Sozialpolitik*, Tübingen: Mohr/Siebeck, 1988, p. 478).
35 In Weber's words, 'These concepts of collective entities which are found both in common sense and in juristic and other technical forms of thought, have a meaning in the minds of individual persons, partly as of something actually existing, partly as of something with normative authority. This is true not only of judges and officials, but of ordinary private individuals as well. Actors thus in part orient their action to them' (Weber, *Economy and Society I*, ibid., p. 14).
36 *SJS*, op. cit., p. 161, note.
37 M. Weber, 'Über einege Kategorien der verstehenden Soziologie' in *Gesammelte Aufsätze zur Wissenschaftslehre*, Tübingen: J.C.B. Mohr (Paul Siebeck), 1988, pp. 425–74 (author's translation).
38 Ibid., p. 440. The same expression can be found in Weber, *Economy and Society I*, op. cit., p. 14, 'Both because of its precision and because it is established in general usage, the juristic concept is taken over [by sociology], but it is used in an entirely different meaning.'
39 See, in French, W. Feuerhahn, 'Sociologie, économie et psychophysique', *Revue Française de Sociologie* (2005), 46, 783–97.
40 See *SJS*, op. cit., p. 36.
41 Ibid., p. 37ff.
42 See ibid., p. 44, 'It is only as a normative system that the State can have these qualities that the psychological approach seeks in vain to attribute forcibly to a fictitious social psychological reality: the *objectivity* of this structure, which is fundamentally opposed to the subjectivity of mental processes (which are the only data that psychological analysis has at its disposal), and which is nothing other than *objective* validity, i.e. independent of the will and desires of the subjects, of a normative order.'
43 This does not mean that Kelsen's position in his 1922 text can be assimilated to that of Stammler, whom Weber criticizes for attributing a power of causal explanation to legal norms.
44 *SJS*, op. cit., p. 163.
45 H. Kelsen, *Hauptprobleme der Staatsrechtslehre*, 2nd edn, Aalen: Scientia Verlag, 1984, preface, p. xvii (quoted in M. Pascher, *Einführung in den Neukantianismus*, Munich: Wilhelm Fink Verlag, 1997, p. 157).
46 Weber, *Gesammelte Aufsätze zur Soziologie und Sozialpolitik*, op. cit., pp. 478–49.
47 Ibid.

Chapter 5

Kelsen, Weber and the problem of the emergence of the State

Michel Troper

There is a widespread belief that Kelsen strongly opposed legal sociology. That belief is based on Kelsen's critique of the claim by legal sociologists of his time that legal sociology being a science of facts is the only true 'scientific legal theory'.[1] For Kelsen, this was obviously unacceptable because, within the framework of legal positivism, norms are different from facts and cannot be derived from facts. Legal sociologists, such as Hermann Kantorowicz or Eugen Ehrlich, were thus guilty of the same fallacy as natural law philosophers. Kelsen was, however, prepared to accept the possibility of a plurality of legal sciences.[2] Legal science and legal sociology are different because the object of the former is legal norms while the object of the latter is a set of natural facts that are parallel to the law, but there are some necessary links between them. The most obvious of such links results from the observation that 'in order to be an object of a sociology of law the human behavior must be determined by the idea of a valid order'.[3]

Yet, we can find some other links and use legal theory as an instrument to understand not only norms but also social facts. This chapter is an attempt to investigate a historical problem, the emergence of the State in the legal and political language of the sixteenth and seventeenth centuries and explain it by means of legal theory.

I will undertake this in two stages. I will begin with Kelsen's theory of the unity of law and State, which has greater affinity than one might think with Weber's conception of the State. I will then seek to indicate that, despite, or perhaps because of, its weaknesses, it can potentially illuminate the problem of the emergence of the State.

Kelsen's theory of the unity of law and State

Kelsen's theory of the unity of law and State is well known and it is sufficient to summarize his main arguments. His is first and foremost a negative theory directed against the traditional theory and aiming at dissolving some of its aporias. According to the traditional theory, law and the State are two distinctive entities and it is, therefore, necessary to analyse their relation. In particular, the theory examines which is superior and Kelsen easily shows that it leads to a logical difficulty: if one views the State as the sole source of law, then it cannot be bound by law; but, on the other hand, the State can only be a source of law if it has been empowered by some legal rules and, in that case, it is limited by those rules. The traditional theory of law is, therefore, constrained to make a bizarre construction and view the State as being at the same time bound and unbound by law or as being bound by its own law.

In addition, such a distinction between the law and the State is based on the assumption that the State is a fact, but if this were the case, it could not produce law because law can only derive from law. This is the reason why legal theory, such as that of Jellinek, has been forced to attempt a vision of the State as an object that could be viewed from both points of view, that of the social sciences and that of legal science. But such an attempt was bound to fail. Thus, Kelsen criticized Jellinek, stressing that each science constructs its own object, so that the social sciences and legal science would not study one and the same object, viewed from different angles, but two different objects. Thus, if the State is viewed as a social reality, a fact, it cannot create law, nor can law create the State out of a legal vacuum, i.e. without being empowered.[4]

On the other hand, it is impossible to find a definition of the State as a fact separate from the law, which would be independent from legal concepts. Kelsen analyses several attempts to define the State in sociological or psychological terms and shows that every such definition presupposes a legal concept.[5] The most important of such analyses is a comment on Max Weber's famous definition of the State as 'an entity that successfully claims a monopoly on the *legitimate* use of violence'. He stresses that this monopoly is obviously not a *de facto* monopoly, because there are many acts of violence that are not committed by the State; it is only a monopoly of the legitimate use of violence. 'Legitimate' here does not mean that the use of violence by the State is just or in accordance with certain fundamental values. It means that acts of violence are performed according to legal rules. This corresponds to what Weber called 'rational legitimacy'. However, the State is an abstraction and, thus, incapable of exercising violence. Only human beings can exercise violence, but the acts accomplished by some individuals are imputed to the State and this is only made possible by way of legal rules that prescribe which acts by which individuals will be imputed to the State.

Yet, while it is impossible to give a purely sociological definition of the State, it is also impossible to define it in purely legal terms. If we look at the traditional definition by the three elements (a people, a territory, a public government), we can see that it is impossible to define these elements taken one by one without a tautology: a people is not an objective entity that could be defined independently of the State; the people of France cannot be defined by some common psychological, religious or ethnic characteristic, but only as the class of human beings who are subject to the French State or, in other words, to the same legal order; similarly, the territory of the State can only be defined as that portion of space that is subject to a particular State or, in other words, to the legal order of that State; moreover, it is the State that decides on the content of the class of subjects that constitute the people or on the limits of the portion of space that constitutes its territory; lastly, the public government is the government of the State or the highest power in the legal order and what constitutes the government of a State is also decided by the State. Thus, these three elements cannot define the State because they are themselves defined by the State and, since we can in each case substitute in the *definiens* the words 'legal order' or 'law' for 'the State', they are just two names for one and the same reality. 'State' is only the name given to the legal order when we want to personify it.

Finally, the traditional dualist theory is closely linked to the idea that law is a product of the will. While every rule is posited by an act of the will, every act of the will does not produce a rule. A rule may be produced only by those acts of the will that have been accomplished according to a rule, which, in turn, has also been posited by a higher act of the will and so on. If the highest rule has been produced by the State, one is compelled to interpret it as the expression of the will of the State, but the will is a psychological phenomenon that only exists in human beings. Thus, either we construe a myth of the State as a sort of superman endowed with a capacity to will, or we only consider the wills of certain human beings as the will of the State. However, these wills form a unity not because of some common psychological feature, but only because they are all imputed to the State by some legal rules. It is the legal rules that make the State.

Understanding the State and the legal order as one offers a number of significant advantages, two of which Kelsen emphasized. The first, and most obvious, is that it eliminates the problem of their mutual relation. The second advantage is that, by unmasking the ideology inherent in the dualist theory, it reveals that the law and the State are nothing but an organization of force. The ideological function of the dualist theory is twofold. On the one hand, by presenting the State as separate from the law, it opens the possibility that the State is subject to the law. The State then appears, not as simple force or violence, but as a *Rechtstaat*. On the other hand, viewing the State as being outside the law implies that it has its own superior interests, which justify, on occasion, the exception to, or even suspension of, legal rule. The dualist theory is, thus, another version of the doctrine of reason of State (*raison d'Etat*).[6]

Unmasking the ideological character of the dualist theory reveals that the State or the law is nothing but power. As Kelsen famously wrote on several occasions:

> Whoever looks for an answer to the eternal question of what stands behind the positive law will never find, I fear, either an absolute metaphysical truth or the absolute justice of natural law. Who lifts the veil and does not shut his eyes will find staring at him the hideous Gorgon head of power.[7]

The image of the Gorgon, and the underlying presumption that the law is the veil of power, can be interpreted in two different ways. First, it can simply mean that law is the form of which the real substance is not justice but power. But it can also be understood in the light of Weber's definition of the State. If the State is the entity that successfully claims a monopoly on the *legitimate* use of violence, and if violence is legitimate when it is exercised as prescribed by rules, then the State is the entity that exercises power by means of rules, laid down in conformity to other rules. In other words, the State only exists when there is a hierarchy of norms and the description of the structure of the law is a political analysis, because it unveils the mode in which the State operates.

This analysis shows the profound mistake in the argument made against Kelsen's monist theory: that it tends to obscure the hard fact that the State is made not only of law but also of bureaucrats, police, guns and prisons. On the contrary, he clearly shows that bureaucrats and police can be understood as part of the State precisely because rules have created them, given them powers and prescribed that their actions be imputed to the State.

However, it seems that this analysis is capable of further development when certain difficulties of Kelsen's theory become apparent. The most evident derives from the fact that we can certainly replace the words 'the French State' with 'the French legal order', but we cannot replace 'the international legal order' by the 'international State', or 'the medieval legal order' by 'the medieval State' because there is no such thing as an international State and the feudal system of the Middle Ages was different from the government that we call a State. Kelsen is, thus, constrained to introduce into his definition a new element: centralization. Some legal orders are centralized, i.e. specialized organs – such as a parliament or an executive – have a monopoly of the production of the most general norms, that are valid for the entire population, on the entire territory, and whose addressees are the subjects; whereas other legal orders, such as the international legal order, are decentralized because the norms are produced, interpreted and applied by the addressees themselves. Thus, the French or the German legal order is a State, but the international legal order is not.

Unfortunately, this distinction does not really help, because the central organs of the legal orders constitute precisely what the classic dualist theory called a 'State'. Kelsen is thus forced to admit that there are two different concepts of the State: the State *lato sensu*, which is identical with the legal order, and the State *stricto sensu*, which is the system of organs that have the power to produce the highest and more general norms. But then we are left with the same puzzle. If law and State are really one and the same thing, then the question of their mutual relation is obviously nonsensical, but the State *stricto sensu* is not the same thing as the law and we are thus confronted with the initial questions: is this State the source of law or is the law the basis of the State? Can the law that it has itself created limit the State?

Thus, Kelsen seems to have failed. However, this failure is a *felix culpa*. It provides what seems to be a fruitful opportunity to analyse the relation between the State *lato sensu* and the State *stricto sensu*. In a brief introduction to the second edition of his *Der soziologische und der juristische Staatsbegriff*, Kelsen remarks that the latter concept presupposes the former.[8]

He probably understood this as a purely logical or conceptual connection because you cannot think of the State *stricto sensu* without conceiving it as the set of those organs that produce the norms that are at the top of the entire legal order, i.e. at the top of the State *lato sensu*. Nevertheless, we can also view it as a real historical and possibly also causal connection.

The unity of law and State as an explanation for the historic emergence of the State

For the most part, Kelsen's general theory is clearly ahistorical in the sense that he is not interested in the development and change in the structure of the legal system and writes as if the description he gives were valid for all systems that qualify as legal systems, defined as immanent orders of constraint. This is particularly problematic as far as the State is concerned. While the very general definition of the law as an immanent order of constraint is applicable to very different systems – national legal systems, international law, feudal law or the law of primitive societies – it is less effective when applied to the State as identical to the law. Even if we consider only centralized legal systems, we must conclude that such centralized legal systems did not exist at all times, because the power to produce the highest norms in the system can only exist when and where there is a hierarchy of norms and the existence of a hierarchy is not universal.

This is much more obvious when we consider, not the State *lato sensu*, but the State *stricto sensu*. Although historians may differ regarding the exact point at which the process of the formation of the State *stricto sensu*, the modern State, began, most of them agree that it did not exist in every period of history and that the process was not completed until the seventeenth or eighteenth centuries.

I will consider the following hypothesis: if we define the legal system, and, thus, the State *lato sensu*, not merely as an immanent order of constraint, but by the formal characteristics identified by Kelsen, as a hierarchy that is both static and dynamic, then the emergence of the State *lato sensu*, the hierarchy of norms, can explain the emergence of the State *stricto sensu*.

We can start from this observation that the hierarchy of norms appeared gradually in Western Europe, particularly in France, in the sixteenth and seventeenth centuries and that the modern State *stricto sensu* also appeared during that period. This is not enough to allow us to speak of a causal connection, but the connection becomes clearer when we view the State as a specific mode of exercising power through law, i.e. by means of a hierarchy of norms. This is already apparent in Weber's conception of rational legitimacy, but also reflects the distribution of power that results from the hierarchy of norms.

The hierarchy of norms allows a central authority to produce general norms empowering lower authorities to produce more detailed or more local norms. Thus, the central authority can exercise power through these authorities. Power is being delegated without being lost, because the lower authorities are bound by the general rules they apply, and they can also be subject to controls. At the same time, the lower authorities benefit from the hierarchy in two ways: their decisions are rationally justified because they can always claim that they only apply higher norms, yet the power they exercise is real because the higher norm may have given them some discretion in the application of the rule, and because the norms that they apply have been expressed in a document that can always be subject to interpretation.

On the other hand, power is exercised by means of some intellectual constructs. Kelsen often stressed the ideological character of several legal doctrines, for instance, the distinction between public and private law, that serves as an argument against a socialist economy, or the *Rechtstaat* that presents the State as both creator of law and bound by law. They are ideologies in the Marxist sense: they are false theories but they serve a political function because they help justify certain political situations or actions.

However, this view of ideology misses an important point: these theories, as descriptions of positive law, even if they serve some political or economic interest, and even if they are based on false premises or lack consistency, cannot be considered false if they reflect the actual practice of legal actors, such as law makers or courts. Kelsen recognized that law is not governed by logic, because a legal system is mainly dynamic. The validity of a court decision does not depend on the validity of an inference of its content from the content of a higher norm, but only on the fact that the court has been empowered to make that decision.[9] Therefore, a correct description of the law should be a description of the actual reasoning of the courts, something that cannot be done without mentioning the use of such concepts as the division between public and private law or the *Rechtstaat*.

The law, thus, appears to be an instrument of power to the extent that it is a system not only of norms but also of concepts that are the material for legal argumentation. The State *stricto sensu* is an instrument of power, not merely because it uses soldiers and prisons – something which many other political systems also do – but also because the violence that it exercises is claimed to be legitimate in two different ways: on the one hand, as Weber clearly showed, its decisions are logically deduced from higher norms; on the other hand, these decisions are justified by a set of arguments based on a small number of specific concepts, such as sovereignty, personality of the State, continuity of the State or representation. Kelsen's critique of these arguments as ideological misses the point that they are actually necessary to the exercise of power in the political system that we call 'the State' and that we cannot describe the State without describing and analysing them.

They are truly 'constitutive' of the State. 'Constitutive' generally means 'essential' and most lawyers would agree that all States are sovereign and no entity that is not a State is fully sovereign. However, the term can also be understood in Searle's sense of a constitutive rule, one that defines the game that is being played.[10] In the present case, we can see that in the modern State authorities use arguments resting on the theory of sovereignty in order to justify their decisions. This is one of the principles that define the game of the State.

The hypothesis can, therefore, be reformulated in the following way: the emergence of the hierarchy of norms in the sixteenth century has given rise to the emergence of the constitutive principles of the State *stricto sensu*, particularly the modern concept of sovereignty. This implies that this development will not be considered from the point of view of the history of political thought or from that of a history of institutions, but from the point of view of legal argumentation on the assumption that the hierarchy of norms is a specific style of legal argumentation that requires the use of a concept of sovereignty.

The word 'sovereign' has been understood in many ways. Carré de Malberg distinguishes among three concepts:

> In the original sense, the word 'sovereignty' refers to the supreme character of the State's power. In a second sense, it refers to the whole range of the powers included in the State's authority and it is therefore synonymous with that authority. Thirdly, it is used to characterize the position occupied within the State by the highest organ of the State's authority and, in that sense, sovereignty is the same thing as the power of that organ.[11]

Carré de Malberg rightly stresses that the French language is poor and contains only one word for these three concepts of sovereignty, while the German language has three words, one for each of these senses. *Souveranität* corresponds to sovereignty in the first sense, i.e. the supreme character of the State on the international as well as on the domestic level. *Staatsgewalt* is the power of the State in the second sense. *Herrschaft* is the power of domination by an organ.

However, Carré de Malberg's distinction does not provide a sufficient account of some sentences that we find in constitutional and political discourse. For example, 'the sovereign is the French people' or, 'sovereignty belongs to the people'.[12] Such a sentence obviously does not mean that the French people *is* the State and effectively acts on an international level, nor that it exercises a power of domination, and certainly not that the people alone can really exercise a range of powers. These propositions do not refer to any reality and they are only used to justify other sentences: for example, in French legal discourse 'sovereignty belongs to the people' was used during the Third Republic to justify 'Parliament is sovereign' or 'the law is sovereign'. It meant that Parliament exercised a sovereignty that was not its own, but that belonged to the people and was exercised *in the name of* the people, or that the law expressed the will of the sovereign people. In this context, when imputed to the people, the word 'sovereignty' is thus used in a fourth sense: it refers to the quality of a being in whose name some power, in any one of the first three senses, is exercised. Indeed, the theory of sovereignty generally implies a distinction between the essence and the exercise of sovereignty. Because of the hierarchy of norms, what is imputed to a sovereign is not only legislation or decisions in international affairs, but also every single act, presumed to have been performed in virtue of a delegation. This is why, for example, justice is rendered in European countries 'in the name of' the French, Italian or German people as it was before 'in the name of the king'. To Carré de Malberg's three concepts, we must, therefore, add a fourth sense: the doctrine of sovereignty is a principle of *imputation* and a sovereign in that sense is the entity presumed to possess the essence of a sovereignty exercised by others in its name and, thus, to be the author, direct or indirect, of every single norm in the system.

Using this distinction among four different concepts of sovereignty, we can see that, whereas sovereignty in the Middle Ages is discernible only in two senses of the word independence – from the Pope or the Emperor, and the quality of being an authority whose decisions cannot be legally challenged – it is only in the sixteenth century that it exists in the full four senses.

Thus, in the Middle Ages, the adjective 'sovereign' applied not only to the King but to any supreme authority who could make a decision in the final instance, such as barons or courts, and had no superior. In fact, it is still used in this weak sense in the French language in relation to superior courts, such as the *Cour de Cassation* or the *Conseil d'État*, that make final decisions; and even in relation to a panel of university professors, which is also called sovereign, because the grades given by the panel cannot be reviewed on the merits.

In the late Middle Ages, the word 'sovereign' had also a stronger meaning: the sovereign exercised *Herrschaft* or domination. However, nobody claimed at that time that this implied *Staatsgewalt* or the unlimited power to decide, by legislation or otherwise, all human affairs and to be the sole source of law.[13] Although the King gradually came to exercise powers similar to those of the Roman Emperor – particularly the power to make general laws and to render justice – he could only legislate on certain matters and he did not have a monopoly of legislative or judicial power.

As we already have seen, legislation was not entirely an expression of the King's will and human affairs were regulated for the most part not by the King, but by custom, the courts or Canon law.

Since there was not one single legal order, this entailed that all rules and decisions could not be imputed, in the last instance, to the King's will. Indeed, at the level of customary rules, most cannot be imputed to anyone's will. As in Yan Thomas' characterization of the Roman Republic 'there could be no sovereignty – imputation of all decisions to one single center – in a system where the powers of every organ rested on an autonomous foundation'.[14] Thus, sovereignty in the full sense of the word did not exist until the sixteenth century.

But, from the sixteenth century onwards, sovereignty became much closer to Carré de Malberg's analysis and corresponded to the four concepts. First, as was already the case in the Middle Ages, the King claimed to possess a power that was supreme in the sense that there was no other power above his own, so that neither the Pope nor the Emperor could produce legislation on temporal matters that would be binding in the realm.

Second, also, as in the Middle Ages, he was the highest authority within the realm. Thus, it is not surprising that the Latin expressions used for sovereignty were the same as in the medieval period, *summa potestas* by Grotius or *majestas* by Bodin. But these terms had once only conveyed the idea of a relative superiority not of an absolute supremacy, and did not imply that the bearer of that *potestas* or *majestas* had the power to do anything they pleased.

What was different from the Middle Ages, then, was the type and the range of powers that the King could exercise. Now the terms acquired new meanings, and the King's power could extend to all human affairs.

Lastly, the fourth concept of sovereignty, imputation, also appeared in the sixteenth century. Previously, such an idea had been inconceivable, because of the plurality of legal orders, but now institutions did not rest on separate basis and all possible legal norms were finally either laid down by the King, or by an authority explicitly or implicitly delegated by him or tacitly authorized. Imputation was, thus, simply an expression of the hierarchy of norms.

It is remarkable that the concept of imputation can refer both to the ascription of an attribute or an action to a person and to the relation between two norms. Kelsen clearly shows that it is one and the same relation.[15] The statement that a crime is imputed to a person means that she is legally considered to have committed the crime and that a sanction can be inflicted upon her. Imputation is therefore the relation between crime and sanction. This relation is not a causal one, because it is not necessarily the case that when someone has committed a crime she will be punished. It is a relation created by a norm that states that if a crime has been committed then the person who committed it ought to be punished. But, more broadly, imputation is the relation between the two elements of the norm 'if x, then y ought to be'. It is the internal structure of the norm.[16]

It follows that the concept also helps to characterize the structure of the whole legal system, because a higher norm empowering an authority to produce a lower norm can be read 'if the authority x makes a decision then that decision is legally valid', for example 'if a court finds that one of the parties to a contract did not consent, then the court ought to declare the contract void'. The relation between the higher and the lower norm is a relation similar to that between crime and sanction and we can say that the lower norm is imputed to the higher and the latter to an even higher norm. In the end, they are all being indirectly imputed to the highest norms and to their author. Indeed, when norms are considered a produce of the will, as in the modern State, lower norms are presumed to be willed not by the authority that immediately produced it but by the highest authority in whose name it has acted.

But this highest authority, whether it is the individual who actually produces the highest norms or an abstract entity, such as the people, the nation or the State, to whom the norms are imputed, and who nevertheless is presumed to have willed them, has not been empowered by a higher norm or a higher authority. One cannot, therefore, avoid the conclusion that he possesses in virtue of his own nature a quality that enables him to exercise the supreme power. That quality is sovereignty.

Sovereignty thus appears to be a concept that one is bound to encounter whenever there is a hierarchy of norms that are thought of as produced by the will.

It can best be understood by analogy with Kelsen's theory of the *Grundnorm*. It is well known that, for Kelsen, the validity of every norm is based in a higher norm, which, in turn, is based in an even higher one and so on until one reaches the highest norm in the system. Since it is the highest there is no higher norm on which it could be based and, yet, if it is not valid, it cannot serve as the basis for the validity of the lower norms. This is the reason why we have to presuppose that the highest norm is valid on the basis of a *Grundnorm*, which states, 'the highest norm is valid'. Everybody is, of course, perfectly aware of the fact that there is no such norm and Kelsen does not pretend that there is. On the contrary, he calls it a fiction. But this fiction is necessary because, without it, we could not treat any norm as valid.

There is, however, a difference between the theory of sovereignty and that of the *Grundnorm*. Kelsen's theory, except in the late period, rests on an ontology of norms, conceived as ideal entities, that are not and cannot be produced by the will, because they belong to the sphere of 'ought' whereas the will is a fact and belongs to the sphere of 'is'. The validity of a norm can only be based on another norm, not on a fact. When an authority wills a rule, that rule is not valid because of the will, but only because the higher norm that empowered that authority has prescribed that if the authority expresses the will to create a rule, then the rule is valid and binding. Thus, Kelsen was able to avoid imputing the *Grundnorm* to a will. But in a system where norms are produced by the will, and where there is 'no imperative without an imperator', as Kelsen later acknowledged, one is bound to presuppose that the highest norms have been willed by a sovereign.

That there is a necessity, because of the hierarchy of norms, to use the argument of sovereignty as a principle of imputation, is shown clearly in the eighteenth-century struggles between the King and the *Parlements*. The *Parlements* claimed the right to refuse the registration of the King's ordinances when they conflicted with their interpretation of the 'fundamental laws of the realm'. The *Parlements* claimed to 'discover' these fundamental laws in ancient customs and practices. This was clearly an attempt to extend the hierarchy by creating a new level above the King. Since they exercised wide discretion in the interpretation of fundamental laws, this was a means to participate in the exercise of legislative power, without admitting it. However, even if this interference in the legislative power was disguised as judicial review, the idea that the King's power could be checked was difficult to reconcile with the doctrine that the King was sovereign. The most efficient way to attempt such reconciliation was to claim that since the *Parlements* were delegated by the sovereign, when they exercised a check on the King, they still acted in the name of the sovereign.[17] When they refused the registration of a law, they did not oppose the King's will, because, they claimed, such a law only expressed the King's apparent will, the will of the individual who happens to be on the throne, not the real will of the King as an institution. The real will was thus expressed by the *Parlements*. The unity of the system was thus preserved and this solution carries two further benefits. It provided a possible answer to the question 'Why cannot the King, if he is sovereign, change the fundamental laws of the realm?'. The answer could be 'the King as an individual cannot, but the king as an institution definitely could, but, thanks to the *Parlements*, he is wise enough not do it'. On the other hand, it provides a solution to the problem of checks to the power of the sovereign. The difficulty lies in the idea that a sovereign that is checked is not sovereign. The solution lies in replacing the idea of external checks, as with those that were found in various institutions, such as the Church, the '*corps intermédiaires*' or the courts, by internal checks that form an integral part of the sovereign. Sovereignty thus remains unlimited, but each of its components is limited. This type of arrangement is the core principle of constitutional government.

We can see now why this concept is central to the modern State. We do not find it in some older political systems like the feudal system and we can use it in the same way as political theory to characterize what is specific about the modern State. But it is more than that: political authorities use it as an instrument of government and they are constrained to use it because of the hierarchy of norms.

It is therefore not surprising that lawyers easily presuppose that there is a sovereign. Sovereignty has not been invented by Bodin or by anybody else, just as Kelsen did not invent the *Grundnorm*, no more than he could have discovered it in positive law. He only claimed that it was an assumption or presupposition of any lawyer who purports to treat something as valid law and that he, Kelsen, merely brought this hidden assumption to consciousness.

Conclusion

We can thus draw several lessons from Kelsen's comments, if we follow them to their logical consequences. First, from a methodological point of view, they show that legal theory is not as distinct and separate from sociology as one might think. On the contrary, the description of the structure of the legal system is at the same time a description of the structure of the State and the ways in which it operates. And legal theory provides this analysis without having to resort to some form of '*zwei Seiten Theorie*'. The State is not something with two sides. If it is a legal phenomenon, it can certainly be analysed from a sociological point of view, but also from a legal point of view.

Second, the contribution that legal theory can make to an analysis of the state is twofold: as Kelsen has clearly shown, the modern State (the State *stricto sensu*) is a set of institutions exercising political power in the form of the law, i.e. by means of commands, prohibitions and authorizations. These commands and authorizations are rationally justified because they have been issued according to higher rules and are, therefore, considered to be binding. On the other hand, political power in the State is also justified substantially by using specific theories, such as sovereignty, separation between office and holder, representation or personality and continuity of the State. But legal theory can also show that these constructions are also closely related to the form of the legal system, because they emerge as the best – and sometimes as the only possible – justifications for the exercise of ultimate power. They are, thus, the result of constraints generated by the hierarchy of norms: since every single legal norm in the system is directly or indirectly imputed to a unique entity, a King, the nation or the people. And since there is no higher legal norm that empowers this entity, one has to assume that this authority acts *suo jure*, because of a special quality called sovereignty. If sovereignty is a constitutive character of the concept of a State, then it can safely be said that the State emerges from the hierarchy of norms.

Notes

1. Ehrlich, quoted by R. Treves, 'Hans Kelsen et la sociologie du droit', *Droit et Société* (1985), 1, 15–23, p. 17f.
2. Ch. Eisenmann, 'Science du droit et sociologie dans la pensée de Kelsen', in B. Battifol, et al. (eds), *Méthode sociologique et droit*, Paris: Dalloz, 1958, p. 60ff.
3. H. Kelsen, *General Theory of Law and State*, New York: Russell & Russell, 1945, p. 176.
4. H. Dreier, *Rechtslehre, Staatssoziologie und Demokratietheorie bei Hans Kelsen*, Baden-Baden: Nomos Verlag, 1986.
5. H. Kelsen, *Der soziologische und der juristische Staatsbegriff; Kritische Untersuchungen des Verhältnisses von Staat und Recht*, 2nd edn, Tübingen: J.C.B. Mohr (Paul Siebeck), 1928.
6. H. Kelsen, 'Gott und Staat' in E. Topitsch (ed), *Aufsätze zur Ideologiekritik*, Berlin: Luchterhand, 1984, pp. 29–55 (original publication 1922–23).
7. As quoted by R. Metall, *Hans Kelsen. Sein Leben und Werk*, Vienne: Verlag Franz Deuticke, 1969, p. 30, Kelsen had already used the image of the Gorgon in *Veröffentlichungen der Vereinigung der Deutschen Staatsrechtslehrer*, Berlin: Gruyter, 1927, vol. 3, pp. 54–55.
8. Kelsen, *Der soziologische und der juristische Staatsbegriff*, op. cit.
9. H. Kelsen, *General Theory of Norms*, M. Hartney (trans), Oxford: Clarendon, 1991; L. Gianformaggio, *In difesa del sillogismo pratico ovvero alcuni argomenti kelseniani alla prova*, Milano: Giuffrè, 1987.
10. J. R. Searle, *Speech Acts: An Essay in the Philosophy of Language*, Cambridge: Cambridge University Press, 1969, p. 33.
11. R. Carré de Malberg, *Contribution à la théorie générale de l'Etat; spécialement d'après les données fournies par le droit constitutionnel français*, Paris: Sirey, 1920; reprint of CNRS, 1962, new edition, Paris: Dalloz, 2003, Vol. I., p. 79 (original publication 1920).
12. Constitution of 1958, art 3.
13. Helmut Quaristsch rightly speaks of the 'über die Unmögligkeit "mitttelaterlicher" Souveränität' (H. Quaritsch, *Souveränität: Entstehung und Entwickung des Begriffs in Frankreich und Deutschland von 13 Jh. bis 1806*, Berlin: Duncker & Humblot, 1986, esp. p. 34).
14. Y. Thomas, 'L'institution de la majesté', *Revue de Synthèse* (1991), 3–4, 331–86, p. 385.
15. H. Kelsen, *Essays in Legal and Moral Philosophy* (selected and introduced by Ota Weinberger), Dordrecht, Boston: Reidel, 1973, Ch. VII, 'Causality and Accounting', p. 154ff.
16. 'Ce sont deux faits qu'unit l'un à l'autre l'imputation juridique: non pas l'acte créateur de droit et la conduite conforme au droit, mais le fait que l'ordre juridique érige en condition et le fait qu'il érige en conséquence' (H. Kelsen, *Théorie pure du droit*, Paris: Dalloz, 1962, re-edition of the French translation, from the 2nd German edition, by Ch. Eisenmann, LGDJ, 1999, p. 144).
17. F. Di Donato, *La rinascita dello Stato – Dal conflitto magistratura-politica alla civilizzazione istituzionale europea*, Bologne: Il Mulino, 2010.

Part III

Hans Kelsen, Max Weber and rights

Chapter 6

The State under the rule of law? The relationship of State and law in the work of Hans Kelsen and Georg Jellinek

Gerhard Donhauser

Introduction

Hans Kelsen (1881–1973) developed his position with regard to the validity of law and the relation between *law* and *State*, not only in dealing with positions of natural law, but also with previous approaches of legal positivism. Georg Jellinek (1851–1911) developed a very influential theory of legal positivism in the Germanic tradition of the late nineteenth and early twentieth centuries. Like Kelsen, Jellinek had spent important years in Vienna in the last decades of the Austro-Hungarian monarchy. Both authors came from Jewish families, though they were not religious themselves (to make his professional development easier in anti-Semitic Vienna, Kelsen converted to Protestantism in 1912 but took an agnostic stand in religious questions).[1] Both Jellinek and Kelsen were jurists and both habilitated at the University of Vienna. Their work made significant contributions to the philosophy of law and constitutional law ('*Staatsrecht*'). In particular, their considerations on *law* and *State* would prove very influential. Jellinek belonged to the circle around Max Weber, and so it is appropriate to include this contribution in the present volume.[2]

This chapter will begin by identifying, in general terms, the central claims of Hans Kelsen's *Pure Theory of Law* with regard to law and State. It will then contrast these with the relevant arguments of Georg Jellinek. In this way, it will be possible to illuminate a somewhat forgotten aspect of the history of legal science. Also, in the midst of the second decade of the twenty-first century, it is appropriate to consider the current relationship between *State* and *law* in Europe or the United States. The chapter will conclude with the question of how the respective positions of Kelsen and Jellinek remain a pertinent resource for theoretical reflection.

Is, ought, basic norm[3]

Is and ought

Hans Kelsen made a rigorous attempt, particularly in his analysis of theories of Natural Law,[4] to completely decouple law from politics (as well from ethics and morality[5]). 'The science of law', writes Kelsen, 'endeavours to comprehend its object "legally", namely from the viewpoint of law'.[6] Kelsen's *Pure Theory of Law* starts out from the (Kantian[7]) fundamental distinction between 'is' and 'ought'.[8] The 'statement that something is', has a 'completely different meaning [...] than the statement that something ought to be', and Kelsen emphasizes the 'logical dualism of is and ought'; the fact that something 'is' does not mean, 'that something ought to be or ought not to be', and vice versa.[9]

Kelsen was born in 1881. He studied law in Vienna where he made, in 1911, his habilitation in constitutional law (*'Staatsrecht'*) and philosophy of law. In 1919, he became Full Professor at the University of Vienna. After the First World War, Kelsen became head of the commission entrusted with developing a constitution for the new Austrian republic, and his influence in the creation of the Federal Constitutional Law (*'Bundes-Verfassungsgesetz'*) of 1920 is evident. He also became a member of the newly established Constitutional Court. In 1930, Kelsen became Professor of International Law at the University of Cologne. In 1933, he had to leave Germany because of persecution by the National-socialist regime. He taught international law at Geneva until 1940. Then, he went to the United States where he became Full Professor for Political Sciences at the University of Berkeley.[10]

Norms

According to Kelsen, 'the legal order' is 'a system of norms regulating human behaviour'.[11] 'Norms' order 'that something *ought* to be or *ought* to happen'.[12] They are 'created by human action [...], whether [...] by willful settlement in a formalized process or in respect of custom'.[13] From Kelsen's point of view, 'law' or 'legal order' is inseparably bound to the idea of the State and the 'State' is, reciprocally, 'a Legal Order' and, in this respect, is equated with 'the State Governed by Law (*Rechtsstaat*)'.[14]

Kelsen states that norms are 'acts of will', described 'in the form of an indicative statement'.[15] These 'rules of law to be formulated by the science of law can only be ought-statements'.[16] So, descriptive sentences are used to describe legal norms, not legal norms themselves. Consequently, 'the "ought" in the rule of law has only a descriptive character'.[17] In this respect, Kelsen's terminology might appear surprising because it differs from the customary (linguistic as well as philosophical) use of language.[18]

In this context, we may restrict ourselves to the observation that Kelsen distinguishes 'legal norms' from 'rules of law' as the latter (because they are only describing law) 'do not impose obligations nor confer rights upon anybody', while the former, 'enacted by the legal authority', '[impose] obligations and [confer] rights upon the legal subjects'. Thus, '[t]he statements formulated by the science of law [...] may be true or false', while 'norms enacted by the legal authority [...] are neither true nor false, but only valid or invalid'.[19]

'Ought' is used here to relate to legal norms as such and to relate to the statements described by the science of law. To clarify the problem, Kelsen explains that both 'the norm as well as the statement about the norm are formulated as ought-statements, but' they 'have different meanings'. Only if the sentence 'Thieves ought to be punished by a prison sentence' is 'laid down by the legislator' is a 'norm' constituted. 'The ought has' then 'a prescriptive meaning'. If the same sentence is found as a statement about the norm in a textbook on criminal law, it is also an ought-sentence, but the 'ought does not have a prescriptive meaning' in this case.[20] In this respect 'an ought-sentence may be as well a norm as a statement about a norm'.[21]

This terminology gives rise to some logical questions, because it remains uncertain which type of sentence is to be specified as the exclusive means of expression for a norm. According to Kelsen, the type of sentence is less important than its author to answer this question. In his view, 'norms' are not only acts of the will of a legal authority, but also the legal 'meaning of empirical facts'.[22] And how is 'meaning' unlike an 'effect' of a 'language movement [*Sprachbewegung*]'?[23] Indeed, this idea is also considered within the *Pure Theory of Law* by defining 'the norm' as a 'scheme of interpretation'. 'To put it differently: The judgment that an act of human behaviour, performed in time and space, is "legal" (or "illegal"), is the result of a specific, namely normative, interpretation'.[24]

But we have to focus on one aspect of norms, namely that of validity. According to Kelsen, the specific ought of 'norms' is based on the fact that they are created by a 'legal authority', a 'legislator'. 'By the word "validity"' Kelsen 'designate[s] the specific existence of a norm'. This '"existence" of a positive norm [. . .] is not the same as the existence of the act of will. A norm can be valid, even if the act of will whose meaning the norm is, no longer exists'. After a legislative norm, for example a law, is passed, the members of the legislative body 'turn in their decisions to the regulation of other affairs'.[25] '[T]he validity of a norm is an *ought* and not an *is*', according to Kelsen. So 'the validity [*Geltung*] of a norm' has to be distinguished 'from its effectiveness [*Wirksamkeit*]'. Kelsen calls a norm *effective* if it is 'actually applied and obeyed'.[26] In Kelsen's view, validity and effectiveness coincide only insofar as '[e]ffectiveness is a condition of validity in the sense that effectiveness has to join the positing of a legal norm if the norm is not to lose its validity'. In other words, 'A minimum of effectiveness is a condition of validity'.[27]

The 'basic norm'

'Why', asks Kelsen, 'is a norm valid, what is the reason for its validity?'. Such a 'reason for the validity of a norm' could 'only be the validity of another norm', not a fact.[28] This results from Kelsen's basic idea that the 'is' and the 'ought' are strictly separate. In contrast to theorists of natural law, but also to an important representative of legal positivism, such as Georg Jellinek,[29] the so-called 'normative power of the factual' is not, for Kelsen, the reason for validity.

'A norm which represents the reason for the validity of another norm is figuratively spoken of as a higher norm in relation to a lower norm'.[30] On this basis, it is possible to develop hierarchies of norms, and it is, in principle, possible that 'the search for a reason of a norm's validity' could 'go on indefinitely'.[31] To avoid such an infinite regress, it seems to be necessary to presuppose a 'highest norm':

> It must be *presupposed*, because it cannot be 'posited,' that is to say: created, by an authority whose competence would have to rest on a still higher norm. This final norm's validity cannot be derived from a higher norm, the reason for its validity cannot be questioned.[32]

This 'highest norm' Kelsen calls the 'basic norm' (*Grundnorm*). 'All norms whose validity can be traced back to one and the same basic norm constitute a system of norms, a normative order'.[33] To presuppose such a 'basic norm' seems to be indispensable from a logical point of view if one 'consider[s] as law exclusively positive law' and refuses to base the validity of norms 'upon a higher, meta-legal norm'.[34] In epistemological terms, we might remember an Aristotelian consideration here, '[F]or if it is necessary to know the prior premises from which the demonstration proceeds, and if the regress ends with the immediate premises, the latter must be indemonstrable'.[35] Most likely, the 'basic norm' can be interpreted as some kind of 'regulatory hypothesis' according to Kant or even as hypothetical precondition, a regulative principle.[36]

What is, one could ask, the content of the 'basic norm'? It does not have any content:

> [f]or the basic norm is limited to authorize a norm-creating authority, it is a rule according to which the norms of its system ought to be created. [. . .] The basic norm supplies only the reason for the validity, but not at the same time the content of the norms constituting the system.[37]

So 'the legal norm belong[s] to the legal order whose norms are created according to' the 'basic norm. Therefore any kind of content might be law'.[38]

Normative power of the factual

Georg Jellinek and the Allgemeine Staatslehre (General Theory of the State)

Amongst other things, Kelsen's *Pure Theory of Law* can also be seen as some kind of negative answer to Georg Jellinek's *Allgemeine Staatslehre* (published in 1900).[39] Although Jellinek is not very well known, his analyses of law and State had great influence upon German thought from the late nineteenth century until far into the twentieth century. Jellinek studied law and philosophy at the Universities of Vienna, Heidelberg and Leipzig. In Leipzig, he was awarded doctorates in philosophy (1872) and law (1874); in 1879 he made his habilitation in Vienna in legal philosophy. Afterwards, he lectured there, first as an Associate Professor

(*Privatdozent*), and from 1883 as an Adjunct Professor. In 1889, he became Full Professor of Law and State (*Staatsrecht*) at the University of Basel, and in 1891 he became Full Professor of Law and State as well as International Law at the University of Heidelberg. In Heidelberg, Jellinek belonged to the circle around Max Weber. In 1907, he became Rector of the University of Heidelberg, the first Jewish holder of that post[40] (though he converted to Protestantism in 1910).

Jellinek's approach to the philosophy of law was one of legal positivism.[41] According to Jellinek, law does not have natural causes. Law is the 'ethical minimum' with which people are able to agree within a certain society. The 'ethical minimum' signifies:

> [o]bjectively [. . .] the conditions for the preservation of society, as far as they depend on human will, i.e. the minimum of ethical norms for existence; subjectively, it is the minimum of moral activity and disposition that is demanded from the members of society.[42]

So, law is a human creation, and this conviction can be seen as the common basis of legal positivism, for all the differences in detail. However, in contrast to Kelsen, Jellinek's legal positivism is not conceived as a purely legal conception of law. For Jellinek includes the social and political contexts of law as integral elements of the conception of positive law.

Hence, Jellinek regards the State from two aspects, or as two functions, which are characteristic of the State as a political and a legal entity. According to Jellinek's *General Theory of the State*, 'these two functions should be strictly distinguished', mixing the 'juridical nature of the state [. . .] with its social reality' is inadmissible.[43]

Against this background the State, equipped with 'original sovereignty', seems to be (socially) a 'unit [*Verbandseinheit*]' as well as (legally) a 'corporation [*Körperschaft*]'.[44] Jellinek defines 'Sovereignty' as 'power of absolute enforcement of the own will'. This power is, according to Jellinek, only suited to the State.[45] A State in this sense is characterized by 'state authority' (in classical terms 'sovereignty'[46]), as well as by a territory ('*Staatsgebiet*') and by a people ('*Staatsvolk*').[47] This, Jellinek's so-called 'doctrine of three elements' ('*Drei-Elementen-Lehre*'), is widely accepted, at least in the science of international law.[48]

As distinct from Kelsen's exclusive focus on the juridical aspects of law and the State, which also marked his elaboration of a theory of democracy,[49] Jellinek sought to express the complexity of the phenomenon of the State by adopting a broader conceptual approach.[50] Nevertheless, Jellinek attributes a primary function of social and legal order to the State. To perform this function, the State has to have actual and legal power at its disposal.[51] In contrast to Kelsen, who assumed the primacy of law over the State, in Jellinek's view, law is preceded by the State.[52] Also, as opposed to Kelsen, Jellinek assumes that the effectiveness of law is, in the end, dependent on its recognition by the legal subjects.[53] So, for Jellinek, the establishment of legal structures is synonymous with a kind of domestication of political power, 'The transformation of initially pure actual power of the state into legal power always occurs by means of the additional idea that this factual power had a normative nature so that something should be as it is'.[54]

Law, ethics and the State

Jellinek's description of the interaction between the creation of law by the State and the recognition by its legal subjects, as a condition of a potentially enduring effectiveness of legal norms, obviously differs from Kelsen's position. For Kelsen, the validity of legal norms depends primarily on a certain kind of legislation. It should be supported by the effectiveness of the positive law, but the latter is not as important as the technically correct creation of norms, based on constitutional norms for the enactment of legislation. Further, according to Kelsen, effectiveness is not confined to the recognition of legal norms by legal subjects. Law can also be valid on the basis of legal enforcement; in general, legal power is defined by compulsion – not only in Kelsen's view.[55] In contrast, Jellinek's approach avoids a purely legal conception of the State and law. Instead, it involves the adoption of a sociological and psychological perspective, and is centred upon the question of which legal norms could be accepted within a society. In Kelsen's opinion, law may have any possible content which, from a legal-technical point of view, appears correct. The question is whether – from a sociological and social-psychological perspective – a legal norm can have any possible content, merely on the basis of a legislator willing to express this content, and pour it, *lege artis*, into the mould of a legal norm; and who is able to enforce this norm.[56] Theoretically, this is surely possible, if only within the bounds of the worst type of despotism. Nevertheless, one may question how long a despotic regime will be able to maintain its hold on power if the oppressed subjects categorically deny this regime. As the writer and psychoanalyst Manès Sperber (1905–1984) makes clear, it is the tyrant's subjects who empower him to become their ruler.[57] It may be that great fear and intimidation hinder any resistance and condemn any revolution to failure; or they may lead, in the case of a successful overthrow, to even more repressive conditions.[58]

These considerations could be exemplified by numerous historical and contemporary forms of despotism and, presumably, establish arguments for both positions. This is, perhaps, related to these arguments merely reflecting different perspectives rather than constituting opposed and contradictory positions. This might have to do with the fact that they do not express primarily fundamental contradictions, but rather different perspectives. However, according to Jellinek, law would obtain its *Geltung* (validity in a legal-technical sense) on the basis of a technically correct creation of legal norms, but it would only become *gültig* (valid in a sociological sense) if legal norms correspond to the everyday understanding of most people concerned with those norms.[59] Legal norms, which correspond with what is seen as usual, familiar and part of the conventional practice of the majority of society, stand, according to Jellinek, a good chance of implementation. Of course, this orientation implies some kind of anti-emancipatory approach, and Jellinek does not even conceal that:

> Therefore the distribution of power within a community, may it be seen as ever so unfair at a later period, because of the exploitation of the ruled by the ruling classes, is obtainable in a full legal sense, not only because it is enforced by power but also because it is accepted by the subjects.[60]

Normally, alterations of a legal system proceed slowly, according to Jellinek. This view seems to be similar to well-known considerations on the development of human mentalities over a long period, as expressed in Fernand Braudel's concept of *longue durée*.[61] In Jellinek's view, radical changes of legal systems – for instance, as a result of political revolutions – rarely happen, one example being the French Revolution (1789).[62] Apart from that, 'law' appears as the 'ethical minimum' on which one can agree within a society.[63]

For Jellinek, ethical and legal norms are not separable within a society inasmuch as law has always been oriented towards relevant concepts of ethics or morality. Confusion may be created by the fact that Jellinek uses the term 'ethics' here. After all, he is speaking about morality; morality is characterized by norms; while ethics, according to the Aristotelian tradition, is conceived as a theory of the good life. Therefore, ethics is an integral part of the selection, practice and perfection of certain ideals of human behaviour. By avoiding extreme emotional states, through this practical ethics, the possibility of happiness (*eudaimonia*)[64] became attainable. This Aristotelian conception has, however, been increasingly supplanted, historically, by an avowedly normative ethics, with utilitarianism as its most diametrically opposed variant.[65] Jellinek, however, assumed a distinct position between the ancients and the moderns, in which the predominant ethical and moral orientations within society would find expression in legal norms. For Jellinek, the passage from ethical and moral orientations to the content of a legal norm is predicated upon an underlying minimal ethical and moral consensus. This position is, however, only one element among a series of other more demanding conditions for the continued acceptance of a legal system. In particular, the State, for Jellinek, has itself to demonstrate its own willingness to establish 'changes of the will of the State' through 'constitutional forms'.[66]

Here, Jellinek commences from a certain conception (perhaps a stage of development) of the phenomenon 'State': the liberal state under the rule of law. This form of State lacked any significant inherence in the existing institutional structure of either the Austro-Hungarian or German Empires of the late nineteenth and early twentieth centuries. The institutional structures of both imperial States were distant from a conception of a modern constitutional system with, for example, the separation of powers and a constitutional court.[67] The representatives of both Empires considered their respective States to be authoritarian with welfare components, and, thus, without relation to a community in which 'the conviction of the' importance of 'binding itself to its law' would be paramount.[68] For Jellinek, it is precisely this conviction which demarcated the 'modern State':[69]

> A pure, formal-juridical consideration of the state can never reach an understanding of material restrictions upon the activities of a state. It is incapable of acknowledging any barriers other than those which the state places upon itself, but it is unable in any way to categorize the content of this activity of the putting into place of barriers. The existence of such barriers has been proved only by the progress of the understanding of the restriction of the state for its own purposes.[70]

The State[71]

A concept and its elements

Jellinek and Kelsen conceived the relationship between law and the State from distinct methodological orientations. This, in turn, requires further consideration of the meaning of the term 'State', and of the actual and potential interaction between law and the State in the early twenty-first century.

In opposition to 'realistic theories' of international politics,[72] one can assert that the State is neither a ubiquitous nor a universal phenomenon. The term 'State' is essentially different from other structures of political and legal institutionalization, as, for example, the *polis* of ancient Greece or the medieval communities of northern Italy in the twelfth century. The 'State' arose at a distinct moment in the early modern period[73] in Europe.[74]

The pertinence of Jellinek's analyses re-emerges from their definition of the modern State as constituted by the elements of sovereignty, people and territory.[75] Jean Bodin, one of the most influential theorists of the State in the sixteenth century, focused on sovereignty as the central aspect of a State's power. He defined it as 'absolute power, owned by the state, with an indefinite period'.[76]

The later conception of the State by Thomas Hobbes further extended the initial theory of Bodin, with its concerted reflection upon the person of the sovereign. Hobbes' concept of the sovereign as 'that great Leviathan [. . .] that mortal god to which we owe, under the immortal God, our peace and defense',[77] is predicated upon the idea of a voluntary subjugation of originally free human beings under a single sovereign. These individuals relinquish their liberty for the security provided by the sovereign. The type of social contract, through which the sovereign is conferred with these powers by these previously free human beings, has been held to be a 'contract of subjugation', because the subjects, once they had agreed the contract, are regarded as being without permission to revoke it. This prohibition on revocation is the counterpart of the absolute power of the sovereign.[78]

Also, Hobbes' reference to 'terror' as an instrument of power seems to be remarkable. '[B]y terror' the sovereign shall be 'enabled to conform the wills of them all [the subjects of the State] to peace at home and mutual aid against their enemies abroad'.[79] The conceptual connection between sovereignty, peacekeeping and a certain idea of security seems to be paradigmatically elaborated here. We should note the context of the English Civil War (1642–49) as a specific motive for Hobbes' concept of State and sovereignty,[80] though the concept of sovereignty still seems to be so significant for the idea of the *State* far beyond this historical context. Although the figure of the sovereign has transformed – at least in many European States and in North America – from absolute monarchy to people's sovereignty, the concept of sovereignty itself, as developed by Bodin and Hobbes, remained a central point of the self-image of States and their executive authorities far into the twentieth century.[81] On behalf of alleged, or real, threats to the *security* of States, the idea of *sovereignty* seems to be promoted nowadays in connection with the so-called 'War against Terrorism' – against the achievements of the State under the rule of law.[82]

As a historical construct, *the State* has run through various transformations. One of great importance has undoubtedly been the rise of people's sovereignty.[83] But apart from that, it seems that the State never had this kind of sovereignty attributed to it by Bodin or Hobbes. At best, the authorities of States could exercise sovereign power against their subjects because of their monopoly on the use of force. Towards other States, in the late twentieth and early twenty-first centuries, and also towards other political players, this sovereignty has always been limited; the independence of States has been similarly reduced.[84] Indeed, after various devastating crises during the twentieth century, States seem to be less independent from other political players than ever. In particular, transnational corporations operating under a globalized financial system, along with rating agencies, are decisive political players today, much more powerful than any State.[85] Moreover, *the State* has transferred to others many of its former activities, particularly administrating and financing educational and cultural institutions, but also, increasingly, the field of social welfare.[86] Yet, the so-called monopoly on force has persisted as an important instrument of government authorities – and against its promise of bringing peace was, and is, generating violence itself.[87] Not least because of this, the monopoly on force has been the pivot of many of the quarrels concerning the State under the rule of law over the centuries.[88]

State under the rule of law

Today a 'state under the rule of law' may be seen as a 'state', which 'realizes law, stated by a representative body of the people according its constitution, subjugated to the control of independent judges'.[89] This kind of State: first, is a democratic State; second, has put the principles of separation of powers[90] into practice; and, third, has a constitution. Factually, points one and two are probably nowhere entirely put into practice. But, as a concept, all three aspects diverge considerably from the concept of *State* developed in early modern times. As regards the question of constitution, a lot depends on definitions.

One may assume that almost any political community will have some rules and that those rules also can be imposed in case of a conflict. Such rules can also be called 'the legal order' of a community, and, according to Kelsen, such an order is 'a system of norms regulating human behaviour'.[91] To create legal norms, other norms are necessary, namely 'norms regulating the creation of general norms'. These norms 'rule [...] the creation of general norms [...] by determining by which organs and which procedures general norms have to be created'.[92] These 'norms regulating the creation of general norms' may be called the *constitution* of the political community, and, from a legal-technical perspective, one will easily be able to agree with this position.

The proponents of constitutional systems and the wider European juridico-political transformations of the eighteenth and nineteenth centuries were characterized by the demand for the creation of constitutions as 'formally issued singular law'.[93] This law should definitively settle how to create legal norms systematically, but first of all it should establish institutions of the State and their powers in a binding way. Anyway, the idea of a constitution had, and has, much to do with the idea, as a priority, of a State 'binding itself to its law'.[94] In other words, a constitution should settle a binding, more or less extensive 'basic legal order' of a political community, especially a State.[95]

Kelsen was of the opinion that State and law could not be separated, and that therefore any State was a State under the rule of law. But, even though Kelsen was an enduring supporter of (representative) democracy,[96] law can have, according to him, any possible content, and so there is nothing said about contents of a State under the rule of law. Jellinek, as we have seen, definitely had concrete opinions about the content of a State under the rule of law. In particular, as noted above, the concept of a State 'binding itself to its law' was important for Jellinek.

Maybe we might finally ask the question whether there could be found more elements of content of a State under the rule of the law, from a legal-positivistic point of view. One perspective for such an approach could be to focus on historical developments (in the tradition of enlightened legal theory[97]) with regard to Jellinek's idea of a self-binding State. Thought could be given to some procedural standards, such as a right of due process, judicial independence and the principle '*in dubio pro reo*' or the presumption of innocence.[98]

It could be worthwhile seeing whether there could also be established a connection to Ronald Dworkin's idea of specific 'moral rights' not based on nature but on legal-historical developments as expressed in the Constitution of the United States.[99] But, also, Jellinek's concept of validity in a sociological or psychological sense (*Gültigkeit*) could help to identify content for a State under the rule of law beyond the doctrines of natural law. This approach could also correspond to traditions of enlightened legal theory and philosophy. After all, they form the basis for the concrete structures of State under the rule of law which are nowadays thoughtlessly put at risk with reference to some scenarios of threat and permanent appeal for 'security'.

Notes

1. G. Donhauser, 'Das Konzept des Atheismus. Kelsen und Mauthner', in C. Jabloner, T. Olechowski and K. Zeleny (eds), *Secular Religion. Rezeption und Kritik von Hans Kelsens Auseinandersetzung mit Religion und Wissenschaft*, Vienna: Manz, 2013, pp. 165–84.
2. See, for example, A. Anter, 'Max Weber und Georg Jellinek. Wissenschaftliche Beziehungen, Affinitäten und Divergenzen', in S. L. Paulson and M. Schulte (eds), *Georg Jellinek. Beiträge zu Leben und Werk*, Tübingen: Mohr Siebeck, 2000, pp. 67–86; S. Breuer, *Georg Jellinek und Max Weber. Von der sozialen zur soziologischen Staatslehre*, Baden-Baden: Nomos, 1999.
3. For the following considerations, see G. Donhauser, *Türhüter. Wie Recht wird, was es ist*, Vienna: New Academic Press, 2013, pp. 49–61.
4. About personal as well as philosophical conflicts between Kelsen and Schmitt see, for example, H. Dreier, 'The Essence of Democracy – Hans Kelsen and Carl Schmitt juxtaposed', in D. Diner and M. Stolleis (eds), *Hans Kelsen and Carl Schmitt. A juxtaposition*, Gerlingen: Bleicher, 1999, pp. 71–79; R. Gross, '"Jewish Law and Christian Grace" – Carl Schmitts Critique of Hans Kelsen', in Diner and Stolleis (eds), *Hans Kelsen and Carl Schmitt. A juxtaposition*, ibid., pp. 101–13; C. Jabloner, 'Legal Techniques and Theory of Civilization – Reflections on Hans Kelsen and Carl Schmitt', in Diner and Stolleis (eds), *Hans Kelsen and Carl Schmitt. A juxtaposition*, ibid., pp. 51–60.
5. For questions of terminology, see the section 'Law, ethics and the State', below.
6. H. Kelsen, *Pure Theory of Law*, M. Knight (trans), from the 2nd revised and enlarged German edition, East Orange: Clark, 2005, p. 70.
7. I. Kant, *Kritik der reinen Vernunft*, in W. Weischedel (ed), I. Kant, *Werkausgabe*, vol. III, 12th edn, Frankfurt am Main: Suhrkamp, 1992, pp. B 375f./A 318ff., p. 325.
8. In Kelsen's opinion, the difference between *is* and *ought* has evolved through history, but '[we are] not immediately aware of it' (Kelsen, *Pure Theory of Law*, op. cit., p. 5). For a historical point of view, see R. Brague, 'Zur Vorgeschichte der Unterscheidung von Sein und Sollen', in T. Buchheim, R. Schönberger and W. Schweidler (eds), *Die Normativität des Wirklichen. Über die Grenze zwischen Sein und Sollen*, Stuttgart: Klett-Cotta, 2002, p. 21ff.
9. H. Kelsen, *Reine Rechtslehre*, 2nd edn, 1960, Vienna: Nachdruck, 2000, p. 196, note 19.
10. See H. Kelsen, 'Autobiographie' (1947), in M. Jestaedt (ed), *Hans Kelsen im Selbstzeugnis*, Tübingen: Mohr Siebeck, 2006, pp. 31, 38, 57ff., 70ff. and 81ff.
11. See Kelsen, *Pure Theory of Law*, op. cit., p. 4; see, also, G. Kucsko-Stadlmayer, 'Rechtsnormbegriff und Arten der Rechtsnormen', in R. Walter (ed), *Schwerpunkte der Reinen Rechtslehre*, Vienna: Manz, 1992, p. 21ff.
12. Kelsen, ibid., p. 4.
13. R. Thienel, 'Der Rechtsbegriff der Reinen Rechtslehre – Eine Standortbestimmung', in H. Schäffer, W. Berka, H. Stolzlechner and J. Werndl (eds), *Staat – Verfassung – Verwaltung. Festschrift anlässlich des 65. Geburtstages von Prof. DDr. Dr. h.c. Friedrich Koja*, Vienna and New York: Springer, 1998, p. 181.
14. See Kelsen, *Pure Theory of Law*, op. cit., pp. 286ff. and 312ff.; see, also, K. Groh, *Demokratische Staatsrechtslehrer in der Weimarer Republik*, Tübingen: Mohr Siebeck, 2010, p. 119ff; J. Vollmeyer, *Der Staat als Rechtsordnung*, Baden-Baden: Nomos, 2011, p. 73ff.
15. See Kelsen, ibid., pp. 5 and 7.
16. Ibid., p. 78.
17. See ibid., p. 79.
18. See, for example, E. Morscher, 'Die Sein-Sollen-Dichotomie im Logischen Empirismus und im Rechtspositivismus', in C. Jabloner and F. Stadler (eds), *Logischer Empirismus und Reine Rechtslehre. Beziehungen zwischen dem Wiener Kreis und der Hans Kelsen-Schule*, Vienna and New York: Springer, 2001, pp. 59 and 61.

19 Kelsen, *Pure Theory of Law*, op. cit., p. 73.
20 See H. Kelsen, 'Recht und Logik', *Forum* (1965) 12, 143, 421–25, 495–500, p. 498.
21 H. Kelsen, *Allgemeine Theorie der Normen*, K. Ringhofer and R. Walter (eds), Vienna: Manz, 1979, p. 121.
22 See Kelsen, *Reine Rechtslehre*, op. cit., p. 61, note.
23 See, also, W. Welsch, *Vernunft. Die zeitgenössische Vernunftkritik und das Konzept der transversalen Vernunft*, Frankfurt am Main: Suhrkamp, 1995, p. 283 (referring to Jacques Lacan).
24 Kelsen, *Pure Theory of Law*, op. cit., p. 4.
25 Ibid., p. 10.
26 Ibid.
27 See, ibid., p. 11.
28 Ibid., p. 193.
29 See the section 'Normative power of the factual', below.
30 Kelsen, *Pure Theory of Law*, op. cit., p. 193.
31 Ibid., p. 194.
32 Ibid., p. 195.
33 Ibid.
34 Ibid., p. 205.
35 Aristoteles, *Analytika hystera* [*Analytica posteriora*], in A. I. Bekker (ed), *Aristotelis Opera*, Vol. I (1960) 71 (72b 20 ff), in the German translation by G. Zekl, in *Aristoteles: Erste Analytik. Zweite Analytik*, Hamburg: Meiner, 1998, p. 321ff.
36 Also Kelsen, *Allgemeine Theorie der Normen*, op. cit., p. 206ff.
37 Kelsen, *Pure Theory of Law*, op. cit., p. 197.
38 Ibid., p. 199.
39 Similarly in O. W. Lembcke, 'Staats(rechts)lehre oder Rechts(staats)lehre? Zum Rechtspositivismus bei Jellinek und Kelsen', in R. Schmidt (ed), *Rechtspositivismus: Ursprung und Kritik. Zur Geltungsbegründung von Recht und Verfassung*, Baden-Baden: Nomos, 2014, pp. 83–134, p. 103.
40 See, for example, C. Keller, 'Biographische Ansichten. Georg Jellinek in seinen Brifen an Victor Ehrenberg', in Paulson and Schulte (eds), *Georg Jellinek. Beiträge zu Leben und Werk*, op. cit., pp. 87–101; K. Kempter, 'Judentum, Liberalismus, Nationalismus. Biographische Prägungen von Georg Jellineks politischer Persönlichkeit', in Paulson and Schulte (eds), *Georg Jellinek. Beiträge zu Leben und Werk*, op. cit., pp. 53–66. In respect of Weber and Jellinek, see, for example, Anter, 'Max Weber und Georg Jellinek', op. cit.; Breuer, *Georg Jellinek und Max Weber*, op. cit.
41 For a differentiated perspective, see M. Sattler, 'Georg Jellinek als Positivist? Überlegungen zur wissenschaftstheoretischen Einordnung seines Denkens', in Paulson and Schulte (eds), *Georg Jellinek. Beiträge zu Leben und Werk*, op. cit., pp. 345–58.
42 G. Jellinek, *Die sozialethische Bedeutung von Recht, Unrecht und Strafe*, 2nd edn, Berlin: O Häring, 1908, p. 45.
43 See G. Jellinek, *Allgemeine Staatslehre* (Unveränderter Nachdruck des fünften Neudrucks der dritten Aufl. Aus dem Jahr 1928), Berlin: Springer, 1966, p. 138ff.
44 See ibid., pp. 180ff. and 183.
45 See ibid., p. 180.
46 See the section 'A concept and its elements' below.
47 See Jellinek, *Allgemeine Staatslehre*, op. cit., p. 389ff.
48 See, for example, R.-O. Schultze, 'Staat', in D. Nohlen and R.-O. Schultze (eds), *Lexikon der Politikwissenschaft. Theorien, Methoden, Begriffe*, vol. 2, Munich: C.H. Beck, 2010, p. 1012ff.
49 See, for example, G. Donhauser, 'Freiheit im Rechtsstaat. Zentrale Themen, Perspektiven und Grenzen von Kelsens Demokratiekonzept', in C. Jabloner et al. (eds), *Gedenkschrift Robert Walter*, Vienna: Manz, 2013, pp. 101–22, p. 101f.

50 See Jellinek, *Allgemeine Staatslehre*, op. cit., p. 73ff.
51 Ibid., p. 361 ff.
52 See, also, Lembcke, 'Staats(rechts)lehre oder Rechts(staats)lehre?', op. cit., p. 124ff.
53 See Jellinek, *Allgemeine Staatslehre*, op. cit., p. 333ff. See, also, Lembcke, ibid., p. 88ff.
54 See Jellinek, ibid., p. 342.
55 For further evidence, see, for example, G. Donhauser, *Angst und Schrecken. Beobachtungen auf dem Weg vom Ausnahmezustand zum Polizeistaat in Europa und den USA*, Vienna: New Academic Press, 2015, p. 172.
56 For a critical view of the figure of the legislator, see, for example, Donhauser, ibid., p. 256ff.
57 M. Sperber, *Zur Analyse der Tyrannis. Ein sozialpsychologischer Essai*, W. W. Hemecker (ed), with an epilogue by E. Marian, Graz: Leykam, 2006, p. 80 (original publication 1937).
58 About fear as a device of politics, see, for example, Donhauser, *Angst und Schrecken*, op. cit., p. 187ff.
59 See Jellinek, *Allgemeine Staatslehre*, op. cit., pp. 334 and 344; Lembcke, 'Staats(rechts) lehre oder Rechts(staats)lehre?', op. cit., pp. 90ff. and 94ff.
60 Jellinek, ibid., p. 343.
61 See F. Braudel, 'Histoire et sciences sociales. La longue durée', *Annales* (1958), 13, 4, 725–53.
62 See Jellinek, *Allgemeine Staatslehre*, op. cit., p. 347ff.
63 See the section 'Georg Jellinek and the *Allgemeine Staatslehre (General Theory of the State)*' above; also, Jellinek, *Die sozialethische Bedeutung von Recht, Unrecht und Strafe*, op. cit., p. 45.
64 See Aristoteles, *Ethikà Nikomácheia*, I, 1, 1095a 18ff., in German translation by E. Rolfes, G. Bien (ed), 4th edn, Hamburg: Meiner, 1985, p. 4.
65 For further detail, see G. Donhauser, *Psychologie und Philosophie*, Vienna: ÖBV, 2015, p. 376ff.
66 See Jellinek, *Allgemeine Staatslehre*, op. cit., p. 33.
67 See, for example, A. J. Noll, 'Georg Jellinek's Forderung nach einem Verfassungsgerichtshof für Österreich', in Paulson and Schulte (eds), *Georg Jellinek. Beiträge zu Leben und Werk*, op. cit., pp. 261–76.
68 See Jellinek, *Allgemeine Staatslehre*, op. cit., p. 371ff.
69 Ibid., p. 371ff. See, also, Lembcke, 'Staats(rechts)lehre oder Rechts(staats)lehre?', op. cit., p. 97.
70 Jellinek, ibid., p. 239.
71 For the following considerations, see Donhauser, *Angst und Schrecken*, op. cit., pp. 137–50.
72 See, for example, M. Fischer, 'Feudal Europe, 800–1300: Communal Discourse and Conflictual Practices', *International Organization* (1992), 46, 2, 427–66.
73 This term is quite ambiguous. See, for example, K. Vocelka, *Geschichte der Neuzeit. 1500–1918*, Stuttgart: UTB, 2010, p. 17ff; R. Koselleck, *Zeitschichten. Studien zur Historik* (with a contribution by H.-G. Gadamer), Frankfurt: Surhkamp, 2000, p. 225ff.; H. A. Oberman, *Zwei Reformationen. Luther und Calvin – Alte und Neue Welt*, Berlin: Siedler Verlag, 2003, esp. pp. 75ff. and 171ff.
74 See, for example, M. van Creveld, *The Rise and Decline of the State*, Cambridge: Cambridge University Press, 1999, pp. 1–188; M. Foucault, *Die Ordnung der Dinge. Eine Archäologie der Humanwissenschaften*, Frankfurt: Suhrkamp, 1993, p. 372ff.; R. Koselleck, *Kritik und Krise. Eine Studie zur Pathogenese der bürgerlichen Welt*, 7th edn, Frankfurt: Suhrkamp, 1992, esp. pp. 11–39; P. Veyne, *Foucault: Die Revolutionierung der Geschichte*, Frankfurt: Suhrkamp, 1992, p. 37ff.; M. Foucault, *Überwachen und Strafen. Die Geburt des Gefängnisses*, Frankfurt: Suhrkamp, 1994; T. Biebricher, 'Macht und Recht: Foucault', in S. Buckel, R. Christensen and A. Fischer-Lescano (eds), *Neue Theorien des Rechts*, Stuttgart: Utb Gmbh, 2006, pp. 139–61; R. L. Dreyfus and P. Rabinow, *Michel Foucault. Jenseits von Strukturalismus und Hermeneutik*, 2nd edn, Weinheim: Beltz Athenäum, 1994, pp. 163ff.

and 183ff.; H.-H. Kögler, *Michel Foucault*, 2nd edn, Stuttgart/Weimar: Metzlersche J.B. Verlagsb, 2004, p. 83ff. For discussion of the *polis*, see Donhauser, *Angst und Schrecken*, op. cit., p. 137ff., referring to Thukydides, *Geschichte des Pelopponesischen Krieges*, translated and introduced by G. P. Landmann, 1993, p. 1078ff.; Herodot, J. Feix (ed), *Historien*, Vol. 2, 5th edn, Zürich: Artemis & Winkler, 1995, p. 1090ff. See, also, S. v. Reden, 'The well-ordered *polis*: Topographies of civic space', in P. Cartledge, P. Millett and S. v. Reden (eds), *Kosmos: Essays in Order, Conflict and Community in Classical Athens*, Cambridge: Cambridge University Press, 1998, pp. 170–90, p. 170ff.; G. Böhme, *Der Typ Sokrates*, 2nd edn, Frankfurt: Suhrkamp, 1998, p. 47. For political and legal structures of the feudal system, see M. Bloch, *Die Feudalgesellschaft*, Stuttgart: Klett-Cotta, 1999 (original French publication 1939), particularly pp. 175ff. and 201ff.
75 See, for example, Schultze, 'Staat' op. cit., p. 1012ff.
76 See J. Bodin, *Sechs Bücher über den Staat*, Vols I–III, B. Wimmer (trans), P. C. Mayer-Tasch (ed), München: Beck, 1981, p. 205. See also Creveld, *The Rise and Decline of the State*, op. cit., p. 176ff.; and P. C. Mayer-Tasch, *Jean Bodin. Eine Einführung in sein Leben, sein Werk und seine Wirkung*, Düsseldorf: Parerga, 2000, p. 43ff.
77 See T. Hobbes, *Leviathan*, N. Malcolm (ed), Vol. 2: *The English and Latin Texts I*, Oxford: Clarendon, 2012, Ch. 17, p. 260.
78 See I. Fetscher, 'Einleitung', in T. Hobbes, *Leviathan oder Stoff, Form und Gewalt eines kirchlichen und bürgerlichen Staates*, 6th edn, edited and introduced by I. Fetscher, Frankfurt: Suhrkamp, 1994, pp. IX–LXVI, p. XXVIff.
79 Hobbes, *Leviathan*, op. cit., p. 260.
80 See, for example, Koselleck, *Kritik und Krise. Eine Studie zur Pathogenese der bürgerlichen Welt*, op. cit., p. 18ff.
81 Even Bodin does not make a decision to determine the person of the sovereign; cf. for example, R. Hoke, *Österreichische und deutsche Rechtsgeschichte*, Vienna: Böhlau, 1992, p. 181.
82 See, in particular, Donhauser, *Angst und Schrecken*, op. cit., pp. 170ff. and 226ff.
83 See, also, for example, Creveld, *The Rise and Decline of the State*, op. cit., p. 191ff.
84 For a definition of 'liberty' as 'independence', see, for example, G. W. F. Hegel, *Vorlesungen über die Philosophie der Geschichte*, in G. W. F. Hegel, E. Moldenhauer and K. M. Michel (eds), *Werke*, Vol. 12, 3rd edn, Frankfurt: Suhrkamp, 1992, pp. 56–74.
85 See Creveld, *The Rise and Decline of the State*, op. cit., p. 336ff.; E.-O. Czempiel, *Weltpolitik im Umbruch. Das internationale System nach dem Ende des Ost-West-Konflikts*, 2nd edn, München: C. H. Beck, 1990, p. 133ff.; M. Herkenrath, *Transnationale Konzerne im Weltsystem. Globale Unternehmen, nationale Wirtschaftspolitik und das Problem nachholender Entwicklung*, Wiesbaden: VS Verlag für Sozialwissenschaften, 2003. For consideration of the role of rating agencies as political players, see, for example, J. Rosenbaum, *Der politische Einfluss von Rating-Agenturen*, Wiesbaden: VS Verlag für Sozialwissenschaften, 2009; T. J. Sinclair, *The New Masters of Capital: American Bond Rating Agencies and the Politics of Creditworthiness*, Ithaca: Cornell University Press, 2005.
86 See, for example, D. Benner (ed), *Bildung zwischen Staat und Markt*, Weinheim: Beltz, 1996; L. Lassnigg, *Bildungspolitik zwischen Ökonomisierung und öffentlichem Gut? Fakten, Widersprüche, Kontroversen*, Vienna: IHS, 2003; T. Stutchey, *Die Finanzierung von Hochschulbildung. Eine finanzwissenschaftliche Analyse und ihre ordnungspolitischen Konsequenzen*, Baden-Baden: Nomos, 2001.
87 See, for example, Foucault, *Überwachen und Strafen. Die Geburt des Gefängnisses*, op. cit.; C. A. MacKinnon, *Towards a Feminist Theory of the State*, 2nd edn, Cambridge, MA: Harvard University Press, 1991; W. Benjamin, 'Zur Kritik der Gewalt', in R. Tiedemann and H. Schweppenhäuser (eds), *Walter Benjamin Gesammelte Schriften*, Vol. II.1, Frankfurt: Suhrkamp, 1991, p. 179ff; for the latter, see, also, H. Bredekamp, 'Von Walter Benjamin zu Carl Schmitt, via Thomas Hobbes', *Deutsche Zeitschrift für*

Philosophie (1998), 46, 6, 901–16; G. Agamben, *Ausnahmezustand*, Homo sacer II. 1, U. Müller-Schöll (trans), Frankfurt: Suhrkamp, 2004, p. 67ff. See, also, Donhauser, *Türhüter. Wie Recht wird, was es ist*, op. cit., p. 44ff.

88 See Donhauser, *Angst und Schrecken*, op. cit., p. 139ff.
89 See Dudenredaktion (ed), *Duden. Deutsches Universalwörterbuch*, 5th rev edn, Mannheim, 2003, p. 1285.
90 See J. Locke, W. Euchner and H. J. Hoffmann (eds), *Zwei Abhandlungen über die Regierung*, 2nd edn, Frankfurt: Suhrkamp, 1983, pp. 291–307; C.-L. Montesquieu, *Vom Geist der Gesetze*, K. Weigand (trans), Stuttgart: Philipp Reclam, 2006, p. 216ff.
91 See, Kelsen, *Pure Theory of Law*, op. cit., p. 4.
92 See, Kelsen, *Reine Rechtslehre*, op. cit., p. 203.
93 D. Grimm, 'Konstitution, Grundgesetz(e) von der Aufklärung bis zur Gegenwart', in H. Mohnhaupt and D. Grimm, *Verfassung. Zur Geschichte eines Begriffs von der Antike bis zur Gegenwart. Zwei Studien*, Berlin: Duncker & Humblot, 1995, pp. 100–41, p. 102.
94 See Jellinek, *Allgemeine Staatslehre*, op. cit., p. 371ff.
95 See, for example, L. K. Adamovich, B.-C. Funk and G. Holzinger, *Österreichisches Staatsrecht*, Bk. 1: *Grundlagen*, Vienna: Springer, 1997, p. 16ff. See, also, J. Elster, 'Die Schaffung von Verfassungen: Analyse der allgemeinen Grundlagen', in U. K. Preuß (ed), *Zum Begriff der Verfassung. Die Ordnung des Politischen*, Frankfurt: Fischer, 1994, pp. 37–57, p. 38.
96 See, Kelsen, *Reine Rechtslehre*, op. cit., p. 289ff; see, also, Groh, *Demokratische Staatsrechtslehrer in der Weimarer Republik*, op. cit., p. 119ff.; Vollmeyer, *Der Staat als Rechtsordnung*, op. cit., p. 73ff. See, also, Donhauser, *Türhüter. Wie Recht wird, was es ist*, op. cit., p. 60ff.; Donhauser, 'Freiheit im Rechtsstaat. Zentrale Themen, Perspektiven und Grenzen von Kelsens Demokratiekonzept', op. cit., p. 110ff.
97 See, for example, P. Blom, *Böse Philosophen. Ein Salon in Paris und das vergessene Erbe der Aufklärung*, München: Carl Hanser, 2013, p. 265ff.; C. Beccaria, *Über Verbrechen und Strafen*, W. Alff (ed and trans), Frankfurt: Insell, 1966; J. v. Sonnenfels, 'Ueber die Abschaffung der Folter', in J. v. Sonnenfels, *Gesammelte Schriften*, Bk. 7, Vienna: Baumeister, 1785.
98 See, also, Donhauser, *Angst und Schrecken*, op. cit., p. 142ff.
99 See R. Dworkin, *Taking Rights Seriously*, rev edn, Cambridge, MA: Harvard University Press, 1997, p. 310ff.

Chapter 7
Human rights and subjective rights: affinities in Max Weber and Georg Jellinek

Kathrin Groh

Introduction

The question of the substantial and striking affinities between Max Weber and Georg Jellinek concerning their conception of individual rights and individual freedom, either in the form of human rights or in the form of so-called 'subjective rights' has never been the subject of systematic consideration, for the relationship between Weber and Jellinek has only ever been examined in a partial manner.[1] In regard to scholarship on Weber concerning human rights, the consensus is that his empirical view of the origins of human rights were completely dependent upon the research of his friend and colleague Jellinek.[2] Retrospectively, Weber confirmed in his speech at the wedding of Jellinek's daughter on 1 March 1911 that he found fundamental encouragement and direction for his own work in Jellinek's writings, in particular, in the fact that Jellinek had established that the need for religious freedom was the origin and genesis of human rights.[3] Although the assumption of Jellinek regarding the significant influence of religion on the development, but especially on the positivity, of human rights has been rejected,[4] in the context of the liberalism of the German Reich it was necessary to loosen the nexus between the idea of human rights and the French Revolution, to render human rights palatable within the parameters of the prevalent German political culture. Jellinek was able to fulfill this necessity. However, according to König, it is Weber's work which enabled Jellinek's assumption to become predominant in German jurisprudence, and facilitated sociological theories regarding political modernization.[5]

Overview of primary texts and secondary literature

Despite the initial character of this relationship, the more detailed comparison of Weber's own poor conception of human rights, or rights to liberty, with Jellinek's orientation towards human rights, and so-called subjective public rights, reveals this connection to be more complex.

Jellinek occupied himself intensively with the genesis of human rights. In his small book *Die Erklärung der Menschen- und Bürgerrechte*,[6] first published in 1895, and with four further editions, he provided essential preparatory work for his theoretical masterpiece *System der subjektiven öffentlichen Rechte* which ultimately covered 366 pages and which was his favourite book.[7] The contemporary doctrine of human rights in Germany accords Jellinek's small book the position of a caesura and a breakthrough in the history of the science of human rights. The German doctrine sub-divides the period of academic disputes regarding human rights into the era before and after Jellinek.[8] His work *System der subjektiven öffentlichen Rechte* also has left deep and lasting traces in the science of public law in Germany. In the discipline of administrative law, Jellinek is regarded as one of the fathers of the modern doctrine of subjective public rights. Even though his book, 'System', was suffused with an overtly theoretical orientation, and did not achieve a wholly favourable reception from his contemporaries,[9] contemporary relevance of the theory of subjective public rights is obvious. Despite the continuous expansion of subjective public rights into more areas of application, their theory and dogmatics apparently remained the same.[10] Some voices from the field of modern administrative law still criticize the statist aftertaste of Jellinek's doctrine in the modern theory of subjective public rights which is, for example, the demand of a so-called 'protecting norm' (*Schutznorm*) that is indispensable to define a subjective public right: the ordinary legislative authority first has to pass a law to explicitly protect the interests of individuals prior to any consideration of the definition of a specific subjective public right. The imposition of this framework upon the ordinary legislator is said to be an obstacle to founding subjective public rights upon human rights themselves for they originate from nature and not from legislation.[11] Nevertheless, nearly every textbook in German administrative law contains the key sentence of Jellinek, where he defines subjective public rights, 'The subjective right in the area of the Public Law consists only of the possibility, to move legal norms in the interest of individuals',[12] which means that it produces the possibility to claim that right against the State by way of legal action.

Moreover, Jellinek is also essential for the German sciences of constitutional law. He grouped the freedom of the citizens from, and in, the State into four 'statuses'. Each status he filled with specific subjective public rights. In the modern German theory of basic rights and human rights, this doctrine, termed the 'doctrine of status' (*Statuslehre*), cannot be ignored. It forms a general legal principle that constitutional theorists always use. However, because of the numerous dogmatic ambiguities in the relationship between status and subjective public rights, Jellinek's doctrine of status is, in contemporary considerations, held to be controversial. One side recognizes it as 'a great example of analytic formation of theory on the field of Basic Rights'.[13] The other side also considers Jellinek's approach entirely successful, terminologically, but qualifies it by recognizing (rightly) that Jellinek's theoretical concept is of no contemporary relevance.[14]

In contrast, Max Weber cannot be accorded a central position in the tradition of human rights or the rights to liberty.[15] To undertake examination of Weber's idea of human rights and rights to liberty in his writings does not even seem plausible. There are merely a few instances, in his extensive complete works, in which Weber refers explicitly, albeit only briefly, to human rights. The extensive and frequent historical and sociological considerations regarding subjective rights are, indeed, concerned with individual rights, for example, property and freedom of contract. However, they concentrate predominantly on the field of civil law, notably the legal relationship of citizens amongst themselves, and not in their interaction with the State. That, of course, is due to the fact that Weber's interest focused upon the development of capitalism. The question of liberty from, and in, the State has a dispersed and fragmentary presence in Weber's texts. It even appears questionable whether these are actually to be read as Weber's contribution to the genesis of modern individualism.[16] Hence, the number of scholars who are concerned with Weber's social studies on human rights, or with the subjective rights, is small. Their aim is to 'excavate', through extensive and patient analysis of the foundations of Weber's work, an 'implicit' sociology of human rights.[17] Alternatively, they try to offer 'first answers' to the question of the universality of human rights through 'reference' to Weber merely to give his work new stimuli.[18] But to find a justification for the universality of human rights in Weber's works does not, initially, seem possible. Weber's writings were imbued with Eurocentrism or, at least, a heuristic kind of ethnocentrism, and he confined his cultural analyses to the Occident. This was accompanied by Weber's espousal of the theory of heterogeneity and the historical contingency of values.[19] Hence, the seeming absence of foundation, in Weber's writings, for the discovery of criteria for the universality of human rights. In his epistemology, Weber's position is one in which a realistic science of ethics does not produce a universalizable, normative ethics.[20] Since Leo Strauss,[21] this Weberian fact-value distinction is held perpetually responsible for the fact that the social sciences were constitutively unable to have developed a sociology of human rights.[22] The sociology of human rights which refers to Weber, therefore, must adopt a circuitous route in order to appropriate Weber for this discourse. The same observation applies to the legal philosophy of human rights 'referring' to Weber. Both academic disciplines seek to connect Weber, at this point of his work, with Kant. The sociological reception of Weberian thought on human rights assumes that Weber, in his cultural analysis, (intentionally) constructed a theory based on Kant's principle of reason, therefore, anticipating a central idea of the modern discourse on human rights.[23] Legal philosophy itself exceeds Weber's work with Kant.[24] Both disciplines retain Weber's relativism of values (*Wertrelativismus*).[25] They insist, paradoxically, that the normativity of Weber's sociology, regarding the discourse on human rights, is Weber's distance towards universalistic norms: this relativism is the preparatory stage for the idea that human rights can be accorded distinct values by different cultures, and the discourse on human rights can become cross-cultural.[26] Moreover, Weber, even within the confines of the specific culture of the West, is said to have advised at least the leaders of the State to pursue a policy of accountability (*Verantwortungspolitik*) that conforms to human rights.[27]

Beyond this set of existing approaches to their work, there are obvious affinities to be found between Jellinek and Weber in the analysis of the genesis of human rights. These affinities and interconnections are located in the deeper layers of their work and personalities. They are to be sought, in particular, in the areas of epistemology, the doctrine of the authority of the State, and the sociology of domination. This is then to be combined with the recognition of their academic or, rather, political utilization in relation to demands of social democracy expressed in the discourse of human rights.

Epistemology: types of knowledge interests and ideals

The political attitude of Weber and Jellinek is to be found within the different nuances of national liberal thought in Germany.[28] Both considered, in their writings, whether the possibility of individual freedom in a community exists: Jellinek sought to define the limits between individual and State within his legal theory of the State,[29] Weber sought to discover, through his sociology of domination, how an autonomous life and action within a society remains possible.[30] Perhaps it follows from the type of knowledge interest of a scientist, which according to Weberian methodology is determined by a value-based relation (*Wertbeziehung*)[31] to the object of his research, not only the determination of previous understandings, but also even an ideal of the scientist himself, which orientates his questions and his methods.[32] This interpretation of Weber is derived from many indications in Weber's writings; for example, his statement that his 'value-idea' or 'his personal belief in values in the mirror of his soul will show the scientist his way'.[33] If one concurs with this assumption, it seems possible to understand the sociology of Weber, in actuality, as plea for a form of bourgeois individualism.[34]

Epistemology, in Jellinek, is shaped by a similar orientation, 'The result of his works depends upon the initial point which one captures and his personal opinions'.[35] Jellinek, therefore, is, in retrospect, surprising with his justification of the modern State 'psychologically and ethically' which, in turn, contains the 'development of individuality' as an integral element.[36] But the presumption that Jellinek should have believed in the individual as the 'criterion for all legal construction'[37] is soon relinquished when one examines Jellinek's construction of the relationship between individual and State. Jellinek rejected the idea of the law of nature which postulated that the State serves the individual and functions as a 'shelter for human rights'. For then, the nationalist Jellinek argued, 'naked individualism' would expunge the higher ideal of the fatherland.[38]

Regarding the genesis of human rights

For Weber and Jellinek, the origin of the idea of human rights in the law of nature was a central theme. They located the idea of human rights at the interface between the law of nature and the positive legal order.[39] Both asked themselves from a historical-genetic perspective, why the already much older idea of unalienable human rights, as the so-called 'Rights of Right', were only gradually enacted in the form of laws, and their comprehensive recognition only arose with the North-American Bills of Rights and the French Déclaration. Jellinek, in his research on human rights, followed the path by which philosophies become laws.[40] Moreover, both were interested in the conditions of possibility of the positivity, and the enforcement, of the idea of freedom. From their extensive historical analysis, both concluded that the ideas of the Enlightenment may have had a powerful presence in history. However, this power was that of a mere idea which in itself was insufficient to become a legally binding norm. Only a combination of ideas and interests which intensify themselves reciprocally would be strong enough to activate the legislator.[41] The point of intensification required a significant section of a population to suffer from pervasive experiences of injustice in order to accelerate the conversion of ideas of the law of nature into a legal or a constitutional order of a State.[42] For Jellinek, the genesis of human rights was to be understood concretely, 'The idea to lay down in law the unalienable and holy birth-rights of the individual has its origins in religion', and 'surely is a fruit of the Reformation and its struggles'.[43] For Weber, the Protestant sects gave:

> rise to an inalienable personal right of the governed as against any power, whether political, hierocratic or patriarchal. Such freedom of conscience may be the oldest right of man – as Jellinek has argued convincingly, at any rate, it is the most basic right of man because it comprises all ethically conditioned action and guarantees freedom from compulsion, especially from the power of the state. The other rights of man or civil rights were joined to this basic right.[44]

However, in his empirical analysis of the genesis of all Rights to Liberty, Weber then modified the initial approach of Jellinek. Travelling through America, Weber had observed other conditions for the successful elimination of situations of unfreedom that were geographical and political, and appended them to the ideals of the law of nature and religious freedom.[45] In his two essays regarding the situation in Russia, Weber then analysed completely different actors to those of the sects as the potential bearers of human rights. This was due to the fact that 'sects in Russia were not able to motivate enough supporters for individualistic ideals'.[46] He thus connected there the goal of individual freedom inextricably with the political idea of liberalism and the economic ethics of the Occidental capitalism, and considered a free society to be achieved only within a specific configuration of material interests.[47]

Subjective (public) rights as the juridification of the idea of human rights

Jellinek's and Weber's studies concerning the genesis of human rights were undertaken as historical and political studies. The underlying emphasis of Jellinek in these studies is a jurisprudential concentration on subjective rights. For Weber, the predominant emphasis is one of a socio-economic perspective on these subjective rights.

While Jellinek was obliged to invent a modern theory of subjective public rights, due to the paucity of existing, preliminary research, Weber was able to resort, in his analysis of capitalism, to the traditional figure of subjective private rights in the theory of civil law. He was, therefore, freed from the requirement for extensive legal or State-theoretical explanations concerning subjective rights. This freedom is the counterpart of an underlying interest in knowledge, and the methodological approach to law as a sociological institution. Therefore, Weber simply identified subjective rights with rights to liberty, and defined them as 'safeguards against specific types of obstruction from third parties, especially also: from the state'. He enumerated, among the most important rights to liberty, the inviolable right to property, the freedom to exercise a trade, the free movement of persons, the freedom of conscience and the freedom of contract.[48] In the conscious absence of a normative theory of subjective rights, Weber was able to nonchalantly construe and justify their impact with normative arguments. If the right of freedom (of contract) was truly based on a formal principle of the law of nature, then this right of freedom would also have formal restraints insofar as this freedom must not be used against its legitimation in the law of nature, 'It is not lawful if one brings himself under slavery whether private or political'.[49]

In contrast, for Jellinek, it was more difficult than for Weber to bring together individual freedom and authority of the State into a legal theory of subjective public rights. The 'bold claim that there have to be moral and legal limits to all earthly authorities' does 'not transform itself automatically into a legal theory of subjective public rights serving as those postulated limits to the authority of the state'.[50] In fact, Jellinek arrived at the same conclusion as Weber, which is that a State of slaves without individual rights was no longer conceivable. But he was not able to support this initial assumption with a purely juridical rationale because he commenced, in his theory of the State, from the primacy of the State over the law. Hence, the State, as sovereign, could not be bound by any law but through a process of self-limitation. Jellinek, therefore, had to postulate the impossibility of a State of slaves as a historically plausible position or rather a pathetic aspiration. That the State would impose upon itself legal limits, and acknowledge the individual as a legal person to whom it accords individual rights to freedom, could only have been construed as a moral duty in Jellinek's theory. This duty, furthermore, arose from the intelligence of the State because, according to Jellinek, 'the modern culture depends on the belief that state authority itself is subject to restrictions and because we are not slaves who are subdued to the boundless omnipotence of the state'. Therefore, 'all civilized nations own a cadre of liberties which are not at the disposition of the arbitrariness of the legislator'.[51] While Hans Kelsen saw remnants of natural law glimmering in this argumentation,[52] Jens Kersten explains Jellinek's preceding doctrine of self-limitation of the State as a variation of the Kantian notion of moral autonomy.[53] However, the set of inviolable liberties that could withstand the legislative authority of the State was minimal in Jellinek's theory. It only explicitly contained individual religious and artistic freedom, economic freedom and the family.[54] This was further qualified by the exceptional position of the State with regard to law: only the sovereign State could impose upon itself legal limits without these being the subject of any obligation.[55]

In Germany, in contrast to America or France, the individual was not a legal subject simply because of its existence as a human being. In Jellinek's theory, the natural liberty of the individual conferred no necessary legal personality unless that freedom was legally protected by the State, 'From the being of the individual arises the historical and logical inevitability only of the duty for, and not the right against the state'.[56] The Germans became legal subjects only through an act by the State, and were complete personalities only in the modern State.[57] Jellinek's doctrine of status was linked to his theories of individual freedom and subjective public rights: at the origin of Jellinek's doctrine of the four statuses – the '*status subjectionis*', the '*status negativus*' or '*libertatis*', the '*status activus*' and the '*status positivus*' – there necessarily existed this legal quality of a person by conferral.[58] The chronological enumeration of those statuses that Jellinek constructed by an inductive, not a deductive method, reflected both the levels of the development of the modern State in Jellinek's theory and the increasing quality of subjective public rights. In particular, we are including the absolute State without individual rights, the liberal State with rights to freedom from the State, the democratic State with political rights and the welfare State with social rights.[59] Winfried Brugger asserts that Jellinek, at this point, had presented the history of the State as a process in which the initial precedence of the State over the individual was progressively transformed by the recognition of the individual's dignity.[60]

Of these four statuses, only the '*status subjectionis*' and the '*status negativus*' are relevant for the following analysis. In Jellinek's status of subjection, the individual was without any rights against the State. But this status of subjection was, for Jellinek, the fundamental relationship between the individual and the State: the individual was subordinated to authority (*Untertan*).[61] Then, the '*status negativus*' was added, in which the individual presided over a sphere from which the authority of the State was excluded.[62] However, the individual's possession of this sphere was not the mere extension of its personhood. In fact, the State had to set the individual free by accepting it as a legal personality within the State's legal system. The decision on the extent of legal personality and, hence, the freedom that the State granted to the individual, remained with the State: individual freedom was created by the State.

Neither his observation that the figure of subjective public right has been displaced from natural law into positive law with the ratification of Bills of Rights,[63] nor his effort to demonstrate the religious origin of liberty rights, encouraged him to construe the pre-State character of individual rights legally – which would have been at variance with the prevailing perspective in this period. But his conformity with the prevailing consensus of his profession was based, at this period of his work, less in conservatism than in a realistic perspective upon the regulative power of laws.[64] From a historical perspective, Germany was not yet prepared for individual rights to take precedence over the State: that which had been achieved in North America had never succeeded in France. Whereas the Bills of Rights were a mere legal restatement of the existing, factual situation, the French people had wanted the acknowledgement of rights which they had not previously possessed, and this intention had failed. This mistake was, for Jellinek, repeated by the Paulskirche in Germany: one needed to have and, therefore, to build a State first before one can be free from the State.[65] However, in another stage of his work, Jellinek's statist arguments shifted from that of a purely chronological to a logical precedence of the State over individual liberty. Thus, he condemned the idea of a sovereign individual founded on human rights as heretical, dangerous and destructive of the State.[66]

The State granted only an abstract notion of personal freedom to individuals. The particular freedoms accorded to the individual, as the specific content of this '*status negativus*', was determined through laws enacted by the State, for it was the legislator's task to maintain the balance between the individuals' and the State's interests. Jellinek's subjective public rights that were contained in the '*status negativus*', and their potential to ensure freedom, were exclusively aimed at the executive, not at the legislator. Therefore, Jellinek only acknowledged a single basic right, namely, the right of freedom against unlawful restraint.[67] The significant number and variety of human rights whose emergence was historicized in Jellinek's book on the Déclaration did not – from a legal perspective – hold any meaning for him in the *System*, because the guarantee of constitutional freedom against unlawful despotism is not a synonym for the idea of the specific fundamental freedoms of human rights and their protection against State legislation.[68] According to him, not even the detailed 'basic rights' positivized in the Constitutions of the German 'Länder' were within the definition of subjective public rights. For Jellinek, in conformity with the prevailing understanding, these rights were only 'principles' which served a programmatic role in the formulation of legislation, and which, due to their indefiniteness, had to be transformed into ordinary law by the legislator.[69] In their State-free sphere, individuals thus always lived with the knowledge that the State – or more precisely the legislative power – could minimize or even completely take away this sphere *ad libitum*.[70] Even if one sought to argue that Jellinek attempted to trace the origin of individualism in a modern State, he attributed a purely legal meaning to this individualism which had little significance throughout the German constitutionalist era.[71] In contrast to Weber, Jellinek was not able to identify the legal boundaries of a State,[72] because a State that voluntarily commits itself to accept a '*status libertatis*' is also equally able to relieve itself of such an obligation at any time.[73]

Another restriction of subjective public rights in comparison with human rights can be identified through an analysis of Jellinek's statist *System*. The State did not grant subjective rights to individuals for mere reasons of philanthropy. In fact, the individuals' status as an 'element' of the State's community, combined with the need to balance the individual and the public good, were the reasons for which national subjects who were citizens were allowed to be privileged in contrast to aliens. Nevertheless, Jellinek accorded the State the capacity to confer legal freedom even to resident aliens. An alien was both a '*subditus temporarius*', and a '*civis temporarius*', albeit in a highly qualified sense in comparison with a national citizen. Thus, Jellinek came to the rather unsatisfactory conclusion that, only 'insofar, [as] the idea of natural law [. . .] has been legally embodied by the drafting of human rights and civil liberties has it [had] a persistent impact on the basic principles of modern state systems'.[74] Weber, however, did not introduce or describe this distinction.

The functionality of human rights and subjective (public) rights

Beyond the recognition of subjective public rights, as individual liberties, the question then arises of whether Weber and Jellinek attributed special functions to individual liberties within a State, a regime or an economic system.

In his remarks on the formation of a capitalist economic system, Weber argued that human rights and basic rights, notably in the form of equality before the law and economic freedom, have been a necessary condition for the expansion of capitalism. Meanwhile, Weber also observed that the origin of one of the basic prerequisites for capitalism, the freedom of contract, preceded the origin of human rights and, thus, would survive their decline. Focusing only on Weber's considerations on subjective rights, and on his sparse remarks concerning the interrelation between freedom and the formation of a capitalist economic system, it may seem – as Hans Joas comments – that Weber has a reduced understanding of human rights,[75] because he merely addressed them under the aspect of their economic function, '[. . .] human rights and civil liberties served as preconditions for the asset's free acting and its striving for liquidation concerning goods and people'.[76] Above all, his chapter considering the different types of formation of subjective rights has to be considered as sociological analysis of the development of contract law in particular. Weber's focus only expanded to recognize the more comprehensive function of human rights, as a guarantee for freedom against the State, if he was concerned with the oppressive power of the bureaucratic State.

For Weber, the domination of bureaucracy in the modern age was inevitable. Bureaucratic domination initially arose out of capitalism and represented that rational organization of administrative power that was for the time being necessary for a capitalist economy to flourish. But then the dynamics of bureaucracy increasingly forced people into an iron cage of bondage to which they, 'like fellaheen had impotently to submit to' – an observation that Weber had adopted from his brother Alfred.[77] Furthermore, the 'rationalization of political and economic fulfilment of demand' restricted the opportunities for 'individually differentiated acting' in a structural way.[78] According to Weber, only those who succeeded in evading the web of bureaucracy and its rationality were able to live with human dignity.[79] Due to the oppressive power of bureaucracy, Weber asked himself, with increasing desperation, whether and how it would be possible to rescue the remnants of the individual freedom of action of humanity. Weber's search for support from within the framework of human rights still remained ambivalent. On the one hand, in his '*Soziologische Grundbegriffe*' he referred to human rights as 'extreme rationalist fanaticism',[80] and as an embodiment of such ultimate values similar to exceptional acts of religious and charitable fervour, which are barely understandable to those who do not share them or those who are less attuned to this orientation. On the other hand, he regarded human rights as the only firm anchor against the bureaucratic regime, although the ideas of 1789 produced a rather arrogant disdain for their 'childishness'.[81] If human rights, in Weber's model, are to be seen as a condition for the possibility that a single human being is provided with an actual and deliberate choice of the substantive values or the 'demons' that he would like to follow,[82] Weber's sociology may be described as a 'Philosophie de la Liberté'.[83] This position gains force, on the one hand, by the fact that Weber personally did not fear an overdevelopment of individualism – a 'too much' of individualism – and, on the other, that he advised his potential audience not to be too afraid of democracy and individualism.[84] Most notably, his essays about the Russian Revolution reveal sympathies for the Russians' struggle for freedom as well as for the more general notion of freedom.[85] Nevertheless, Weber's description of the outlines of the free individual future is rather dismal and gloomy.

In comparison with Jellinek, Weber's opinion concerning the State's authority, incorporated by the administration, was a much more sceptical one. It appears that, in contrast to Weber, Jellinek presented an essentially evolutionary cultural theory.[86] However, he, too, realized that the actual State was turning into a modern State of intervention which took over one field of action after the other. For Jellinek, as well as for Weber, the specific administrative power increased due to the proliferation of laws.[87] Nevertheless, Jellinek, in contrast to Weber, was convinced that the course of history was marked by a constant expansion of civil liberties against the State and, hence, a related expansion of autonomous individualism.[88] The relationship between the State and the autonomous individual would be further enhanced by the State's promotion of culture within the fields of social life to which its powers extended. These fields, controlled and orientated by the State, would enable the autonomous individual to cultivate an ever growing field of freedom of movement and action.[89]

The law of nature and human rights: legitimacy, obedience or acceptance of a legal system

Weber and Jellinek were convinced that a scientific proof for natural law, as an eternal and unchallengeable objective order – a 'Law of the Law' – from which positive law has to derive its legitimacy, could not be established. This was the counterpart of their presentation of the historical contingency and the subjectivity of values: the relativism of all values.[90] Nevertheless, natural law retained an importance in their work in relation to the question how a legal system can be held to have achieved factual validity or binding authority.

For Weber, in conformity with Jellinek, the law of nature which contained the idea of human rights was 'the total sum of all those norms which are valid independently of, and superior to, any positive law and that do not derive their dignity from arbitrary statutes, but provide the very legitimation for the binding force of positive law'.[91] That is why, once positivized, human rights contributed to the legitimacy, and acceptance, of the State, in both its particular form and its legal system. For Weber, the reason for this could be found in the people's faith in the legitimacy of authority. Only that faith established a solid base for an enduring regime and the continued obedience to the commands of those who ruled.[92] The mutual integration of ethical ideals and positive law became a 'natural law' which furnished the justification of the legitimacy of the legal order.[93] For Weber, the specific character of this 'natural law' was particularly evident in periods of the change of regimes and legal systems. In periods in which the legitimacy of an effective legal order was placed into question, 'the natural law is the specific form which is used by the classes revolting against the existing order to give its desire for a new and better legal conceptualisation a boost'. Weber's position overlapped, here, with that of Jellinek's.[94]

The openness of the 'natural' law to the recognition of diverse powers – the potential for it to be exploited at will – led Weber to deny its capacity as a solid foundation for the law.[95] The lack of solidity is accompanied by a particular paradox of the wider process of disenchantment: once human rights have become incorporated and expressed in written law, according to Weber, they lose their special dignity which formerly identified them as being 'the Law of the Law'. Disenchantment arises because legal rationalism, combined with the more general scepticism of the modern intellectuals, prefigured the subsequent corrosion of all meta-legal axioms: the entirety of all written law was demystified as a product of compromises and of interests.[96] However, the State-integrative function of human rights was still retained by Weber, although he accorded it only marginal importance, 'The idea of human rights [. . .] has the power to unite the different classes – in this case, the bourgeois with the proletarian'.[97]

Jellinek, whose intellectual formation was in the context of legal positivism, was surprisingly less austere than Weber. Jellinek described the empirical phenomenon of natural law as 'nothing else than the entirety of those postulations which a gradually changing society demands of law-making powers'.[98] Jellinek sought to reveal the 'ethical *logos*' enshrined in the legal order and, thereby, pre-figured aspects of Weber's theory of legitimacy.[99] When Jellinek broached the issue of the validity and binding force of legal norms, this was not only by reference to the concept of 'the normative power of the factual' (normative *Kraft des Faktischen*), but also by reference to the doctrine of acceptance. In order to obtain approval, and to be obeyed consistently, a legal norm should convince the average citizen through the idea which stands behind it. This idea was, according to Jellinek, represented by the natural law and, thus, by human rights. Hence, for Jellinek, human rights had the power to create a faith which, in turn, would have the ability to permanently stabilize the legal order.[100] In this regard, Jellinek diverged from both Weber's pessimism and characterization of the future dynamics of a positivist, technical jurisprudence, but, instead, welcomed the rise of a new idealism[101] with respect to the search for foundational principles in the law that were, at minimum, psychologically effective.

Human rights as social rights and rights of participation

From this presence of natural law and human rights in their work, the question then arises as to the positions adopted by Weber and Jellinek regarding the actual character of the social question contemporaneous with their theoretical work.

For Weber, one of the consequences of an emergence and development of a capitalist economic system was the institutionalization of the idea of equal freedom as a right to freedom. This was accompanied by the presence of an enduring factual inequality for many, namely, for the propertyless classes. As a consequence, the freedom of the propertyless, working class was only formal, and, in reality, the working class was unfree.[102] How did Weber's 'Philosophie de la Liberté' react?

Weber's sociology of individualism centred upon the interplay between individual and society and was continually inquiring: In what way does society relate to a human being, which form of society needs which type of individual human personality and how does it produce it?[103] Weber's concerns regarding a further loss of freedom and individuality led to his opposition to the recognition of social rights as human rights. He was convinced that socialism would intensify and extend bureaucracy and finally eliminate all individualism.[104] This concern was the expression of a deeper unease about the type of human who would be created by the welfare State: the bureaucracy of a welfare State would enable the birth of persons of a 'mentally dull' type that it could herd like a flock of sheep.[105] Instead of relying on State welfare, in the form of an entitlement to financial support, or to the protection of the rights in favour of the working class, Weber attempted to confront the social problem by developing those characteristics, even within the working class, that make for human greatness – whatever they were.[106] In his essay about the Russian Revolution, Weber clarified what would happen if the path of natural economic selection were to remain orientated toward a welfare State, inspired by natural law, that privileges the 'economically unqualified', 'A strong decline of cultural intensity would be inevitable'. The full realization of this particular path would result in the collapse of capitalism and, without the capitalist economy, the State would cease to exist.[107]

However, Weber justified his negative evaluation of the juridification of the demand for social rights on the level of legal theory. He commenced by dividing natural law into two categories: formal and material natural law. To the category of formal natural law are attributed the contract theories of natural law of the seventeenth and eighteenth centuries and their associated related liberal civil liberties, in particular, the formal freedom of contract and equality before the law. To the category of material natural law are attributed the socialist demands, based on human rights, for social and economic rights to participate and for material justice. According to Weber, both categories of law, formal and material natural law, rested upon different concepts of rationality and, within a definitional framework determined by logic, were mutually exclusive.[108] The *de facto* impact of the social demand for human rights on the positive law was even more central to Weber's critical position: the jurisprudential positivism and its legally trained officialdom, judges and bureaucrats, had created and extended to its fullest extent the certainty of individual expectations of the legal order. The extension of formalism in law and jurisdiction had supplanted subjective despotism and legal privileges: formally rational law and trained legal personnel combined to produce a form of action based upon generalized and logical rules that applied equally to all.[109] However, the factually non-privileged classes now were demanding a material justice.[110] Weber, a rationalist and proponent of the capitalist economic system, whose existence the formal rationalism of a continental legal culture had assisted, was concerned that irrationalism would re-emerge in law and its interpretation, due to social demands for justice and the ideologies of these classes. Those tendencies might prevail which were 'demanding a social right on the groundings of emotive and moral postulates like justice' and, thus, could be regarded as the development of weak judiciary (*Kadijustiz*) based on equity,[111] 'The law has to be kept free from any kind of arbitrariness whether social or ethical'.[112] Weber's acrimonious words against the linguistic form that the Americans and French had chosen, in the course of providing written form for human rights, underline his antipathy to excessive space for discretion in the law: human rights in those two countries were formulated with 'epigrammatic theatrics' using 'postulate-like patters' instead of opting for 'matter-of-fact rules of law'.[113] Jellinek also advocated legal guarantees and civil liberties without embellishment that were not only well-defined in written form, but would be practically enforceable. Therefore, he presupposed that sub-constitutional guarantees of rights to liberty would be sufficient in a State bound by law.[114] Jellinek thus considered the German Reich, which granted rights to liberty through ordinary laws in place of fundamental rights in a Constitution, to confer a greater legal freedom than most States with constitutionally stipulated fundamental rights.[115]

However, the attempt to protect formal freedom against its infiltration by substantive freedom that is particularly orientated towards economic equality in order to prevent an artificial levelling of all human beings was the corollary of contemporaneous elitist, libertarian ideas. Weber was a class-conscious bourgeois who rejected any egalitarian values. This also becomes evident in his articles on the Russian Revolution.[116] Although Weber predicted that the 'natural harmony of interests of free individuals' would be forever annihilated by capitalism,[117] and although, according to his 'female companion', he was engaged in social politics,[118] he was not able to include social democratic and communist demands in his conception of liberalism.[119] Hence, an ambivalence arises from the interpretation of his work. It can equally be held that Weber represents a 'peculiar individualism' without connection to the 'codified egalitarian individualism of a liberalism which is able to be integrated into Declarations of human rights'.[120]

The same ambivalence is present in Jellinek. In order to grant the possibility of equal freedom in a State, irrespective of whether one is poor or rich, formal civil liberties have to be supported legally by material guarantees. Jellinek reflected this equal freedom in the '*status positivus*' of his 'doctrine of status'. In this context, the contemporary 'theory of protecting norms' (*Schutznormtheorie*), which is criticized as being a remnant of statism, is relevant because, especially in the '*status positivus*', it was in the discretion of the legislator to grant an entitlement, as subjective public rights, to welfare services provided by the State. The legislator's intention had to be clearly defined in the relevant norm. If there was a norm regulating certain benefits, but without an indication of the legislator's intention to grant this individual entitlement as a legally enforceable claim to their benefits, the law in question could only be classified within the category of objective law in the interest of the polity which granted the individual benefit merely as a 'reflex'.[121] This benefit, therefore, was a gift from the State to its subjects not a citizens' claim against the State and, thus, not a subjective public right. Jellinek, very pedantic in this approach, categorized all social rights to financial support or to assist the socially deprived within the group of these reflex-laws. In Jellinek's work, the individual remained an 'object of public assistance'. Jellinek condensed the demands for human rights, within the concept of socialism, into a mere 'ethical' obligation for the State.[122] The purpose of the State to foster individuality only obliged Jellinek's State – the Weberian conception of the State simply re-expressed in another vocabulary – to engage in an objective legal 'promotion of culture' in order to encourage the best in humans.[123] Both conceptions directed poor people onto the slippery path of politics through the use of their electoral rights.[124]

Conclusion

The work and orientation of Weber and Jellinek is a reflection of a particular form of liberalism. Jellinek is to be distinguished by the detached manner of the presentation and analysis of the ideal or the legal protection of individual freedom. In contrast, Weber's perspective is shaped by a deeper disenchantment. Both, however, accord a secondary place to individuals and their rights which only occupied a residual position in either a theory of the State (Jellinek) or a sociology of domination (Weber). Human rights were accorded explicit recognition, but in their work their importance was either factually or legally minimized. This is despite their acknowledgement as potential safeguards against bureaucracy and their inherent capacity to enlarge the sphere of existing individual rights. This theoretical approach is the counterpart of the anxiety generated by a potential transition to a welfare State based upon social human rights. The anxiety centres upon their assumption that the increased recognition of social rights undermines liberal principles and individualism. The theoretical 'resolution' of this dilemma involves the detachment of social demands from their expression as social rights and their redirection into political rights and the promotion of culture by the State.

Weber and Jellinek were liberals of their time. At least Jellinek treated the ideal or the legal protection of individual freedom in a rather non-committal way. Weber, in contrast, was resolutely disenchanted. The individuals and their rights were only weaved into either Jellinek's theory of the State or Weber's sociology of domination. Human rights made an impression on them. But in their writings they were either factually or legally reduced, although they should have nevertheless served as safeguards against bureaucracy and should have enlarged their power. Both of them understood the welfare State that was based on social human rights as a threat to liberal principles and to individualism. They were seeking to assuage their social conscience by stressing the importance of political rights and the promotion of culture by the State.

Notes

1 E. Vollrath, 'Max Weber: Sozialwissenschaft zwischen Staatsrechtslehre und Kulturkritik', *Politische Vierteljahresschrift* (1990), 31, 102–8, p. 102; S. Breuer, *Georg Jellinek und Max Weber. Von der sozialen zur soziologischen Staatslehre*, Baden-Baden: Nomos, 1999, p. 8.
2 H. Joas, 'Max Weber and the origin of human rights: a study of cultural innovation', in C. Camic (ed), *Max Weber's Economy and Society*, Stanford: Stanford University Press, 2005, pp. 366–82, p. 366.
3 Marianne Weber, *Max Weber. Ein Lebensbild*, Tübingen: Mohr, 1926, pp. 484 and 366.
4 M. Heckel, 'Die Menschenrechte im Spiegel der reformatorischen Theologie', in *Gesammelte Schriften, Band II*, Tübingen: Mohr, 1989, pp. 1122–93, p. 1141. Already in the lifetime of Jellinek this book caused misunderstandings. G. Jellinek, *Die Erklärung der Menschen- und Bürgerrechte. Ein Beitrag zur modernen Verfassungsgeschichte*, 2nd edn, Leipzig: Duncker & Humblot, 1904, p. ix.
5 M. König, 'Max Weber', in A. Pollmann, and G. Lohmann (eds), *Menschenrechte. Ein interdisziplinäres Handbuch*, Stuttgart: Metzler, 2012, pp. 57–59, p. 59.
6 G. Jellinek, *Die Erklärung der Menschen- und Bürgerrechte. Ein Beitrag zur modernen Verfassungsgeschichte*, 1st edn, Leipzig: Duncker & Humblot, 1895.
7 G. Jellinek, *System der subjektiven öffentlichen Rechte*, 2nd edn, Tübingen: Mohr, 1905.
8 W. Schmale, *Archäologie der Grund- und Menschenrechte in der frühen Neuzeit*, München: Oldenbourg, 1997, pp. 52–57; M. Stolleis, 'Georg Jellineks Beitrag zur Entwicklung der Menschen- und Bürgerrechte', in S. L. Paulson, and M. Schulte (eds), *Georg Jellinek. Beiträge zu Leben und Werk*, Tübingen: Mohr Siebeck, 2000, pp. 103–16, pp. 103–4.
9 O. Mayer, 'Rezension Georg Jellinek, System der subjektiven öffentlichen Rechte 1892', *Archiv des öffentlichen Rechts* (1894), 9, 280–88, p. 281; F. Tezner, 'System der subjektiven öffentlichen Rechte von Prof. Dr. Georg Jellinek', *Zeitschrift für das Privat- und öffentliche Recht der Gegenwart* (1894), 21, 107–254, p. 124.
10 H. Bauer, *Geschichtliche Grundlagen der Lehre vom subjektiven öffentlichen Recht*, Berlin: Duncker & Humblot, 1986, p. 11ff.; in contrast, J. Kersten, 'Einleitung', in J. Kersten (ed), *Georg Jellinek, System der subjektiven öffentlichen Rechte (1905)*, Tübingen: Mohr Siebeck, 2011, pp. 7–52, p. 21.
11 H. Bauer, ibid., pp. 77–83.
12 Jellinek, *System der subjektiv öffentlichen Rechte*, op. cit., p. 51.
13 R. Alexy, 'Grundrecht und Status', in Paulson and Schulte (eds), *Georg Jellinek. Beiträge zu Leben und Werk*, op. cit., pp. 209–25, p. 221; R. Alexy, *Theorie der Grundrechte*, 2nd edn, Frankfurt a.M.: Beck, 1994, p. 244.
14 W. Pauly, 'Georg Jellineks "System der subjektiven öffentlichen Rechte"', in Paulson and Schulte, ibid., pp. 227–44, pp. 229–30 and 244; M. Sachs, 'Die Einteilung der Grundrechte', in K. Stern (ed), *Staatsrecht der Bundesrepublik Deutschland, Band III/1: Lehren der Grundrechte*, München: C.H. Beck, 1988, pp. 388–476, pp. 427–30.

15 König, 'Max Weber', op. cit., p. 57.
16 C. Colliot-Thélène, 'Les modes de justification des droits subjectifs', in C. Colliot-Thélène (ed), *Études Weberiennes*, Paris: Presses Universitaires de France, 2001, pp. 259–78, p. 274.
17 König, 'Max Weber', op. cit., p. 59.
18 W. Brugger, 'Sozialwissenschaftliche Analyse und menschenrechtliches Begründungsdenken. Eine Skizze im Anschluss an Max Weber', *Rechtstheorie* (1980), 11, 356–77, p. 358; W. Brugger, *Menschenrechtsethos und Verantwortungspolitik. Max Webers Beitrag zur Analyse und Begründung der Menschenrechte*, Freiburg: Karl Alber, 1980, p. 5.
19 For example, M. Weber, *Wissenschaft als Beruf*, 6th edn, Berlin: Duncker & Humblot, 1985, p. 27ff.
20 M. Weber, 'Die "Objektivität" sozialwissenschaftlicher und sozialpolitischer Erkenntnis' (1904), in J. Winckelmann (ed), *Gesammelte Aufsätze zur Wissenschaftslehre*, Tübingen: Mohr Siebeck, 1985, pp. 145–214, p. 147f.
21 L. Strauss, *Naturrecht und Geschichte*, Stuttgart: Koehler, 1953, p. 44.
22 B. Turner, 'Outline of the theory of human rights', in B. Turner (ed), *Citizenship and Social Theory*, London: Sage, 1993, pp. 162–90, pp. 171 and 172.
23 M. König, *Menschenrechte bei Durkheim und Weber. Normative Dimensionen des soziologischen Diskurses der Moderne*, Frankfurt/M.: Campus, 2002, pp. 85 and 94.
24 Brugger, *Menschenrechtsethos und Verantwortungspolitik*, op. cit., p. 276f.
25 Weber, *Max Weber. Ein Lebensbild*, op. cit., pp. 94 and 339; Weber always neglected to fully acknowledge that he was a relativist.
26 König, *Menschenrechte bei Durkheim und Weber*, op. cit., pp. 11 and 78; Brugger, *Menschenrechtsethos und Verantwortungspolitik*, op. cit., p. 172.
27 W. Brugger, 'Max Weber und die Menschenrechte als Ethos der Moderne', in J. Schwartländer (ed), *Menschenrechte und Demokratie*, Kehl: Engel, 1981, pp. 223–40, pp. 225–26 and 233, refers to M. Weber, *Politik als Beruf* (1919), 5th edn, Berlin: Duncker & Humblot, 1968, pp. 57–65.
28 Weber, *Max Weber. Ein Lebensbild*, op. cit., pp. 124–28 and 237; J. Kersten, *Georg Jellinek und die klassische Staatslehre*, Tübingen: Mohr, 2000, pp. 25–26.
29 Jellinek, *Die Erklärung der Menschen- und Bürgerrechte*, op. cit., p. 62, 'To identify the valid limitations between oneself and the community is the highest problem which is to be resolved by observing the human community'.
30 H. P. Müller, *Max Weber. Eine Einführung in sein Werk*, Köln: Böhlau, 2007, p. 109.
31 Weber, 'Die "Objektivität" sozialwissenschaftlicher und sozialpolitischer Erkenntnis', op. cit., p. 182.
32 König, *Menschenrechte bei Durkheim und Weber*, op. cit., pp. 15–16.
33 Weber, 'Die "Objektivität" sozialwissenschaftlicher und sozialpolitischer Erkenntnis', op. cit., pp. 181–82.
34 Müller, *Max Weber. Eine Einführung in sein Werk*, op. cit., p. 258; Weber, *Max Weber. Ein Lebensbild*, op. cit., p. 319.
35 G. Jellinek, *Die sozialethische Bedeutung von Recht, Unrecht und Strafe*, 2nd edn, Berlin: Häring, 1908, p. 6.
36 G. Jellinek, *Allgemeine Staatslehre*, 3rd edn, Berlin: Häring, 1914, p. 254.
37 G. Jellinek, 'Georg Jellinek. Ein Lebensbild', in *Ausgewählte Schriften und Reden, Band I* (1911), Aalen: Scientia, 1970, pp. 7–140, p. 10; also E. Troeltsch, 'Rezension G. Jellinek, Ausgewählte Schriften und Reden (1911)', *Zeitschrift für das Privat- und öffentliche Recht der Gegenwart* (1912), XXXIX, 273–78, p. 277.
38 G. Jellinek, 'Adam in der Staatslehre' (1893), in *Ausgewählte Schriften und Reden, Band II* (1911), Aalen: Scientia, 1970, pp. 23–44, p. 35ff.
39 For Weber, see König, 'Max Weber', op. cit., p. 58.
40 Jellinek, *Die Erklärung der Menschen- und Bürgerrechte*, op. cit., pp. viii–ix; G. Jellinek, 'Die

Erklärung der Menschen- und Bürgerrechte. Antwort an Émile Boutmy', in R. Schnur (ed), *Zur Geschichte der Erklärung der Menschenrechte*, Darmstadt: Wissenschaftliche Buchgesellschaft, 1964, pp. 113–28, pp. 116–17; W. Brugger, 'Historismus und Pragmatismus in Georg Jellineks "Erklärung der Menschen- und Bürgerrecht"', in B. Hollstein et al (eds), *Handlung und Erfahrung*, Frankfurt: Campus, 2011, pp. 217–46, p. 220ff.

41 M. Weber, *Gesammelte Aufsätze zur Religionssoziologie/1*, Tübingen: Mohr, 2005, p. 252; Weber, *Max Weber. Ein Lebensbild*, op. cit., p. 348; M. Weber, 'Kirchen und Sekten in Nordamerika', in M. Weber, *Soziologie, Universalgeschichtliche Analysen, Politik*, J. Winckelmann (ed), Stuttgart: Alfred Kröner Verlag, 1992, pp. 382–97, p. 392.

42 Jellinek, 'Die Erklärung der Menschen- und Bürgerrechte', op. cit., pp. 127–28; Jellinek, *Die Erklärung der Menschen- und Bürgerrechte*, op. cit., pp. 34–35 and 50–51.

43 Jellinek, *Die Erklärung der Menschen- und Bürgerrechte*, op. cit., p. 46.

44 M. Weber, 'Wirtschaft und Gesellschaft', in *Max Weber Gesamtausgabe, Abt. I: Schriften und Reden, Band IV*, Tübingen: Mohr Siebeck, 2005, p. 678; see, further, B. Nelson, 'Max Weber, Ernst Troeltsch, Georg Jellinek as Comparative Historical Sociologists', *Sociological Analysis* (1975), 36, 229–40, pp. 235–36; J. M. Ouédrago, 'Sociologie religieuse et modernité politique chez Max Weber', *Revue européenne des sciences sociales* (1996), 34, 25–49, p. 32ff.

45 M. Weber, 'Wirtschaft und Gesellschaft', in *Max Weber Gesamtausgabe, Abt. I: Schriften und Reden, Teilband III: Recht*, Tübingen: Mohr Siebeck, 2010, pp. 356–57.

46 M. Weber, 'Zur Lage der bürgerlichen Demokratie in Rußland', *Archiv für Sozialwissenschaft und Sozialpolitik* (1906), 22, 234–353, p. 280.

47 Weber, 'Zur Lage der bürgerlichen Demokratie in Rußland', ibid., pp. 350–53.

48 Weber, 'Wirtschaft und Gesellschaft', in *Max Weber Gesamtausgabe, Abt. I: Schriften und Reden, Band IV*, op. cit., pp. 678–79; M. Weber, 'Wirtschaft und Gesellschaft', in *Max Weber Gesamtausgabe, Abt. I: Schriften und Reden, Teilband III: Recht*, op. cit., p. 308.

49 Ibid., p. 308.

50 H. Hofmann, 'Zur Herkunft der Menschenrechtserklärungen', *Juristische Schulung* (1988), 841–48, p. 844.

51 Jellinek, *System der subjektiv öffentlichen Rechte*, op. cit., pp. 28 and 86; Jellinek, *Allgemeine Staatslehre*, op. cit. (1914), pp. 234–36, 374 and 483.

52 H. Kelsen, *Allgemeine Staatslehre*, Berlin: Springer, 1925, p. 41; P. Goller, 'Georg Jellinek und Edmund Bernatzik', *Zeitschrift für öffentliches Recht* (1999), 475–528, p. 509ff.

53 Kersten, 'Einleitung', op. cit., pp. 29–30.

54 Jellinek, 'Adam in der Staatslehre', op. cit., p. 44.

55 Jellinek, *Allgemeine Staatslehre*, op. cit., pp. 475–85.

56 Jellinek, *System der subjektiv öffentlichen Rechte*, op. cit., p. 82.

57 Ibid., p. 29.

58 Ibid., p. 86.

59 G. Jellinek, 'Die Entstehung der modernen Staatsidee' (1894), in *Ausgewählte Schriften und Reden, Band II* (1911), Aalen: Scientia, 1970, pp. 45–63.

60 W. Brugger, 'Georg Jellinek als Sozialtheoretiker und Kommunitarist', *Der Staat* (2010), 49, 405–34, p. 407; M. J. Sattler, 'Georg Jellinek (1851–1911). Ein Leben für das öffentliche Recht', in H. Heinrichs et al (eds), *Deutsche Juristischen jüdischer Herkunft*, München: Beck, 1993, pp. 355–68, p. 356; Kersten, 'Einleitung', op. cit., p. 39.

61 Jellinek, *System der subjektiv öffentlichen Rechte*, op. cit., p. 119; Jellinek, *Allgemeine Staatslehre*, op. cit., p. 426; W. Pauly, and M. Siebinger, 'Staat und Individuum. Georg Jellineks Statuslehre', in A. Anter (ed), *Die normative Kraft des Faktischen. Das Staatsverständnis Georg Jellineks*, Baden-Baden: Nomos, 2004, pp. 135–51, pp. 142–43; K. Friedrichs, 'Rezension zu Georg Jellinek, System der subjektiven öffentlichten Rechte (1905)', *Deutsches Literaturblatt* (1906), 18, 91–92.

62 Jellinek, *System der subjektiv öffentlichen Rechte*, op. cit., p. 87.
63 Jellinek, *Die Erklärung der Menschen- und Bürgerrechte*, op. cit., p. 2.
64 In other parts of his work, Jellinek adopted a state-centred perspective, Jellinek, *System der subjektiv öffentlichen Rechte*, op. cit., p. 9.
65 Jellinek, *Die Erklärung der Menschen- und Bürgerrechte*, op. cit., pp. 55–57.
66 Jellinek, *System der subjektiv öffentlichen Rechte*, op. cit., p. 119; Jellinek, *Allgemeine Staatslehre*, op. cit. , p. 205.
67 G. Jellinek, *System der subjektiven öffentlichen Rechte*, op. cit., pp. 103–5.
68 K. Hofmann, 'Zur Herkunft der Menschenrechtserklärungen', *Juristische Schulung* (1988), 841–46, p. 844.
69 Jellinek, *System der subjektiv öffentlichen Rechte*, op. cit., pp. 96–97.
70 Ibid., pp. 336–39. In doing so, the State was at least ethically obliged to protect freedom as far as possible, Jellinek, *Allgemeine Staatslehre*, op. cit., p. 481.
71 Troeltsch, 'Rezension G. Jellinek, Ausgewählte Schriften und Reden (1911)', op. cit., p. 278.
72 Jellinek, *System der subjektiv öffentlichen Rechte*, op. cit., p. 85: attributing legal personality to an individual is an ethical demand on the state.
73 G. Jellinek, *Gesetz und Verordnung: staatsrechtliche Untersuchungen auf rechtsgeschichtlicher und rechtsvergleichender Grundlage*, Aalen: Scientia Verl., 1964, p. 199; Jellinek, *Allgemeine Staatslehre*, op. cit., pp. 326–27 and 234; a critical position already emerges in G. Meyer, 'Rezension G. Jellinek, System der subjektiven öffentlichen Rechte 1892', *Deutsche Literaturzeitung* (1892), 1691–93, p. 1693.
74 Jellinek, *System der subjektiv öffentlichen Rechte*, op. cit., p. 116; cf. pp. 51–53, 56–67, 87, 201 and 359; Jellinek, *Allgemeine Staatslehre*, op. cit., p. 408; see, further, W. Henke, *Das subjektive öffentliche Recht*, Tübingen: Mohr, 1968, p. 44; W. Brugger, 'Georg Jellineks Statuslehre: national und international', *Archiv des öffentlichen Rechts* (2011), 136, 1–43, p. 5.
75 Joas, 'Max Weber and the origin of human rights: a study of cultural innovation', op. cit., p. 376.
76 Weber, 'Wirtschaft und Gesellschaft', in *Max Weber Gesamtausgabe, Abt. I: Schriften und Reden, Band IV*, op. cit., p. 679.
77 M. Weber, *Gesammelte Politische Schriften*, München: Drei Masken Verlag, 1921, p. 320; Weber, *Max Weber. Ein Lebensbild*, op. cit., pp. 420–21.
78 Weber, 'Wirtschaft und Gesellschaft', in *Max Weber Gesamtausgabe, Abt. I: Schriften und Reden, Band IV*, op. cit., p. 678.
79 Weber, 'Zur Lage der bürgerlichen Demokratie in Rußland', op. cit., p. 227.
80 Joas, 'Max Weber and the origin of human rights: a study of cultural innovation', op. cit., p. 336; Weber was surely thinking of the French Enlightenment version of human rights.
81 Weber, 'Wirtschaft und Gesellschaft', in *Max Weber Gesamtausgabe, Abt. I: Schriften und Reden, Band IV*, op. cit., p. 836; M. Weber, 'Parlament und Regierung im neugeordneten Deutschland', in *Gesammelte Politische Schriften*, op. cit., pp. 126–260, p. 152. M. Weber, 'Zur Politik im Weltkrieg', in *Max Weber Gesamtausgabe, Abt. I: Schriften und Reden, Band 15*, Tübingen: Mohr Siebeck, 1984, p. 466. It would be a grave self-delusion to believe that 'without having these achievements of the time of "Human Rights", we (even the most conservatives amongst us) are capable of living'. Also M. Weber, 'Brief an Keyserling, 21st of June 1911', in E. Baumgarten, *Max Weber – Werk und Person*, Tübingen: Mohr Siebeck, 1964, p. 429.
82 Weber, *Wissenschaft als Beruf*, op. cit., p. 37.
83 F. Draus, 'Max Weber et la Liberté', *Revue européenne des sciences sociales* (1995), 33, 123–43, p. 127.
84 Weber, *Gesammelte Politische Schriften*, op. cit., pp. 150–52; Weber, 'Zur Lage der bürgerlichen Demokratie in Rußland', op. cit., pp. 347–51.

85 M. Weber, 'Rußlands Übergang zur Scheindemokratie', in *Gesammelte Politische Schriften*, op. cit., pp. 107–25, p. 107.
86 G. Jellinek, *Der Kampf des alten mit dem neuen Recht*, Heidelberg: Winter, 1907, p. 56; Jellinek, *System der subjektiven öffentlichen Rechte*, op. cit., p. 89.
87 A. Anter, 'Georg Jellineks wissenschaftliche Politik. Positionen, Kontexte, Wirkungslinien', *Politische Vierteljahresschrift* (1998), 39, 503–26, pp. 510–11.
88 Jellinek, *System der subjektiv öffentlichen Rechte*, op. cit., pp. 71 and 84; W. Brugger, 'Existenz, Freiheit und Ordnung. Von Werner Maihofer zu Georg Jellinek und zurück', in S. Kirste and G. Sprenger (eds), *Menschliche Existenz und Würde im Rechtsstaat*, Berlin: BWV, 2010, pp. 152–69, p. 162.
89 Jellinek, *System der subjektiv öffentlichen Rechte*, op. cit., pp. 86–87; Jellinek, *Allgemeine Staatslehre*, op. cit., p. 254. Jellinek argues in a dialectical manner: the expansion of the State's activities leads to both the emergence of human association and the emergence of individual differentiation.
90 G. Jellinek, 'Rezension zu Viktor Cathrein, Naturrecht und positives Recht', *Deutsche Literaturzeitung* (1902), 10, 8 (March), 628–29.
91 Weber, 'Die formalen Qualitäten des revolutionär geschaffenen Rechts. Das Naturrecht und seine Typen', in M. Weber, *Wirtschaft und Gesellschaft: Grundriss der verstehenden Soziologie*, Tübingen: Mohr, 5. Aufl., 1976, pp. 497–503, p. 497; K. V. Friedman, *Legitimation of Social Rights and the Western Welfare State: A Weberian Perspective*, Chapel Hill: University Press, 1981, p. 39.
92 Weber, 'Wirtschaft und Gesellschaft', in *Max Weber Gesamtausgabe*, Abt. I: *Schriften und Reden, Band IV*, op. cit., pp. 16, 19, 122ff., 549 and 822ff.
93 Ibid., pp. 19–20. Also G. Fitzi, *Max Weber*, Frankfurt: Campus, 2008, p. 71.
94 Weber, 'Die formalen Qualitäten des revolutionär geschaffenen Rechts', op. cit., p. 497; Jellinek, *Allgemeine Staatslehre*, op. cit., pp. 344–45.
95 Weber, ibid., p. 502; Müller, *Max Weber. Eine Einführung in sein Werk*, op. cit., p. 236ff.
96 Weber, 'Die formalen Qualitäten des revolutionär geschaffenen Rechts', op. cit., p. 502; Weber, 'Wirtschaft und Gesellschaft', in *Max Weber Gesamtausgabe*, Abt. I: *Schriften und Reden, Teilband III: Recht*, op. cit., pp. 316ff. and 345–48.
97 Weber, 'Zur Lage der bürgerlichen Demokratie in Rußland', op. cit., pp. 253–54.
98 Jellinek, *Allgemeine Staatslehre*, op. cit., pp. 344–45; Jellinek, *Der Kampf des alten mit dem neuen Recht*, op. cit.
99 Troeltsch, 'Rezension G. Jellinek, Ausgewählte Schriften und Reden (1911)', op. cit., pp. 274–76; Anter, *Die normative Kraft des Faktischen*, op. cit., pp. 521–22.
100 Jellinek, *Allgemeine Staatslehre*, op. cit., pp. 333–34, 344–45, 349–50 and 353; Kersten, *Georg Jellinek und die klassische Staatslehre*, op. cit., pp. 372–74.
101 W. Windelband, 'Geleitwort zur Originalausgabe', in Jellinek, *Ausgewählte Schriften und Reden, Band I*, op. cit., pp. V–XII, p. VIII.
102 Weber, 'Wirtschaft und Gesellschaft', in *Max Weber Gesamtausgabe*, Abt. I: *Schriften und Reden, Teilband III: Recht*, op. cit., pp. 367–68 and 425–26.
103 Müller, *Max Weber. Eine Einführung in sein Werk*, op. cit., pp. 17–18.
104 Weber, 'Parlament und Regierung im neugeordneten Deutschland', in *Gesammelte Politische Schriften*, op. cit., p. 141.
105 Ibid., pp. 234–53, pp. 347–51.
106 D. Beetham, *Max Weber and the Theory of Modern Politics*, Cambridge: Polity Press, 1985, p. 43. M. Weber, 'Parlament und Regierung im neugeordneten Deutschland', in *Gesammelte Politische Schriften*, op. cit., pp. 137–38.
107 Weber, 'Rußlands Übergang zur Scheindemokratie', op. cit., p. 307; Weber, 'Zur Lage der bürgerlichen Demokratie in Rußland', op. cit., p. 336.
108 König, *Menschenrechte bei Durkheim und Weber*, op. cit., p. 107.
109 Weber, 'Wirtschaft und Gesellschaft', in *Max Weber Gesamtausgabe*, Abt. I: *Schriften und*

Reden, Band IV, op. cit., p. 678; F. Loos, 'Max Webers Wissenschaftslehre und die Rechtswissenschaft', *Juristische Schulung* (1982), 87–93, p. 88.
110 Weber, 'Wirtschaft und Gesellschaft', in *Max Weber Gesamtausgabe, Abt. I: Schriften und Reden, Band IV*, op. cit., p. 511.
111 Ibid., p. 512; M. Weber, 'Parlament und Regierung im neugeordneten Deutschland', in *Gesammelte Politische Schriften*, op. cit., p. 142.
112 M. Weber, '"Römisches" und "Deutsches" Recht', in *Max Weber Gesamtausgabe, Abt. I: Schriften und Reden, Band 4, Teilband I*, Tübingen: Mohr Siebeck, 1993, pp. 526–34, p. 534.
113 Weber, 'Die formalen Qualitäten des revolutionär geschaffenen Rechts', op. cit., p. 496.
114 Jellinek, 'Die Erklärung der Menschen- und Bürgerrechte', op. cit., pp. 122ff. The formulations of the French Déclaration are conducive for great speeches, but are of little practical effect. Jellinek, 'Die Entstehung der modernen Staatsidee', op. cit., p. 53.
115 Jellinek, *Die Erklärung der Menschen- und Bürgerrechte*, op. cit., p. 4.
116 Beetham, *Max Weber and the Theory of Modern Politics*, op. cit., p. 55.
117 Weber, 'Zur Lage der bürgerlichen Demokratie in Rußland', op. cit., p. 280.
118 Weber, *Max Weber. Ein Lebensbild*, op. cit., pp. 132–35.
119 Friedman, *Legitimation of Social Rights and the Western Welfare State: A Weberian Perspective*, op. cit., p. 50ff.
120 W. Hennis, *Max Webers Fragestellung. Studien zur Biographie des Werks*, Tübingen: Mohr, 1987, p. 212.
121 Jellinek, *System der subjektiv öffentlichen Rechte*, op. cit., pp. 68–71.
122 Ibid., pp. 73, 114–15 and 135; Brugger, 'Historismus und Pragmatismus in Georg Jellineks "Erklärung der Menschen- und Bürgerrecht"', op. cit., p. 240: the ideology of individual self-interest.
123 Jellinek, *Allgemeine Staatslehre*, op. cit., p. 263; Jellinek, 'Die Entstehung der modernen Staatsidee', op. cit., pp. 60–61.
124 For Jellinek's view, see Brugger, 'Georg Jellineks Statuslehre: national und international', op. cit., p. 17.

Part IV

Hans Kelsen, Max Weber and the character of law

Chapter 8

Max Weber and Hans Kelsen: formal rationality and legitimacy of modern law

Michel Coutu[1]

Introduction

The relationship between the thought of Hans Kelsen and that of Max Weber is certainly complex, but altogether fascinating and rich in lessons for the sociology of law. In the following study, we cover two central questions in this regard: the proximity of the concept of law in Kelsen's pure theory to Weber's ideal type of the formal rationality of law; and, consequently, a particular vision of the legitimacy of contemporary law shared by both authors and based foremost on the idea of legality.

We will observe that, for both Kelsen and Weber, the basic scientific project remains that of an objective science despite the complete heterogeneity of the field of study: the normative science of law for Kelsen, empirical sociology (including of 'law') for Weber. The 'purity' of the scientific project entails, as Kelsen clearly explains, the radical rejection of any consideration external to the object, whether ethical, axiological, political or ideological, which too often pervades its study and prevents its understanding.

Hence, Kelsen's constant preoccupation with maintaining firmly at a distance the interference of ethics (in particular, all variants of natural law theory, including its modern and classical forms) and of legal politics (conservative or revolutionary), which create obstacles between knowledge and its object. Hence, also, Weber's continuous effort toward axiological neutrality and setting aside the value judgments which have generally coloured efforts to gain knowledge of social relations.[2] This effort, common to the two authors, originates with their adherence to Neo-Kantianism and to the aprioretic category of objective knowledge, which for both Weber and Kelsen is based upon the radical contrast between the 'is' (*Sein*) and the 'ought' (*Sollen*).

The formal rationality of modern law: a parallel between Weber and Kelsen

In large part, Weber focuses his interest in the *Sociology of Law* on the processes of rationalization which foster the logical coherence and systematization of law. The

Weberian method is based on two types of questions: first, what are the essential characteristics of a completely rationalized, meaning formally rational, law? Second, what are the factors which support the emergence of this kind of formal and rational law? To clearly understand the analysis developed by Weber in response to these two questions, we examine the antinomy, which is paramount, between formal and substantive rationality. To do this, a parallel between Weber and Kelsen will be outlined in order to highlight the basic traits of formally rational law.

The antinomy of form and substance

Weber uses a typology based on the distinction, as regards the methods of legal technique,[3] between four ideal types of rationality in the creation and application of law: a formally irrational character in the absence of control by reason;[4] a substantively irrational one when the recourse to general norms is lacking;[5] a substantively rational one in cases where the applicable legal rules are elaborated according to 'ethical imperatives, utilitarian and other expediential rules, and political maxims';[6] and, lastly, law is formally rational if 'the legally relevant characteristics of the facts are disclosed through the logical analysis of meaning and where, accordingly, definitely fixed legal concepts in the form of highly abstract rules are formulated and applied'.[7]

This typology of modes of creation and discovery of law has only a heuristic value. A rational utopia, it does not directly reflect empirical reality. The ideal-typical constructions can therefore be considered as a methodological artifice, which permits Weber to compare legal systems between very different societies.[8]

In order to better define the scope and practical interest for the study of contemporary law of the dichotomy of form and substance, it is helpful to isolate the essential components of these two ideal types of legal rationality. To do this, we will clarify the concept of formal legal rationality by bringing together the conceptions of Weber and of Kelsen.

The formal rationality of law

Continental European law represents, for Weber, in its fundamental structure characterized by logical systematization, the purest type of formally rational legal order.[9] In this sense, formal law, viewed from the Weberian perspective, corresponds in many ways to the legal order as conceived by the pure theory of Kelsen.[10] The proximity of these concepts has been raised, with strong justification, by a number of authors;[11] in our opinion it supports a complementary use of Kelsen with Weber, in favour of a clearer demonstration of the essential characteristics of formal legal rationality. From this perspective, this demonstration combines the following elements:

(a) *Logical coherence*: for Weber, the legal order is a system characterized by coherence, logical clarity and by 'an integration of all analytically derived legal propositions'.¹² Kelsen refers to the 'logical unity of the legal order', which shows that it can be described by non-contradictory propositions of law.¹³

(b) *Completeness*: Law, Kelsen asserts, directly or indirectly, qualifies all human behaviour, and as a consequence, has no lacunae.¹⁴ For Weber, this absence of holes is, if not a real property, at least a necessary postulate for the formal analysis of law:¹⁵ in this way, the legal order is built as a 'gapless "legal ordering" of all social conduct'.¹⁶

(c) *Deductive character*: according to Weber, the use of the syllogism,¹⁷ the rejection of analogical procedures,¹⁸ and the move beyond a purely analytical method,¹⁹ are the necessary conditions for the development of the formal rationality of law; each legal decision thus appears as the '"application" of an abstract legal proposition to a concrete "fact situation"'.²⁰ In the domain of legal theory, deduction also characterizes the relationship which the science of law establishes between illicit behaviour and a sanction, and which Kelsen designates by the concept of 'imputation'.²¹

(d) *Methodological specificity*: the systematization of law in the sense of formal rationality requires the development of a specific method, which is distinguished from the procedures used by non-legal sciences, and is not identified with moral or political discourse.²² It is clear that the postulate of methodological specificity leads powerfully to the autonomization and the professionalization of the legal order. For Weber, the most rigorous formal sublimation is based on an abstract method of logical interpretation of meaning.²³ From the Kelsenian point of view, legal science studies juridical norms by formulating legal propositions based on hypothetical judgments, which apply the principle of imputation; this is distinguished from the principle of causality characteristic of the natural sciences, while the hypothetical quality of judgment is contrasted with the categorical imperatives of morality or ideology.²⁴

(e) *Axiological neutrality*: from this perspective, the progression of formal rationality of law is linked to the rejection of ideological considerations and value judgments.²⁵ Kelsen insists on the fact that the pure theory of law must avoid making such judgments, and refuse 'to serve any political interests by supplying them with an "ideology" by which the existing social order is justified or disqualified'.²⁶ As we have seen, for Weber, a fundamental characteristic of formal law is the putting aside of extrinsic considerations (among them religious and political considerations) in the systematization of legal norms.

(f) *Formal legitimation*: formally rational law bases its legitimacy on the principle of legality and procedural regularity, and not on a substantive criterion of legitimation, such as natural law. In the Weberian perspective, 'the axioms of natural law have lost all capacity to provide the fundamental basis of a legal system'.²⁷ For Kelsen, the validity of normative systems rests in the final analysis on a fundamental norm:²⁸ it is either material and static – this is the case of moral or natural law systems, where the validity is based on the content of the fundamental norm – or it is formal and dynamic – when validity is evaluated independently of any substantive consideration, this is the case of the positive legal order, in which:

> A legal norm is not valid because it has a certain content, that is, because its content is logically deducible from a presupposed basic norm, but because it is created in a certain way – ultimately in a way determined by a presupposed basic norm.[29]

For both Weber and Kelsen, the logical and systematic formalization of law, even when most advanced, inevitably has certain limitations, which result at once from the restrictions inherent in any rationalization, and the necessary support of elements arising from substantive rationality. Self-sufficiency of the legal system remains unattainable because, despite the tendency toward logical closure, the formalization of law rests on extra-legal presuppositions.[30] From this point of view, even the most abstract legal concepts are derived from considerations which, at their origin, appear substantively rational.[31]

Here we can follow the analysis of Kelsen, who traces the limits of a 'pure' theory of law. Any legal order is characterized by the partial indeterminacy of its norms: hierarchically pre-eminent norms cannot solve all of the details of their application, and this, therefore, requires an interpretation. In terms of material content, the superior norm presents itself, in fact, as a frame to be filled, which leaves a certain margin of appreciation to the interpreter. The judicial discovery of law is, therefore, not at all a simple conclusion on the content of a norm: it instead takes part in the process of law creation as an act of will and not of knowledge.

Substantively rational criteria often intervene in a decisive manner in this process: since even in a highly formalized system, the judicial act is based just as much, if not more, on legal politics as on the science of law, it requires the use of non-juridical norms 'such as norms of morals, of justice, constituting social values which are usually designated by catch words such as "the good of the people," "interest of the state," "progress," and the like'.[32] Because, in this way, the preference given to one method of interpretation is based on a choice of values, the concept of legal certainty, understood as the prediction of the decision of a judicial body, must be illusory.[33] If, when describing the ideal of the formal coherence of law, Weber refers in certain passages to the 'automatism' of the judge's decision[34] or to the character of the judicial apparatus as a 'technically rational machine',[35] he clearly shows, by comparing the judicial trial to the game of skat in the *Critique of Stammler*,[36] that foreseeability of a specific ruling often remains completely uncertain.[37] While insisting generally on the importance of the development of the formal qualities of law, Weber nevertheless admits that decision makers must take socio-political or socio-ethical points of view into account under certain circumstances, 'if they do not want to make a mockery of the administration of justice'.[38]

'The inevitable conflict between an abstract formalism of legal certainty and [the] desire to realize substantive goals'[39] is an aporia which sets the limits on any effort to make law coherent. The rationalization of the legal order, which may take very different paths in no way oriented in principle toward the progression of formal systematization, at times emphasizes logical closure, and at times teleological considerations: if these play a significant role in formally rational law, they are nevertheless relegated to the background; though it is clear that contemporary Western law is increasingly influenced by substantive rationality, which, for Weber, 'signifies a weakening of legal formalism out of considerations of substantive expediency'.[40]

The formal ('legal-rational') legitimacy of modern law

One of the most controversial aspects of the legal and political sociology of Weber rests on the relationship established between the *formal rationality* of law and the type of legitimacy characteristic of modernity, the belief in the *legality* of domination. In contrast with substantively rational law, formally rational law, as we have seen, is characterized by the rejection of imperatives (of an ethical, religious, utilitarian or political nature) external to the legal sphere, in favour of the discovery of legal solutions according to the logical interpretation of abstract norms. From this point of view, the dominant characteristic of a legal order founded on formal rationality is based on *axiological neutrality*, a corollary of the idea that 'law is a rational technical apparatus, which is continually transformable in the light of expediential considerations' rather than concerns related to values.[41] Legal domination is identified with submission to objective and impersonal rules which are formally valid, and which only command obedience with respect to a rationally-defined field of application; all law remains conceived of in this way as a 'consistent system of abstract rules which have normally been intentionally established'.[42] As an ideal type, legal domination rests – unlike historically previous modes of domination – on the proximity, or even the identity of the legal and political orders.[43]

The classification of Weber in the camp of adherents to legal positivism, common to various authors, is accompanied by a critique of the dangers of a concept of legitimacy based on legality as its sole criterion. Following Jürgen Habermas, 'in general, [Weber] conceives modern law and legal domination so narrowly that the need for a principled mode of justification is shaded out in favour of sheer positivism'.[44]

In light of the above, it is pertinent to contrast the respective points of view of Weber and of Kelsen regarding the problem of the legitimacy of law. This will illustrate the complexity of Weber's thought, which is open to emphasis and extension in opposing directions, while highlighting the specificity of his reasoning, which cannot be reduced to that of Kelsen.

To this end, we will first discuss the demise of natural law, meaning the loss of the effectiveness of value rationality as the basis for belief in the legitimacy of the legal and political order; second, we will examine the postulate of the identity of law and the State for Kelsen, in contrast with Weber's analysis.

The demise of natural law

Following Weber, natural law concepts are no longer able to ensure the foundation and legitimacy of the legal order. At first glance, this assertion feeds directly into an ideological current which was dominant in Weber's contemporary Germany. As Troeltsch has explained,[45] German thought, in the nineteenth century, developed in an original way, in contrast with 'Western European' thought – not only Anglo-Saxon but also French – which was strongly attached to the rationalist ideal of natural law. The Romantic counter-revolution, including the Historical School of Law, rejects the pure abstraction of a universal Humanity founded on the equal dignity of Reason and the pretence of deduction on the model of the physical and mathematical sciences, of the fundamental principles of law;[46] 'cold rationalism' and the supposed 'atomism' of theories of natural law, were contrasted with the organic concept of the public spirit (*Gemeingeist*),[47] as well as the celebration, against the egalitarian principle, of exceptional personalities capable of carrying the spiritual life of the community to its most elevated degree and of assuming political leadership.[48] The reflection of the Historical School, of the Romantic Movement in general, thus leads to the almost complete disappearance of the idea of a universal natural law in Germany, law being subsequently constituted as an entity external to the moral sphere.[49]

If it remains realistic to assume that this intellectual atmosphere had a certain influence on Weber, it is nevertheless important to emphasize that the rejection of natural law representations does not result for him in a romantic trajectory toward an organically dominated vision of the world. Weber, in fact, does not hesitate to include the dogma of the Historical School in the movement of natural law theories, while noting their destructive impact on the deductivist axiomatics of Modern natural law of the rationalist type, 'natural law of the historically real' surely affirms a supra-positive principle in the pre-eminence of customary law, reflection of the *Volksgeist*, which becomes the 'only natural, and thus the only legitimate, source from which law and culture can emanate'.[50] As Radbruch would later remark, the Historical School, which appears at first to be a resolute enemy of natural law, in fact develops a romantic legal philosophy, conservative in essence, and which posits the organic formation of law by the national spirit, on the basis of a definitive value judgment.[51]

In fact, the necessary abandonment of the idea of natural law as the foundation of legitimacy of contemporary law comes for Weber from two principal considerations: the first, epistemological, finds its source in the Kantian antinomy between the 'is' (*Sein*) and the 'ought' (*Sollen*); the other, essentially sociological and historical, is supported by the differentiation between the spheres of activity and values, which renders impossible any unitary conception of a supra-positive law. We focus here only on the first element.

As we have already mentioned, the Weberian theory of science has as its centre of gravity the dualism of the *Sein* and the *Sollen*.[52] It is in fact necessary to avoid – regardless of the difficulty of an effective search for scientific objectivity – 'the [. . .]

confusion of the scientific discussion of facts and their evaluation [. . .]'[53] From this perspective, it is not the infinite historical diversity of worldviews which renders the contrast between science and faith necessary as a matter of principle: it is instead a transcendental condition of knowledge, the opposition of fact and value, which makes any single inference of 'generally valid ultimate value-judgments'[54] impossible.

Again, Weber generally rejected this qualification, which appeared to him improper in light of his decisionist philosophy of values,[55] because his epistemological positions can justly be described as *relativist*;[56] for Raymond Aron, the Weberian theory of science, in fact, represents an absolute relativism, which is radically sceptical of any philosophy, as no axiological choice is objectively capable of receiving a superior value.[57]

In the Weberian perspective, the science of law is also constructed with reference to the opposition of the 'is' and the 'ought'.[58] As an object of study, law in fact can be understood either as *Sein* or as *Sollen*. The norms of law which legal dogmatics analyse possess no tangible reality in themselves; they come from the ideal sphere of the ought-to-be:[59] the abstract legal order of legal theory does not necessarily relate to the world of concrete social activity.[60] By contrast, a legal science of the 'is', being founded on an essentially sociological approach to law, is interested only in the obligatory rules of behaviour, considered *from a sociological viewpoint* to have the quality of legal phenomena,[61] and which in general are empirically observed by agents. However, this does not mean that the knowledge of the ideal sense of juridical norms remains without interest for the sociologist of law: on the contrary, he or she will find there a heuristic tool which is often essential for causal-empirical explanation. Legal norms – once internalized by agents as maxims of behaviour – become vectors orienting social activity, with an effectiveness which is variable but often, Weber emphasizes, 'exceptionally important'.[62] The sociologist or historian, when trying to circumscribe empirically observable law of a given era, is generally obliged to resort to a dogmatic construction of the legal norms. Such a construction is only an ideal-typical representation: it is based on the probability of a certain correspondence between the effective behaviour of agents and the theoretically valid legal norm.[63] Of course, in a significant number of cases, the real behaviour will remain without a direct relationship to the ideal-typical representation: it will then be necessary to ask why the formally applicable rule lacks the quality of 'living law'.[64]

To clearly distinguish legal dogmatics from both the empirical science of law, as well as from axiological reflection on the ultimate value of legal norms (or 'legal politics'), Weber gives the example, in his critique of Stammler,[65] of different perspectives according to which an article of the Civil Code may become an object of analysis. *Conceptually*, this is a matter of determining the legally mandatory scope, following the logical (or conventional) relationships which case law establishes between legal propositions and concepts. *Empirically*, as we have just examined, it is necessary to evaluate the correspondence with the probability of a resulting real behaviour. Finally, the discussion of the normative justification of this position, with respect to ethical, religious, economic and utilitarian principles, etc. belongs to a purely *political* or axiological dimension.

Weber thus strongly contrasts, in a manner similar to Kelsen, the investigations based on the dogmatic science of law with those belonging to the politics or 'metaphysics' of law. Following Weber, legal science remains without an answer before the question, 'should there be a law and *should we* create' precisely this legal rule?[66]

Thus, theories of natural law, which rest on no scientific foundation, create an inextricable confusion between *Sein* and *Sollen*. As Kelsen wrote, 'no logical reasoning permits one to pass from that which is to that which should be, from natural reality to moral or legal values'.[67] It follows that the idea of justice, as an absolute, immutable and eternal principle, holds no content which can be determined by science. Justice here appears definitively as an 'irrational ideal'.[68]

But did Weber consider, as Kelsen does, natural law axioms to be only 'useful lies', ideological postulates 'destined to hide a disagreeable reality'?[69] To answer this question, it is essential to consider the different standpoints from which Kelsen and Weber examine natural law. The emphasis Kelsen places on natural law remains, above all, negative: the point is mainly to condemn, from the perspective of the 'Tribunal of Science',[70] the various concepts of natural law by rooting them out to the very last (eventually in the form of an 'ethical minimum'), in order to allow the creation of a pure theory without concessions, meaning a uniquely positivist theory of law. When Kelsen refers to the content of natural law axioms and their socio-historical scope, his intent is always to support this epistemological condemnation by demonstrating that the various theories of justice are incapable of escaping the principle of non-contradiction and are apt to serve completely opposing political and material interests.[71]

Weber's view of natural law concepts is more favourable, because he examines their influence on human activity not as a pure theoretician, but as a sociologist of law. From the perspective of historical sociology, Weber clearly outlines the importance of natural law axioms, in particular, with respect to the formal rationalization of law: it is only because of the historical process of rationalization that natural law theories – similarly to religious concepts – are rejected, following the disenchantment of the world, in the irrational sphere.

In other words, the demise of natural law in contemporary society does not result from an epistemological condemnation, which mostly interests the philosopher or the theoretician of science: after all, relativist scepticism, present from Ancient times, never prevented the concepts of the 'law of law' from playing a fundamental role in history. If natural law can no longer serve as a basis for belief in the legitimacy of the legal and political order, this is above all the result of the differentiation and the growing autonomy of spheres of (political, economic, legal, etc.) activity, and their ethical neutralization.[72] The decisive and final entry of rationality into each of these autonomous fields of action creates the conditions where 'all metajuristic axioms in general have been subject to ever continuing disintegration and relativization'.[73]

The identity of law and the state

Following Kelsen, the State, as an organization of domination or an apparatus of constraint, represents essentially a system of obligatory norms, a normative order.[74] However, according to Kelsen again, once we recognize a normative order in the State, there is no longer a possibility of contrasting it, as an institution, with the law, 'the state as an acting person is not a reality but an auxiliary construction of legal thinking [. . .]'.[75] Any distinction between the State apparatus of constraint and the legal system becomes theoretically inadmissible. Any distinction between the power of the State and that of the law appears equally superfluous: the power of the State is actually nothing more than the effectiveness of the legal order, meaning the fact that the norm becomes an effective motive of human behaviour. Contrasting effectiveness (property of the '*is*') and validity (property of an '*ought*'),[76] Kelsen bases this validity of the State legal order on the presupposition of an original norm (*Ursprungsnorm*) which institutes its authority and renders legitimate its creation of juridical norms.[77]

As noted by Norberto Bobbio, the State represents, in fact, the legal order which corresponds for Kelsen to the full legalization of domination for Weber.[78] The elements which, for Weber, characterize the essence of legal domination are actually on display with Kelsen, as attributes of the State legal order. The Head of State should, thus, be considered as no more than a State organ which essentially fills legal functions; the legal and political order bears an impersonal character, all being subordinated to it and surpassed by it, including the officials: they 'perform a function determined by the legal order, according to the principle of division of labor'.[79] Keslen insists on the importance of the bureaucratization of State activities, a consequence of the growing centralization of the legal order: the passage from the *jurisdictional State* to the *administrative State*, which is devoted to the direct attainment of State goals, requires a bureaucratic apparatus of considerable size to be put in place.[80] We also note that Kelsen, like Weber, sees in the bureaucratic system the guarantee of true execution of the will of the State which is partially lacking in other forms of administration.[81]

These convergences between Weber and Kelsen should nevertheless not lead one into error: the position of Weber, considered in its entirety, cannot be assimilated to that of Kelsen. There is, rather, in terms of the epistemology of State law, a fundamental incompatibility between the two. For Kelsen, in fact, the principle of identity of law and State constitutes a necessary presupposition for any adequate knowledge of the juridical and political order. For Weber, the reduction of the political unit in its most rationalized form, the State, to an objective and impersonal legal order serves only the ends of construction of an ideal type, which shows in all its clarity the pure type of legal domination: but this is precisely a pure form which historical reality never translates in a univocal way.[82] Epistemologically, Weber situates himself clearly – to speak in Kelsenian terms – in the perspective of the dualist theory of law and the State.

Kelsen most certainly wished to read in Weber – who delivered in his opinion 'the most significant sociological production since Simmel' – the demonstration, if implicit and unintentional, of the postulate of the identity of law and State.[83] Kelsen bases his argumentation on the introductory chapter in *Economy and Society*, regarding the basic concepts of sociology. Without analysing the detail of the argument here, it is worth noting that Kelsen starts from the following observation: the concept of the State for Weber is an ideal type, an intellectual construction of an activity which is oriented in a rational way, used as a scheme for interpreting the behaviour of actors. From this point of view, the State is the direction taken by a group of activities, not these concrete activities considered alone. To rationally construct the meaning of this complex of activities, sociology, which cannot purport – according to Kelsen – to have the status of an autonomous discipline, must take account of the maxims of behaviour which orient action toward a determined goal and which are therefore constitutive of an 'ought'; in doing this, sociology must necessarily consider the State understood as a legal order, and 'see with the eyes of jurists, to be able to see anything at all'.[84] The juridical-normative point of view remains thus decisive for the knowledge of the State.

Despite its logical rigour, Kelsen's analysis appears undeniably like a unilateral and reductive reading of Weber, marked by a normativist perspective. In epistemological terms, the Weberian position is largely similar to the dualist perspective which Jellinek adopted in his *Allgemeine Staatslehre*. Jellinek argued that the State could be considered on two distinct planes, describing it either as a social formation or as a legal institution and that as a result the science of the State is divided into two different disciplines, social on the one hand, legal on the other.[85] Imagining the State from the sole point of view of the science of law represents an unacceptable, if frequent, error, typical of theories of natural law. A profitable study, Jellinek added, must necessarily be based at once on social science and on the legal theory of the State.[86]

In the explanation which he devotes to the modern State in *Economy and Society*, Weber, while adopting a sociological perspective, emphasizes that the legal concepts related to the State phenomenon must be taken into account. In a manner similar to Jellinek, Weber notes that 'the term "state" is used both for the legal concept and for the social phenomena to which its legal rules are relevant'.[87] The collective representations which legal thought produces are in part constitutive of an 'ought' which conditions the real activity of agents and thus has 'a powerful, often a decisive, causal influence'.[88] From this, the modern State consists, in large part, of a collective structure which is the representation of a *Sollen*, based on the authority of law.[89]

But the State, contrary to the position defended by Kelsen, can never be reduced only to its legal dimension. From a sociological perspective, a State 'ceases to exist [. . .] whenever there is no longer a probability that certain kinds of meaningfully oriented social action will take place'.[90] A State can actually continue as a legal entity – following, for example, the maintenance of its recognition by other States, as illustrated by the history of international relations – while sociologically as a real structure of activity it has totally lost its quality as a State order, no longer having to any significant degree, the monopoly of legitimate violence in a designated territory. Kelsen is incorrect to see in this essential characteristic of the Weberian definition of the State a simple equivalent of the (juridical) concept of sovereignty. It is actually the sociological foundation of the State which cannot be reduced to a simple legal representation. Of course, in the contemporary State, normally the monopolization of legitimate violence essentially means the regular application of legal norms and, as required, the methods of constraint which are attached to them. This does not mean that the State is essentially identical to the law, a conclusion which Weber would certainly not have drawn; it is, instead, paramount that one disassociate the juridical and sociological conceptions of the State, because otherwise an adequate understanding of the State phenomenon becomes impossible.

Conclusion

As we have explained, there are many convergences between Max Weber and Hans Kelsen which nevertheless must not lead us to ignore – situating ourselves here in the field of legal sociology – certain fundamental differences.

Kelsen takes up a distinction already present for Weber, between the legal norm (*Rechtsnorm*) and the legal proposition (*Rechtssatz*), but he pushes the analysis forward, seeing in the first an act of will (the decision of the legislator or judge, for example) and in the second (the hypothesis posed by the science of law as to the meaning of the norm) an act of knowledge. Thus outlined, this distinction does not appear as clearly in Weber, who highlights the great indeterminacy of the legal norm when it is the object of a specific decision, while at the same time adhering to the traditional understanding of formalist positivism (Pandectism in Germany), which reduces the role of the judge to that of an 'automat' of subsumption. It appears evident to us that the fact of conceiving the norm as a frame to fill, as the *ab initio* holder of a certain level of indeterminacy, represents an element of capital importance, which the sociology of law absolutely must take into account.

In contrast, Kelsen, when he ventures onto the terrain of the social sciences, takes a reductionist view of their fundamental assumptions. This appears clearly when Kelsen introduces the contrast between 'nature' and 'law' and distinguishes between their respective processes of correlation of their elements, through the separate notions of 'causality' and 'imputation'. The category which is problematic here is that of causality. Kelsen, in sum, described it as a univocal correlation between natural processes. In doing so, he does not distinguish between causality in the natural sciences and that which characterizes the cultural sciences and which holds to the meaning aimed at in cultural processes. Overall, Kelsen retains neither the idea of causal pluralism, nor those of 'chances' and 'probabilities' which he nevertheless must have encountered in his study of the texts of Max Weber.

Just as he does not focus on the distinction between nature and culture, Kelsen makes no distinction between the 'law' which is the subject of the pure theory, and the distinct social phenomenon of the same name, which forms the object of the sociology of law. It is evident that, for Kelsen, the law here is the same in both cases, being the law of the State which the pure theory examines through the undeniably useful image of the pyramid of norms.

However, the conception of Weber, which clearly contrasts – in a move completely alien to the Kelsenian construction – *normative* and *empirical* legal orders on the one hand, and *State* and *non-State* law on the other, is much more adapted to the development of the sociology of law as a social science which is largely autonomous with respect to legal dogmatics. This fundamental divergence between Weber and Kelsen strongly influences the incompatibility of the Kelsenian postulate of the identity of law and State which we have evoked, and the Weberian distinction between State and non-State law. We encounter here the problem of 'legal pluralism', for Max Weber, an issue which we cannot develop in this chapter, but which marks an essential distance between the world of legal sociology and the normative sphere, legitimate in its own right, of the pure theory of law.

Notes

1 Special thanks to Alexandra Juliane Law for translating this chapter into English.
2 Although Weber underlines the unavoidability of *value relevance*, an idea absent from Kelsen's theory of law.
3 M. Weber, *Wirtschaft und Gesellschaft*, Tübingen: J.C.B. Mohr, 1922. p. 396 (hereinafter: 'Weber, *Wirtschaft und Gesellschaft*'); English translation: M. Weber, *Economy and Society: An Outline of Interpretive Sociology*, G. Roth, and K Wittich (eds), E. Fischoff, et al. (trans), Berkeley: University of California Press, 1968. p. 654 (hereinafter: 'Weber, English trans.').
4 For example, in the case of discovery of law by consultation of an oracle or other similar means.
5 In this case, the legal solution is identified by recourse to 'concrete factors of the particular case as evaluated upon an ethical, emotional, or political basis', Weber, English trans., op. cit. p. 656; Weber, *Wirtschaft und Gesellschaft*, op. cit., p. 396.
6 Weber, English trans., ibid., p. 357; Weber, *Wirtschaft und Gesellschaft*, ibid., p. 397. For Weber, substantive rationality characterizes many sacred legal systems, including Hindu law, Islamic law and princely and patrimonial law.
7 Weber, English trans., ibid., p. 657; Weber, *Wirtschaft und Gesellschaft*, ibid., p. 396.
8 D. M. Trubek, 'Max Weber on Law and the Rise of Capitalism', *Wisconsin Law Review* (1972), 720–53, p. 727.
9 See Weber, *Wirtschaft und Gesellschaft*, op. cit., p. 397; Weber, English trans., op. cit. p. 657. The formalism of law as outlined by Weber nevertheless only constitutes, as an ideal type, an extreme case, not a factual description of the legal order. See R. Brubaker, *The Limits of Rationality: An Essay on the Social and Moral Thought of Max Weber*, London: Allen & Unwin, 1984, p. 18.
10 It is possible that Weber was aware of the first works of Kelsen (see W. Schluchter, *The Rise of Western Rationalism: Max Weber's Developmental History*, Berkeley: University of California Press, 1981, p. 56n). As for Kelsen, he explicitly recognized his debt to the methodological works of Weber in the preface to the first edition of the *Hauptproblemen der Staatslehre* (1911) (H. Kelsen, *Hauptprobleme der Staatslehre*, in M. J. Jestaedt (ed), *Hans*

Kelsen Werke, II, 1, Tübingen: Mohr, 2008). See N. Bobbio, 'Max Weber und Hans Kelsen', in M. Rehbinder and K.-P. Tieck (eds), *Max Weber als Rechtssoziologie*, Berlin: Duncker & Humblot, 1987, pp. 109–26, p. 110.

11 Aside from Schluchter (see previous note), see R. Treves, 'Hans Kelsen et la sociologie du droit', *Droit et Société* (1985), 15–23, p. 17. Also, M. Rheinstein, *Max Weber on Law in Economy and Society*, Cambridge: Harvard University Press, 1964, pp. xv–ixxii (Introduction), p. lxx. For these authors, the remarks are made only in passing. One can find a substantial analysis of the relations between the thought of Weber and of Kelsen in F. Loos, *Zur Wert- und Rechtslehre Max Webers*, Tübingen: J.C.B. Mohr, 1970, p. 106ff. See also Bobbio, 'Max Weber und Hans Kelsen', op. cit.

12 Weber, English trans., op. cit., p. 656; Weber, *Wirtschaft und Gesellschaft*, op. cit., p. 396.

13 Nevertheless, with respect to the creation of norms as acts of will, contradictions can exist. See H. Kelsen, *Pure Theory of Law*, trans. M. Knight (trans), Berkeley: University of California Press, 1967, p. 205.

14 H. Kelsen, *Reine Rechtslehre. Einleitung in der rechtswissenschaftliche Problematik*, 1st edn, (1934), Aalen: Scientia Verlag, 1994, p. 100; Kelsen, *Pure Theory of Law*, ibid., p. 248.

15 Weber, *Wirtschaft und Gesellschaft*, op. cit., p. 397; Weber, English trans., op. cit., p. 657: 'the law must actually or virtually constitute a "gapless" system of legal propositions, or must, at least, be treated as if it were such a gapless system.' Weber recognized, in his discussion with Kantorowicz, that this had the status of a mere assumption, see M. Weber, 'Diskussionsrede zu dem Vortrag von H. Kantorowicz, "Rechtswissenschaft und Soziologie"', in *Gesammelte Aufsätze zur Soziologie und Sozialpolitik*, Tübingen: J.C.B. Mohr (Paul Siebeck), 1924, p. 479.

16 Weber, English trans., ibid., p. 658; Weber, *Wirtschaft und Gesellschaft*, ibid., p. 397.

17 Weber, English trans., ibid., p. 787; Weber, *Wirtschaft und Gesellschaft*, ibid., p. 457.

18 See Weber, English trans., ibid., p. 407; Weber, *Wirtschaft und Gesellschaft*, ibid., p. 249. For Weber, analogy is characteristic of the mode of reasoning preferred by the *common law*, see Weber, English trans., p. 787; Weber, *Wirtschaft und Gesellschaft*, ibid., p. 457.

19 Following Weber, the analytical procedure consists in the 'breaking up of the complex situations of life into specifically determined elements', Weber, English trans., ibid., p. 796; Weber, *Wirtschaft und Gesellschaft*, ibid., p. 464. Ancient Roman law exhibited an essentially analytical nature. To attain full formal sublimation, legal work must be based on a 'constructive synthetic capacity' meaning systematization (ibid.).

20 Weber, *Wirtschaft und Gesellschaft*, ibid., p. 397; Weber, English trans., ibid., p. 657.

21 Kelsen, *Reine Rechtslehre*, op. cit., p. 22; Kelsen, *Pure Theory of Law*, op. cit., p. 76ff.

22 See R. M. Unger, *Law in Modern Society*, New York: The Free Press, 1976, p. 53.

23 Weber, *Wirtschaft und Gesellschaft*, op. cit., p. 397; Weber, English trans., op. cit., p. 657.

24 See Kelsen, *Reine Rechtslehre*, op. cit., p. 14ff.

25 See the position of Bernard Windscheid, head of the Pandectists, according to whom 'ethical, political or economic considerations are not the business of the jurist *per se*', K. Larenz, *Methodenlehre der Rechtswissenschaft*, Berlin: Springer-Verlag, 1969, p. 30 (author's translation).

26 Kelsen, *Pure Theory of Law*, op. cit., p. 106; Kelsen, *Reine Rechtslehre*, op. cit., p. 17.

27 Weber, English trans., op. cit., p. 874; Weber, *Wirtschaft und Gesellschaft*, op. cit., p.502.

28 Kelsen, *Reine Rechtslehre*, op. cit., p. 62ff.; Kelsen, *Pure Theory of Law*, op. cit., p. 193ff. Compare Loos, *Zur Wert- und Rechtslehre Max Webers*, op. cit., p. 110.

29 Kelsen, *Pure Theory of Law*, ibid., p. 198.

30 See Schluchter, *The Rise of Western Rationalism: Max Weber's Developmental History*, op. cit., p. 92.

31 Rheinstein, *Max Weber on Law in Economy and Society*, op. cit., p. lvii.

32 Kelsen, *Pure Theory of Law*, op. cit., p. 353.

33 Ibid., p. 356; Kelsen, *Reine Rechtslehre*, op. cit., p. 99ff.

34 M. Weber, 'Parliament and Government in a Reconstructed Germany', in M. Weber, *Economy and Society: An Outline of Interpretive Sociology*, Berkeley: University of California Press, 1978, pp. 1381–469, p. 1395.
35 Weber, English trans., op. cit., p. 811; Weber, *Wirtschaft und Gesellschaft*, op. cit., p. 469. See also M. Weber, *The Religion of China*, H. H. Gerth (trans), New York: The Free Press, 1968, p. 149.
36 M. Weber, *Critique of Stammler*, Guy Oakes (trans), New York: The Free Press, 1977, p. 133. See also Weber, 'Diskussionsrede zu dem Vortrag von H. Kantorowicz, "Rechtswissenschaft und Soziologie"', op. cit., p. 478.
37 The concept of legal foreseeability plays an important role for Weber: nevertheless, it does not attempt to anticipate a singular judicial decision, but more generally aims at a certain regularity in the functioning of the legal order. It can be understood in two ways, one centred on dogmatic truth, the other on the empirical validity of a juridical proposition.
38 See M. Weber, '"Roman" and "Germanic" Law', Otmar Foelsche (trans), *International Journal of the Sociology of Law* (1985), 237–46, p. 244.
39 Weber, English trans., op. cit., p. 811; Weber, *Wirtschaft und Gesellschaft*, op. cit., p. 469.
40 Weber, English trans., ibid., p. 882; Weber, *Wirtschaft und Gesellschaft*, ibid., p. 504.
41 Weber, English trans., ibid., p. 894; Weber, *Wirtschaft und Gesellschaft*, ibid., p. 513.
42 Weber, English trans., ibid., p. 217; Weber, *Wirtschaft und Gesellschaft*, ibid., p. 125.
43 See C. Colliot-Thélène, *Le désenchantement de l'État. De Hegel à Max Weber*, Paris: Les Éditions de Minuit, 1992, p. 217.
44 J. Habermas, *The Theory of Communicative Action*, Vol. 1, *Reason and the Rationalization of Society*, Boston: Beacon Press, 1984, p. 262.
45 See E. Troeltsch, 'The Ideas of Natural Law and Humanity in World Politics', in O. Gierke, *Natural Law and The Theory of Society 1500 to 1800*, E. Barker (trans), Cambridge, Cambridge University Press, 1958, pp. 201–2.
46 Ibid., pp. 210–11.
47 See A. Dufour, 'Rationnel et irrationnel dans l'École du droit historique', in *Archives de philosophie du droit*, Vol. XXIII, 1978, pp. 147–74, p. 161ff.
48 Troeltsch, 'The Ideas of Natural Law and Humanity in World Politics', op. cit., pp. 204, 211 and 213.
49 Ibid., pp. 212–13.
50 Weber, English trans., op. cit., p. 867. Weber, *Wirtschaft und Gesellschaft*, op. cit., p. 497. See, also, Kelsen, *Pure Theory of Law*, op. cit., p. 227.
51 See G. Radbruch, 'Legal Philosophy', in *The Legal Philosophies of Lask, Radbruch and Dabin*, 20th Century Legal Philosophy Series: Vol. IV, Cambridge: Harvard University Press, 1950, p. 62. See, also, R. Stammler, *The Theory of Justice*, I. Husik (trans), Modern Philosophy Series, New York: The Macmillan Company, 1925, p. 116, who emphasizes that the romantic mythology of the *Volksgeist* implies definitively the equivalence of positive law with the national spirit (the first being a reflection of the second) and consequently renders any critique of the existing legal order unthinkable.
52 See F. Loos, 'Max Webers Wissenschaftslehre und die Rechtswissenschaft', in Rehbinder and and Tieck (eds), *Max Weber als Rechtssoziologie*, op. cit., pp. 169–87, p. 172ff. Colliot-Thélène, *Le désenchantement de l'État*, op. cit., p. 258.
53 M. Weber, '"Objectivity" in Social Science and Social Policy', in E. Shils and H. A. Finch (eds), *Methodology of Social Sciences*, New Brunswick: Transaction Publishers, 2011, p. 60; M. Weber, *Gesammelte Aufsätze zur Wissenschaftslehre*, Tübingen: J.C.B. Mohr, 1988, p. 157.
54 Weber, '"Objectivity" in Social Science and Social Policy', ibid., p. 57; Weber, *Gesammelte Aufsätze zur Wissenschaftslehre*, ibid., p. 154. See Radbruch, 'Legal Philosophy', op. cit., p. 60, 'The claim of natural law to deduce legal rules of universal validity,

unchangeable and definite in content, cannot be deemed refuted purely empirically, by the usual reference to the colorful variety of the legal views of different ages and nations [. . .] The decisive blow against natural law has been struck not by legal history and comparative law but by epistemology; not by the historical school, but by critical philosophy; not by Savigny but by Kant'.

55 See Weber, *Wirtschaft und Gesellschaft*, op. cit., p. 508; Weber, English trans., op. cit., p. 888ff. See on this point, H. Rickert, 'Max Weber's View of Science', R. C. Spiers (trans), in P. Lassman, and I. Velody (eds), *Max Weber's Science as Vocation*, London: Unwin Hyman, 1989, p. 79.
56 See Radbruch, 'Legal Philosophy', op. cit., p. 57n, for whom the three grand figures of legal relativism are Georg Jellinek, Max Weber and Hans Kelsen.
57 R. Aron, *La philosophie critique de l'histoire: Essai sur une théorie allemande de l'histoire*, Paris: Julliard, 1987, p. 289.
58 The capital importance of this antinomy for the science of law was highlighted, first by Georg Jellinek in his general theory of the State (see *Allgemeine Staatslehre*, 3rd edn, Bad Homburg vor der Höhe: Hermann Gentner Verlag, 1960, p. 20ff.) and in his *System der subjektiven öffentlichen Rechte*, Freiburg: J.C.B. Mohr, 1892, p. 23ff. Weber emphasizes from this perspective the methodological interest of the work of Jellinek in his 'Gedankrede auf Georg Jellinek', reproduced in R. König, and J. Winckelmann (eds), *Max Weber zum Gedächtnis. Materialen und Dokumente zur Bewertung von Werk und Persönlichkeit*, Köln: Westdeutscher Verlag, 1963, pp. 13–17, p. 15.
59 M. Weber, 'R. Stammlers "Überwindung" der materialistischen Geschichtsauffassung', in M. Weber, *Gesammelte Aufsätze zur Wissenschaftslehre*, op. cit., p. 349ff. (English translation, p. 130ff.).
60 Weber, *Wirtschaft und Gesellschaft*, op. cit., p. 181 (English trans., p. 311ff.). See, for example, the distinction which Weber explains between the concept of the 'United States' as used by legal science, and the empirical structure of the same name, as considered by the various social sciences: ibid., *Gesammelte Aufsätze zur Soziologie und Sozialpolitik*, p. 463; see also ibid., 'R. Stammlers "Überwindung" der materialistischen Geschichtsauffassung', p. 130ff. Weber argues here against Stammler, who sees in law a form of ordering of social life; see Stammler, *The Theory of Justice*, op. cit., p. 6, '[. . .] legal regulation represents, in the concept of society, the determining form; whereas the common activity of the persons united constitutes the matter of social existence determined by that form'.
61 Following the definition of Weber, rules 'externally guaranteed by the probability that physical or psychological coercion will be applied by a *staff* of people in order to bring about compliance or avenge violation' (Weber, English trans., op. cit., p. 34; Weber, *Wirtschaft und Gesellschaft*, ibid., p. 17).
62 Weber, 'R. Stammlers "Überwindung" der materialistischen Geschichtsauffassung', op. cit., p. 351 (author's translation).
63 Ibid., p. 358.
64 Weber, 'Diskussionsrede zu dem Vortrag von H. Kantorowicz, "Rechtswissenschaft und Soziologie"", op. cit., p. 481.
65 Weber, 'R. Stammlers "Überwindung" der materialistischen Geschichtsauffassung', op. cit., p. 345ff.
66 M. Weber, 'Wissenschaft als Beruf', in Weber, *Gesammelte Aufsätze zur Wissenschaftslehre*, op. cit., p. 600 (author's translation).
67 H. Kelsen, *Théorie pure du droit*, 1st edn, Thévenaz (trans), Neuchâtel: Éditions de la Baconnière, 1988, p. 95 (author's translation). See, also, Kelsen, *Pure Theory of Law*, op. cit., p. 6, 'Nobody can assert that from the statement that something is, follows a statement that something ought to be, or vice versa.'
68 Kelsen, *Reine Rechtslehre*, op. cit., p. 16 (author's translation). H. Kelsen, 'Justice et

droit naturel', in H. Kelsen et al., *Le Droit naturel*, É. Mazingue (trans), Paris: Presses Universitaires de France, 1959, pp. 1–123, p. 63.
69 Kelsen, *Théorie pure du droit*, op. cit., pp. 63 and 102 (author's translation).
70 See the study by Kelsen, 'The Natural-Law Doctrine before the Tribunal of Science', in H. Kelsen, *What is Justice? Justice, Law, and Politics in the Mirror of Science*, Berkeley: University of California Press, 1960, pp. 137–73.
71 Kelsen, *Reine Rechtslehre*, op. cit., p. 16. See also Kelsen, 'Justice et droit naturel', op. cit., p. 103.
72 See Schluchter, *The Rise of Western Rationalism: Max Weber's Developmental History*, op. cit., p. 51.
73 Weber, English trans., op. cit., p. 874; Weber, *Wirtschaft und Gesellschaft*, op. cit., p. 501.
74 See H. Kelsen, *Der soziologische und der juristische Staatsbegriff. Kritische Untersuchung des Verhältnisses von Staat und Recht*, Aalen: Scientia Verlag, 1981, p. 82ff.
75 Kelsen, *Pure Theory of Law*, op. cit., p. 292.
76 On the relationship between effectiveness and validity see ibid., p. 211ff.
77 Kelsen, *Der soziologische und der juristische Staatsbegriff*, op. cit., p. 94.
78 Bobbio, 'Max Weber und Hans Kelsen', op. cit., p. 126.
79 Kelsen, *Pure Theory of Law*, op. cit. p. 299.
80 Ibid., p. 298.
81 H. Kelsen, *La démocratie. Sa nature. Sa valeur*, C. Eisenmann (trans), *Série politique et constitutionnelle*, Paris: Economica, 1988, p. 71 (author's translation).
82 Weber, English trans., op. cit., p. 215ff.; Weber, *Wirtschaft und Gesellschaft*, op. cit., p. 124.
83 Kelsen, *Der soziologische und der juristische Staatsbegriff*, op. cit., p. 156 (author's translation).
84 Ibid., p. 163 (author's translation). On the position of Kelsen, see M. J. Fariñas Dulce, *La sociologia del derecho de Max Weber*, Madrid: Civitas, 1991, p. 154ff., p. 207ff.
85 G. Jellinek, *Allgemeine Staatslehre*, 3rd edn, Bad Homburg von der Höhe: Gentner Verlag, 1960, p. 11.
86 Ibid., p. 12.
87 Weber, English trans., op. cit., p. 14; Weber, *Wirtschaft und Gesellschaft*, op. cit., p. 6.
88 Weber, English trans., ibid., p. 14; Weber, *Wirtschaft und Gesellschaft*, ibid., p. 7.
89 Ibid, '[. . .] one of the important aspects of the existence of a modern state, precisely as a complex of social interaction of individual persons, consists in the fact that the action of various individuals is oriented to the belief that it exists or should exist, thus that its acts and laws are valid in the legal sense.'
90 Weber, English trans., ibid., p. 27; Weber, *Wirtschaft und Gesellschaft*, op. cit., p. 13. See also ibid., p.14 (English trans., p. 28), '[. . .] that a "friendship" or a "state" exists or has existed means this and only this: that we, the observers, judge that there is or has been a probability that on the basis of certain kinds of known subjective attitude of certain individuals there will result in the average sense a certain specific type of action. For the purposes of legal reasoning it is essential to be able to decide whether a rule of law does or does not carry legal authority, hence whether a legal relationship does or does not "exist". This type of question is not, however, relevant to sociological problems.'

Chapter 9

Using Weber's and Kelsen's schemas for legal history

Jean-Louis Halpérin

Max Weber and Hans Kelsen share the common fate of a rather bad reception among legal historians of the twentieth century. Hans Kelsen has been the most ill-treated, notably by advocates of natural law (relatively numerous in the professional group of researchers interested in legal traditions, who have often focused on Roman law or Canon law doctrines in relation to Aristotle's or Aquinas' theories of justice and natural law), who have reproached him for a legal theory which failed to offer the conceptual resources to resist Nazism (a reproach that sounds particularly unfair towards a victim of the Nazi's policy and, in some cases, from conservative lawyers who were not prominent opponents of Nazism or Fascism).[1] Max Weber had, in comparison, a more tangible effect upon legal history, but legal historians were, in common with other jurists, hesitant towards a methodology of legal sociology, and the potential 'confusion' produced by Weber's schemas of legal evolution.[2]

Hence, legal historians have attributed two overlapping limitations to Weber and Kelsen: (a) a narrowly positivist point of view, reputed to be too State-centred (especially with Kelsen's assimilation of the State and legal order) and, for this reason, unable to explain the older legal systems, which preceded the emergence of modern States; and (b) an unscientific interest in a 'world legal history' that seemed universally rejected (with a laudable concern for the peculiarities of every historical context) since the nineteenth century (first, with the polemics between Gans and Savigny, opposing 'universal history' to 'antiquarian micrology' in a context of recourse to Jewish culture against anti-Semitic feelings that can be compared with that to which Kelsen was subjected in the next century;[3] then, with the criticisms addressed to Sumner Maine's evolutionism for over-generalizations about the history of different cultures[4]).

The dominance of this representation, by legal historians, of Kelsen and Weber has, however, begun to recede. While the increasing interest for comparative legal history gives a new meaning to some kinds of 'universal' (or at least 'regional' in Europe, America, Asia or Africa) legal history, the theoretical reflections of Weber and Kelsen about legal sanctions and their representations in the mind of law subjects[5] have been placed in the framework of historical studies of legal cultures. Thus, it seems possible, and even fruitful, to use Weber's and Kelsen's schemas in legal history to confront and perhaps to combine the two approaches of these writers towards past legal systems. At first glance, Max Weber's analysis of the rationalization process of law is more sophisticated and historically anchored than the brief remarks from Kelsen about the emergence and developments of legal orders. However, Kelsen's distinction between legal orders and normative systems provides for a critical reformulation of Max Weber's initial schemas. A second point would be to examine the role of legal science in relation to Weber's and Kelsen's theories. Here, Kelsen appears to be of essential importance through his rejection of the idea of a 'doctrine' that could create norms (the law-making process as the domain of legal writers). Yet, Kelsen's abstract conception of the influence of the constructed legal order upon the normative order is rendered more determinate through Weber's conception of the subjective representation of law and the 'empirical legal order'.

The genesis of legal orders: reading Weber with Kelsen

Max Weber has asked, in different parts of *Wirtschaft und Gesellschaft*, the question of the origins of legal systems and his elaborations were much more devoted to legal history (in a very comparative and comprehensive understanding) than those of Kelsen some decades later. In his famous chapter concerning the fundamental relations between economy and social organization, Max Weber situated a point of departure regarding the legal (or 'juridical') and a sociological approach to legal orders and legal propositions.[6] He makes a link between 'guaranteed law' and 'coercive apparatus' but he recognizes that the monopoly of violence and legal coercion by the State is rather a recent phenomenon. For Weber, extra-state laws have been developed outside the power of State authorities and law does not exist only 'where legal coercion is guaranteed by the political authority'.[7] The next development in the same chapter is devoted to the 'continuum with imperceptible transitions' between law, custom and convention. In these difficult passages, Weber seems to adopt the word 'convention' for regular conduct (*Massenhandeln*), which is not induced by coercion, whereas custom can be enforced by a coercive apparatus. He admits that the boundary between convention and custom is fluid. Therefore, 'it is entirely a question of terminology and convenience at which point of this continuum one shall assume the existence of the subjective conception of a legal obligation'.[8] For Weber, the question concerns the possibility of change in a modern world dominated by regularity and obligation flowing from the effect of repetitive conduct.

One can say that Weber has not established a clear demarcation between law and custom in this part of *Wirtschaft and Gesellschaft*. He deals again with this question in the chapter on the formal characteristics of objective law in some very dense pages, which are difficult to interpret without taking account of the doctrines with which Weber engages.[9] Then – and here legal historians are particularly interested in this discourse – Weber states that 'this kind of law-making is not aboriginal'.[10] He means, probably, that it cannot explain the appearance of legal norms in ancient societies, but curiously his argument is, rather, to say that customary law retains a place 'even in economically or socially complex and advanced societies',[11] such as England or Germany (from a Kelsenian perspective, however, this modern customary law is recognized through the written or the customary constitution, thereby confining the question, for ancient societies, of the presence or absence of this recognition). The question of customary law is of central importance to Weber and, with his contemporaries, he considers that the current theorization of custom is a rather recent (appearing in late Roman law) and an academic construction (with the references to repeated observation, *usus*, and common belief of its binding effect, *opinio necessitatis*). Then, without giving many explanations, he opposes the dogmatic theory formulated by Zitelmann and Gierke to the one that legal sociologists, Lambert and Ehrlich, have developed as a 'violent struggle against customary law', that represents 'a confusion between the legal and sociological methods of analysis'.[12]

Legal historians, familiar with the works of Édouard Lambert and Eugen Ehrlich, would be perturbed by the meaning of the opposition between these 'bad' legal sociologists and the 'good' legal dogmatists: Zitelmann and Gierke. Concerning the French pioneer of comparative law Édouard Lambert, Weber certainly refers to one part of his 1903 *Études de droit commun legislatif ou de droit civil comparé. La fonction du droit civil comparé*, which is devoted to the critique of the Roman and Canon Theory of Custom.[13] Yet, Lambert presents the traditional theorization of custom as a doctrinal construction (in exactly the same manner as at the beginning of Weber's chapter) and makes comparative analysis of the legal writing of Roman jurists, Talmudic rabbis, Hindu priests and Muslim lawyers, according to a method which could have inspired Weber. One can presume that it is Lambert's denunciation of a 'spontaneous' customary law (without the intervention of courts and legal science) – which was also a critique of Geny's theory of the sources of law rehabilitating custom as an autonomous source of law[14] – with which Weber disagreed.

Concerning Ehrlich, the main reference could be the 1906 inaugural lecture *Die Tatsachen des Gewohnheitrechts*.[15] Here the discovery is much more important. The whole problematic of this 42-page text is exactly the same as that developed by Weber in this chapter: how can customs (*Sitte*, as distinguished from ethical norms or *sittliche Normen*) become legal rules? The answer given by Eugen Ehrlich consists, first, in distinguishing legal norms and social (customary) norms (with the affirmation that marriage, sale or succession have appeared a long time before a law of marriage, a law about the contract of sale or legal rules about succession rights), then, in insisting on the role of courts, jurists and legislators (through citing Lambert), and, lastly, (which is a divergence from Lambert) in stating that legal rules are derived from legislative interventions (the State creating new rules through this intervention in society), from norms of decision (formally emanating from courts, legal writings and statutory laws) and from 'pure' customs practised by social groups.[16]

Ehrlich has proposed an original division between three sources of law that has kept an independent place for customary law. Reading this text of Ehrlich, we can ask why Weber (as with Kelsen in the *General Theory of Law and State*, reproaching Ehrlich for confusing social and legal institutions) has thus opposed, on the one hand, the theories of Lambert and Ehrlich (that were not identical) and, on the other hand, the conceptualization of Zitelmann (the former cited with approval by Lambert) and Gierke (the latter being cited by Ehrlich to support his theory). The ambiguity increases when one observes that the next argumentative development of Weber – explaining that the Roman and medieval theory of customary law fits not the appearance of customary law (in a pre-legislative stage), but the relationship between Roman law and local laws in the provinces or common law and local customs in England – were exactly the examples given by Ehrlich.[17] Lambert has devoted more than 500 pages of his book[18] to historical examples chosen from Roman law, Jewish law, Muslim law and Hindu law, and it is difficult to believe that Weber has not been influenced by these arguments.

It seems that Weber has tried to 'rub out' the traces of Lambert's and Ehrlich's influences in his reflections in order to emphasize the greater originality of his further argumentative development. In the following sentences, Weber states that a psychological adjustment can explain how some regularity of conduct (or habituation to an action) can create a consensus among people and the feeling of 'semi or wholly conscious expectations' in favour of a binding effect of the rule resulting from the habitual conduct. This feeling can also explain how these rules can be guaranteed by coercive enforcement and distinguished from customs. But, asks Weber, 'there arises the question of how anything could ever change in this inert mass of canonized custom'.[19] Weber answers that he is not convinced by the Historical School of Law's Theory of *Volksgeist* (such a hypostatized supra-individual organic entity does not exist and cannot change customs), even if unconscious changes can be presented (especially by lawyers?) as an absence of change. Weber no longer considers that external conditions (social and economic determinants probably) can explain the possibility of change of a customary rule. Here, begins a long development[20] about new agreements (*Gemeinschftshandeln, Vergesellschaftung, Zweckrationale Vereinbarung*) among interested people with the decisive help of legal experts. It is Weber's most original contribution to the genesis of legal systems through customs: contrary to Lambert and Ehrlich, Weber considers that decisions of arbiters and judges (more generally the intervention of 'legal experts', including priests, oracles or magicians that Lambert has also considered) are not the only primary source of customary law (even if he recognizes that the judge is 'doing more than merely placing his seal on norms which would already have been binding'[21]). There is a potential for new invented agreements (probably contracts between interested persons, but transactions could happen also in family life or about successions, as exemplified by the *zadruga* community in the Balkan era), sometimes solemnized through oaths, which can be imitated (as with judicial decisions) and, thus, provoke a change in the law (completely integrated in the *Juristenrecht* through judicial precedents). Whereas Lambert continued to invoke a 'legal feeling' (difficult to postulate before the appearance of a legal system),

Weber insists on rational expectations arising from *ad hoc* agreements produced by commercial activity (the persons concluding such agreements sensed the possibility that they would be recognized by the community and thus encourage potential legal enforcement of these new legal rules). In these developments, Weber repeatedly emphasizes that primitive societies contained different ways to invent legal rules (hence, to introduce new legal rules): new orientations of communal activity; creations by legal experts; and even imposition from above through legislation (here, Weber probably envisages Jewish and Muslim law, and agrees with Ehrlich's conception of 'true' statutory laws). Weber is rather unclear about the use he is making here of the distinction between law-making (*Rechtsschöpfung*) and law finding (*Rechtserfindung*, or *Rechtsfindung*, the latter expression having been popularized by Ehrlich) which he has proposed in the preceding developments (in contrast to the distant past, the differentiation between law-making, as the establishment of general rules, and law finding, as the application of these norms, is a contemporary phenomenon).[22] One can suggest that Weber has linked the 'creation' (another meaning of 'law-making' which can be associated with the 'law-finding' decision of the judges) of a legal order (Weber's notion of law-making would be characterized as the 'invention of the law') with the discovery of new rules.

It is in relation to this Weberian framework that Kelsen's work becomes an insightful comparative resource. If Kelsen has not the same historical interest in explaining the birth of law – as he granted a decisive role to the criterion of 'coercion' (or sanction) to find a common link between primitive and modern systems[23] – he has explained that the primary constitutional (or constitutive) norm of a legal order can be a written legislation or a customary rule (authorizing the creation of more detailed rules through customs), flowing from the principle 'law regulates its own creation'.[24] From this Kelsenian perspective, the Weberian explanation of the genesis of legal systems is the attribution of a *sociological* meaning to the appearance of a 'constitution' or a 'constitutive rule' of the 'legal field'. Either this constitutive rule was a written one – a schema that Kelsen has privileged, but that Weber has not neglected in these explanations of either Jewish and Muslim law or of the Law of Twelve Tables in Rome he characterized as primitive legislation implemented *uno actu*[25] – or a customary one, that corresponds to Weber's understanding of new agreements, judicial decisions and the intervention of 'legal' experts. Of course, a customary constitution, allowing for the creation of new legal rules through customs, is impossible to prove with factual evidence, but Weber has proposed certain explanatory elements which furnish a potential to comprehend the moment, in different civilizations, at which 'legal' rules have been distinguished from other 'social' rules (which can be guaranteed by coercion, in contrast to the Kelsenian position).

Post-Weberian works – those of Kelsen, but also Hart's *Concept of Law* with its idea of a transition from a pre-legal to a legal world – are, of course, influencing such an interpretation.[26] However, a particular form of Weber's argument concerning the question of change within customary rules can be seen to have affected Hart, despite Hart's desire to deny any such influence.[27] If we try to combine, in a historical perspective, the insights from Weber, Kelsen and Hart, then this would include the invention of legal techniques (conceived as artefacts by these three positivist theoreticians) and the creation of a legal field that can arise historically from constitutive legislation (the *Torah*, the *Koran* or the Roman Law of Twelve Tables), or through mechanisms of recognition and change of customary rules supported by the action of judges (to recognize these rules and adjudicate trials accordingly) and the intervention of legal experts (able to formally recognize these rules as legal).

Furthermore, such an interpretation can explain why Weber has concluded this chapter on the emergence of legal rules with a repeated emphasis on the role of legal specialists. He seems here to make a distinction about a first stage of primitive law (resulting from individual agreements and judicial decisions which were not consciously considered as legal rules, which Kelsen would have considered 'non-legal' rules in the absence of a constitutive rule about law creation) and a 'formally elaborated law constituting a complex of maxims consciously applied in decisions'.[28] Is this not effectively the Hartian conception of the transition from a pre-legal stage (with 'primary' rules which are already binding) to a legal system (with the adjunction of secondary rules of recognition, change and adjudication)?

In this development, Weber states that the emergence of a 'formally elaborated law' (we shall see later the importance of this phrase) is linked to the decisive co-operation between 'administrators of justice' (one can suppose, against Kelsen's weak arguments, that arbiters and judges have existed prior to a 'legal order') and the 'trained specialists', 'the practitioner of law concerned with adjudication'. According to Weber, 'formal' law requires lawyers or, more exactly, a differentiated group (which does not mean that members of this group cannot be simultaneously priests or 'notables', for example, Roman pontiffs or *lag sagas* in Scandinavian societies, *Schöffen* in Germanic ones), who devote themselves to both supporting the administration of justice (through advising judges) and to making 'legal inventions'. Even if these persons were a type of 'part-time lawyer', the fact that they could constitute a group (Weber is extremely cautious about calling it a 'professional group', the question being discussed in the next chapter of his book) is an indication of the formation of a legal system: Kelsen will say that only law can create legal rules, Weber has considered that only a group of lawyers (or 'pre-lawyers') can recognize (and simultaneously create) a 'legal field' (to use a more sociological expression than 'legal system'). Here is a centrally important subject for legal historians (how can we know that Roman pontiffs or Scandinavian *lag sagas* have developed a 'special knowledge' before the invention of a clearly distinct legal vocabulary?) and also a supplementary explanation of Max Weber's ideal types of 'formalization' and of 'rationalization' of law.

It is well known that at the beginning of his so-called *Sociology of Law* (Chapter VIII, 'fields of substantive law'), Weber seeks to differentiate several kinds of 'legal fields' or of 'legal thought' with the two binary oppositions of rational/irrational and formal/substantive. From a formal perspective, 'irrational law' means law-making which 'cannot be controlled by the intellect' (because it is derived from oracles or magicians), whereas rational law supposes rules of procedure determining the understanding of facts through reason. Concerning the substance of the rules, law is 'irrational' when it is created from singular decisions and 'rational' when it derives from general norms.[29] However, further nuance is introduced by Weber himself when he says that all 'formal law is, formally at least, relatively rational'.[30] Beyond the initial tautological appearance of this phrase, one can suggest that, for Weber, 'formal law' (*formales Recht*) as 'genuine' law, is always, from a procedural perspective (*formell*), relatively rational. If one combines this affirmation with the previous explanation of the relation between lawyers and the emergence of law, one can suggest that, for Weber, primitive law (which means irrational law in a formal perspective, as determined by oracles or magicians) is not 'genuine law', as it could not give birth to a special knowledge known by a specific group (oracles or magicians do not share a common knowledge, because their decisions are not controlled by reason and cannot be presented through the medium of reasoned argument). Reading this text in parallel with Kelsen's conception, it follows that only 'formal' law (i.e. law recognized as such through an intellectual operation) is 'genuine' law, conceived as a specific intellectual operation by particular individuals (likely to form the group of specialists knowing something about law). Such an interpretation also supports the repeated emphasis made by Weber that the historically most remote legal systems are marked by procedural formality. In this way, Weber has effectively removed from the purview of legal history 'primitive' systems where there was no 'formal law' – because there were no rules of procedure to alter customary rules, no development of coherent criteria for uniformity of judicial decision making and no particular group with specialist legal knowledge – and confined the perspective of legal historians to the processes of 'rationalization' of the law.

This ideal type of law rationalization animates Weber's subsequent analysis of legal professionals (distinguishing those educated through practice, as in England, and those educated in universities, as in continental Europe since the revival of Roman law), the influence of the different religious and political regimes (with the examples of Hindu, Muslim, Jewish and Canon laws) or the distinction between patrimonial codifications (such as the 1794 Prussian Code based on the idea of a 'substantive justice') and modern codifications (such as the 1804 Napoleonic Code, compared with the Roman Law of Twelve Tables, as a more complete rationalization based on 'purely' legal elements composed of epigrammatic sentences[31]). While these evolutionary analyses remain extremely pertinent within legal history, they are qualified by the existence of discontinuities in this process – the tendency is not for more and more rationalization, the rationalization process can proceed in different ways, and external factors such as ethical ideas, utilitarian conceptions or political interventions interfere with this process.

Here, again, it is pertinent to combine certain elements from Kelsen and Weber. In his *Pure Theory of Law* (second edition), Kelsen has proposed three criteria to distinguish between decentralized and centralized legal orders – a distinction that is historically important because the former are often 'pre-State' legal orders and the latter legal orders are linked with the modern 'legislative' State. Initially, decentralized legal orders are characterized by a law-making process based upon custom (that is, the behaviour of the individuals who are subjected to the legal order); then, centralized legal orders can be identified through the extensive domain of legislative rules and are opposed to decentralized legal orders where 'individual norms' (so called because they are created during litigation between individuals) are decided by courts in a discretionary way (e.g. in common law systems); and, finally, centralized legal orders are the ones where the norms are enforceable throughout the State, whereas in decentralized legal orders, a plurality of different local laws exist within the same territory.[32]

Kelsen's schema is, thus, not radically distinct from that of Weber's and, hence, opens a similar form of questioning for legal historians. In what manner can the decline of customary rules in relation to the increase of State law be analysed as a 'rationalization' of law (directed by legal professionals to achieve enhanced control of the law-making process)? How can the development of statutory law (and especially codification) be compared with the emergence of the rule of *stare decisis* and the collection of standardized Law Reports, as a parallel means to transform law into a systematized set of rules (a point that Weber seems to have considered and an argument to refute rule-scepticism defended by some American realists)?[33] What is the impact of regional or community-based (e.g. the personal statutes linked with religious affiliations) laws as obstacles to a rationalization (through truly general norms) of the legal system? The fact that the combined reading of Weber and Kelsen can initiate these questions indicates a certain commonality in their approach to the evolution of legal norms: an evolution that supposes the historical invention of legal techniques and the development (often associated with transplants and imitations) of rationalizing processes. Of course, Weber and Kelsen have developed singular and personal perspectives; in particular, Weber's perspective may be too affected by an underlying form of admiration for the Pandectists (as the craftsmen, in nineteenth-century Germany, of this process of legal rationalization) and too prone to accept that lawyers' ideas could directly affect the evolution of norms.

The representation of legal orders: reading Kelsen with Weber

Legal historians, who share the positivist postulate of the differentiation between law as a set of norms and the science of law (*Rechtswissenschaft*) as a collection of statements (*Rechtssätze*), would commence from Kelsen's works and his numerous denunciations of the ideological character of much doctrinal writing. For example, in the first edition of the *Reinerechtslehre* (1934), Kelsen has opposed the 'traditional legal science', with its ideological features to the 'pure theory of law' as a 'true' science of law.[34] In his preface to Charles Eisenmann's French dissertation on the Austrian Constitutional Court (1928), Kelsen states that doctrinal writing could not create legal norms and that legal academics had to desist from this misplaced idea of participation in law-making.[35] In order to avoid the failings of many 'traditional' (in essence, inspired by natural law theories) legal histories, which hold that, without reference to context, statutory law, customs and doctrinal writing are all sources of law-making, the rigorous separation between law and legal science should be retained, even if Kelsen's perspective remains problematic in regard to certain periods of legal history (e.g. the power of Roman *jurisconsults* to create law through their *responsa*).

Although Weber's approach is 'value-free' and equally based on positivist postulates, it seems that, in many of his historical analyses of the evolution of law, the author of *Wirtschaft und Gesellschaft* has closely associated, if not confused, the science of law with legal norms as elements in, and indicators of, this evolution. In his distinction between formal and material rationalization of the law, Max Weber insists on the 'peculiarly professional, legalistic and abstract approach to law', which 'allows the execution of the specifically systematic task, i.e. the collection and rationalization by logical means of all the several rules recognized as legally valid into an internally consistent complex of abstract legal propositions'.[36] If one can consider some codifications (such as the Napoleonic Code as opposed to the casuistic Prussian Code), let alone the collection of (English) precedents, as organized systems of rules, it seems that Weber has, instead, concentrated upon the systematic set of legal propositions (*Rechtssätze*) composed through doctrinal writings. For Weber, the material and logical rationalization of law found its realization in the *Begriffsjurisprudenz* of his contemporary legal colleagues in Germany. The chapter devoted to law teaching – that is initially elaborated from the opposition between the English conception of law as craft with a practitioner's education and the continental approach of law as science, 'sacred' in its origins, though university education, combined with the distinctive features of Roman legal logic – is entirely built on the comparison between different 'legal thoughts', which means different types of legal writing.[37] This chapter ends, again, with the praise of the systematic work of Roman jurists and of the subsequent development (probably thanks to German Pandectism) of legal concepts from Roman origins. Finally, and equally importantly, Weber acknowledges the significant influence of doctrines of natural law upon the process of rationalization and codification of law, in particular, its 'revolutionary' character enabling the legitimation of law-making by new institutions or groups defined by their rebellion against traditional sources of power.[38]

Is it necessary to conclude that, from a Kelsenian perspective, Weber's analysis of the historical importance of legal science is simply to be rejected as entirely flawed? One can tentatively suggest that the perspectives of Weber and Kelsen on the role of doctrinal writing in legal evolution can be combined. First, Kelsen has not been always so critical (or contemptuous) towards the 'traditional' legal science. He has recognized some merits of his predecessors, especially the Historical School of Law for its contribution to the formation of the positivist theory.[39] Paradoxically, Kelsen displayed more affinity with Savigny and greater distance towards German Pandectists than Weber. Second, Kelsen utilized traditional doctrine to reveal its ideological character and to denounce theoretical errors that were instructive for the understanding of the pure theory of law, for example about gaps in legal orders (a subject about which Kelsen has noted the influence of the 'fictive' traditional theory on the Swiss Civil Code, i.e. on a positive norm).[40]

Despite this 'complex of superiority', Kelsen has thus recognized the usefulness of doctrinal 'errors' and the necessity for legal science to take account of the history of juridical thought. Finally, for Kelsen, the 'multi-secular' legal science corresponded to the intellectual needs of jurists and had a particular mission, i.e. to create concepts or 'means' that can be used by practitioners.[41] Hence, Kelsen has not rejected the possibility (how could he have?) that doctrinal concepts could influence the process of law making through statutory norms (as in the case of the Swiss Civil Code) or 'individual norms' (precedents).

From a Weberian perspective, there is no general assumption that legal doctrine was always a source of positive law. If we take the example of Roman law (that Kelsen has considered as a legal order despite the fact that he knew the contribution of Roman jurisconsults to the law-making process), Weber is very cautious and very well informed about the question of norms created by the works of jurisconsults. He considers that the influence of Roman jurisconsults has 'particular' (this designation connoting historically original factors) features: the separation of the Roman process between a preliminary phase before the magistrate and a decisive phase before a single judge (appointed from the 'notables') that has encouraged the involvement of legal professionals to prescribe the *praetor*'s edict and offer advice to single judges,[42] and the official recognition since Augustus of the privilege granted to some jurisconsults to make official *responsa* that could be binding for the judges.[43] From a Kelsenian perspective, it can be said that Roman jurisconsults have been empowered to create law, through customary rules (leading *praetors* and judges to take advice from the professional jurists, especially for the transcription of the *praetor*'s edict that Weber supposes, very accurately, to have been binding at a second stage, and which could support the hypothesis of a norm authorizing the creation of law by this means) or through written norms (the ones conferring the privilege of public *responsa* during the imperial period). Weber knew very well that Roman legal writing (what Romans called 'jurisprudence') was not a source of law during the entire history of Roman law and that we could have a distorted understanding of it because of the 'sacralization' by Justinian's *Digest* of one part of Roman doctrine. In regard to the 'reception of Roman law', provoked by the rediscovery of Justinian's compilations in Italy at the end of the eleventh century – itself the subject, from the emergence of the Historical School of Law in Germany, of an extensive academic and even political discussion – Weber is also very careful to notice that there is no comparable upheaval of legal thought to this reception of Roman law, but that its effects are closely linked with the supportive action of the princes and of the courts.[44]

This cautious attitude about the real impact of legal doctrine on positive norms is equally evident in Weber's approach to Islamic or Chinese law. Weber has clearly recognized that Islamic law was developed through professional jurists – it was a *Juristenrecht* – who were endowed with the mission to give advice to the litigants or the *cadi* judges. However, he considers that the intellectual barrier constituted by a 'sacred law' has made difficult a 'free' interpretation of texts (at least, this interpretation has been strictly channelled through the interpretive rules formulated in each of the Islamic 'schools of law') and that the *muftis* (the jurists who gave consultations) remained confined to the provision of individual decisions, conceived as 'oracles' and lacking many of the prerequisites for systematization (the Islamic legal science remained characterized by 'stereotyped' jurists[45]). For these reasons, Islamic law was rather weakly influenced by legal doctrine, despite the strong presence of legal professionals. If this analysis can be corrected today, or at least nuanced, through more recent enquiries about the role of legal science (*fiqh*) in the selection of the rules of the *Sunna* (the *hadith* resulting from the words and acts of Mohammed, the number of which diverges considerably from one 'school of law' to another), Weber was very attentive to the resemblances (provoked also, he thought, by a significant transplantation of Hellenic and Roman jurisprudence into Islamic law) and differences (because of the early 'secularization' of Roman law) between Roman and Islamic legal science.

In relation to Chinese law, Weber has considered that the absence of a class of professional jurists has hindered the process of rationalizing a legal system (that is supposed to have existed, since Antiquity, through positive rules expressed in statutory codes). Chinese judges, for Weber, were bureaucrats (in some cases advised by Taoist 'magicians'), who decided cases according their ideas of 'material' justice and without the help of a systematized set of abstract rules. From this perspective, the Chinese legal order (which presented minimal features of a 'formal' law through its codes) could not be transformed into a rational system, because of the lack of abstraction created by a professional jurisprudence. This effectively confirms that the Roman model was rather exceptional, and that legal systems could develop without the influence of legal writing.[46] Here, again, if Weber's analysis remains pertinent, he cannot be accused of situating legal doctrine as a universal source of law nor of equating the professional lawyer with an influence upon law-making.

The pages devoted by Weber to the Napoleonic Code confirm this positivist approach to the law-making process and of the contribution of legal doctrine to the rationalization of law. What is important for Weber in the global influence of the French Civil Code is not its supposed legislative 'spirit' inspired by theories of natural law, but the effectiveness (in part, attributed to the personal influence of Napoleon on the law-making process) of a State law that has combined customary rules (which had pragmatic advantages) with 'common sense' axioms.[47] Is there not, here, a veiled criticism of the German Civil Code as limited by the difficulties of systematic abstraction created by the Roman juristic tradition? Beyond this, Weber has never confused positive law (especially that created within modern States) with the influence (not, in principle, disputed by Kelsen, even if it remains of peripheral interest) of legal science.

Within this question of legal science, there is a further possibility to reconcile Weber's and Kelsen's approach to the statements of professional jurists. Kelsen, as a Neo-Kantian theorist, maintains that legal science creates its own methodological object. From this perspective, legal scientists, working on legal propositions and using legal concepts, are 'representing' law in methodological cognition. While the 'pure' theory of law, purporting, through a value-free approach, to describe the legal system, is, for Kelsen, the only 'true' representation of legal systems, nevertheless, other 'representations' could and have existed. Hence, should one not investigate these other 'representations' (and require jurists to 'construe' facts in a legal manner, a Weberian expression, which can then be compared with Kelsen's 'construction' of law) through Weber's historical method?

This subject is made very difficult by the different 'phases' of Kelsen's conception of legal science[48] and, conversely, by the absence of a specific theorization of legal science by Weber. In his first writings, Kelsen creates the impression that he followed the German 'copy theory' of knowledge: legal propositions, made by legal science, could be considered as reproductions (or reformulations) of legal norms. Legal science had only to describe any legal order that was composed of (hierarchical) norms (even if, especially for the more ancient legal orders based on oral customs, the jurists have to enunciate a statement that was only tacit in the past legal system). In his later work, Kelsen focused on the interpretation of legal norms, as acts of will and not (only) of knowledge, opening a plurality of interpretations. The last page of the second edition of the *Pure Theory of Law* is devoted to this 'scientific interpretation' – as differentiated again from the 'authentic interpretation' by law-applying organs, which can only create legal norms – that has to formulate (all) the 'possible meanings' of legal norms.[49] Hence, legal science (even if it follows the method prescribed by Kelsen) is not a single copy of legal norms, but a wider array of proposed meanings. Of course, to be correct (or 'possible'), the statements from legal science have to be 'ascertained by an objective method. The existence of the value of law is conditioned by objectively verifiable facts'.

The orientation of Weber was, of course, different: he tried to distinguish the legal (namely in accordance with the concepts of legal science) interpretation of the meaning of a norm and the 'empirical' interpretation (made by concrete individuals, i.e. all persons subjected to law in order to determine their conduct), the latter being the object of the research of legal sociologists. In his *Critique of Stammler* (an opposition to natural-law theory in which law gave 'form' to concrete societal rules common to Weber and Kelsen), Weber deemed legal interpretation capable of formulating a 'legal truth' (without saying it was the 'authentic' truth stated by law-applying institutions, as for Kelsen, or a 'scientific' truth formulated by the *Begriffsjurisprudenz* that Weber continued to admire).[50] The importance he gave to 'representations' ('the ideas of men about the "meaning" and the "validity" of certain legal representations'[51]) does not exclude an interpretation that acknowledges the importance of legal science in empirical interpretations which creates the distinction between professional interpretation (the culture of lawyers itself open to evaluation) and lay interpretation (the presence of law in popular culture). Is this not Kelsen's position in the *General Theory of Law and State* of 1945, when he refers, concerning Weber, to the 'law as it exists in the minds of men as contents of their ideas'?[52] Here, Kelsen engages directly with Weber's sociology of law in order both to criticize it (citing the example of the criminal whose conduct is not always influenced by his/her representation of law), to admit (perhaps for the first time) that 'human behaviour' could equally be an object of normative jurisprudence (Kelsen speaks of a conduct determined by legal norms, but can we not consider legal science as a set of intellectual conducts 'oriented' by legal norms?) as of legal sociology.[53] For legal historians, this manner of combining Weber and Kelsen indicates the potential to examine the historical development of legal science together with the interpretations and cultural representations of past legal orders.

With which concepts, and with what purpose, can legal historians conduct their analysis of these different legal representations? For Kelsen, these concepts formulated by the 'pure theory of law' – derived from the 'fundamental norm' or from the legal order identified with the State (encompassing both centralized and decentralized legal orders) – are the sole basis for a scientific understanding of what was (or what is) law. In comparison, Weber's interest in German legal science of his period has been less emphasized, despite his statement that 'rational judicial concepts' supply the role of ideal-types for the 'empirical history of law'.[54] If Weber's methodology is predicated upon the 'construction' of ideal-types (and renewal, upon the exhaustion of their potential for understanding) to develop a comprehensive understanding of history and proposed (e.g. in regard to a typology of domination) his ideal-types of his own creation, he considered legal concepts (due to their technical character) to have an enhanced capability for use as ideal-types to understand law.

From a methodological position, Weber simultaneously utilizes sociological concepts (such as the distinction between formal and substantive rationalization of law as ideal-types to comprehend global legal evolution, or the distinction between true codifications and 'legal compilations'[55]) and legal concepts (for the comprehension of the evolution of more complex institutions).

Initially, it appears that Weber has utilized both types of legal concept: he has applied the concept *Rechtsgeschäft* (the concept of legal transaction formulated by German Pandectists) to Roman contracts (whereas Roman jurists have ignored this concept), but has preferred the concept '*imperium*' to characterize the rule of princes (encompassing Frankish kings, English or French medieval princes and even certain African chiefs who imposed a durable form of rule on tribes) and its peculiar (distinguished from domestic power) and inherent power to change the law.[56] Weber has, therefore, avoided the potential difficulties flowing from the attribution of the concept 'State' to ancient polities (or the semantic ambiguity of Kelsen's notion of decentralized legal orders). Furthermore, in an explicit criticism of German jurists (perhaps indebted to Jhering's second phase), especially the legal historians, Weber emphasizes that these legal historians' (affiliated with the Pandecticts) scientific rationalism ('purism') has created a conceptual systematization equally incapable of explaining the emergence of new legal demands (during the nineteenth century) and the character of ancient legal orders (defined as anachronisms).[57] The methodological sophistication of Weber in his comparative analysis – in order to prevent the attribution of deceptive resemblances – provides the possibility to combine the concepts of past legal science with those of contemporary observers. Max Weber and Hans Kelsen have never considered that a particular legal theory was the exact 'reflection' of the corresponding 'legal order' (or even its best representation: otherwise many legal orders of the past, whose development was unaccompanied by burgeoning legal theorization, would be difficult to comprehend) and have acknowledged that contemporary observers' purported description of these legal orders could contain mistakes and ideological errors. Among the tasks of legal history, there was the necessity for a distancing from ideological perspectives (including the idea that legal change was the exclusive province of dominant or emerging classes) and for a sophisticated understanding of the impact of intellectual currents (e.g. the impact of Greek philosophy on the Roman legal science) on the processes of legal change.

Is there one 'empirical legal order' at a determined time in a specific territory, as a single reality independent from the representations of contemporaries and existing as the convergent combination of these different perspectives? This remains an open, and highly uncertain, question. However, Weber's and Kelsen's schemas provide legal historians with the potential conceptual resources from which to initiate an attempted answer to this question.

Notes

1 J.-L. Halpérin, 'De quelques difficultés kelséniennes pour l'historien du droit', in D. de Béchillon, P. Brunet, V. Champeil-Desplats and E. Millard (eds), *L'architecture du droit. Mélanges en l'honneur du professeur Michel Troper*, Paris: Economica, 2006, pp. 477–86, p. 478.
2 W. Gephart, 'Einleitung', in M. Weber, *Wirtschaft und Gesellschaft* in W. Gephart and S. Hermes (eds), *Max Weber Gesamtausgabe*, Teilband 22-3, Tübingen: J.C.B. Mohr, 2010, p. 1.
3 N. Waszek, 'Judaïsme et histoire comparée du droit chez Edouard Gans', *Revue germanique internationale* (2002), 17, 163–75.
4 A. D. J. Marcfarlane, 'Some contribution of Maine to history and anthropology', in A. Diamond (ed), *The Victorian Achievement of Sir Henry Maine. A Centennial Reappraisal*, Cambridge: Cambridge University Press, 2001, pp. 111–42, pp. 140–1.
5 It is noteworthy that this aspect of Weber's sociology of law is practically the only one mentioned by H. Kelsen, *General Theory of Law and State*, A. Wedberg (trans), Cambridge: Harvard University Press, 1945, reprinted Clark: The Law Book Exchange, 2009, pp. 171–78.
6 M. Weber, *Economy and Society*, G. Roth and C. Wittich (eds), Berkeley, Los Angeles: University of California Press, 1978, p. 311.
7 Ibid., pp. 316–17.
8 Ibid., pp. 321 and 325 (for the evolution from the stage of mere usage to the stage of the legal norm).
9 Ibid., pp. 753–55 (in the German new edition, *Wirtschaft und Gesellschaft*, op. cit., p. 430ff).

10 Ibid., p. 753.
11 Ibid.
12 Ibid.
13 É. Lambert, *Études de droit commun législatif ou de droit civil comparé. La fonction du droit civil comparé*, Paris: Giard, 1903, pp. 222–338.
14 C. Petit, 'Lambert en la *Tour Eiffel* o el derecho comparado de la *belle époque*', in A. Padoa-Schioppa, *La comparazione giuridica tra Otto e Novecento*, Milano: Istituto Lombardo, 2001, pp. 53–98, pp. 75–80.
15 E. Ehrlich, *Die Tatsachen des Gewohnheitsrecht*, Leipzig-Wien: Franz Deuticke, 1907. Concerning the knowledge Weber could have of the *Grundlegung der Soziologie der Rechts* published by Ehrlich in 1913, Hubert Treiber, 'Max Weber and Eugen Ehrlich. On the Janus-headed Construction of Weber's Ideal Type in the Sociology of Law', *Max Weber Studies* (2008), 8, 2, 225–46, p. 231.
16 Ehrlich, ibid., pp. 9 and 28.
17 Ibid., p. 35.
18 Lambert, *Études de droit commun législatif ou de droit civil comparé*, op. cit., pp. 214–717.
19 Weber, *Economy and Society*, op. cit., p. 754.
20 Ibid., pp. 755–75.
21 Ibid., p. 758.
22 The two expressions are used also in the presentation of the rational/irrational and formal/substantive distinctions used for the conception of law: ibid., pp. 653–56.
23 Kelsen, *General Theory of Law and State*, op. cit., p. 19.
24 Ibid., p. 126.
25 Weber, *Economy and Society*, op. cit., p. 848. Max Weber has also proposed an interesting explanation of the *imperium* of Roman magistrates, based on their military powers, to create new legal rules: a type of hypothesis regarding the emergence of law from military rules.
26 H. L. A. Hart, *The Concept of Law*, Oxford: Oxford University Press, 1961, p. 91.
27 N. Lacey, *A Life of H.L.A Hart: The Nightmare and the Noble Dream*, Oxford: Oxford University Press, 2004, p. 230.
28 Weber, *Economy and Society*, op. cit., p. 775.
29 Ibid., p. 656.
30 Ibid.
31 Ibid., p. 866.
32 H. Kelsen, *Pure Theory of Law*, M. Knight (trans), Berkeley, Los Angeles and London: University of California Press, 1967 (reprinted The Lawbook Exchange, 2002) pp. 228, 251 and 315.
33 Weber, *Economy and Society*, op. cit., p. 657 on the importance of collecting and collating rules.
34 H. Kelsen, *Die Reine Rechtslehre*, Wien: Deuticke, 1934, p. 17.
35 H. Kelsen, 'Préface', in Ch. Eisenmann, *La justice constitutionnelle et la Haute Cour constitutionnelle d'Autriche*, Paris: Librairie Générale de Droit et de Jurisprudence, 1928, p. x.
36 Weber, *Economy and Society*, op. cit., p. 657.
37 Ibid., pp. 775–805.
38 Ibid., p. 866.
39 Kelsen, *Pure Theory of Law*, op. cit., p. 129.
40 Ibid., p. 247.
41 Kelsen, 'Préface', op. cit., p. x.
42 Weber, *Economy and Society*, op. cit., p. 795.
43 Ibid., p. 798.
44 Ibid., p. 852.
45 Ibid., p. 821.

46 Ibid., p. 818. This question is developed in M. Weber, *Confucianisme et Taoïsme*, C. Colliot-Thélène and J.-P. Grossein (trans, French), Paris: Gallimard, 2000, pp. 214–17.
47 Weber, *Economy and Society*, op. cit., p. 865.
48 S. L. Paulson, 'Four Phases in Hans Kelsen's Legal Theory? Reflections on a Periodization', *Oxford Journal of Law Studies* (1998), 18, 153–66.
49 Kelsen, *Pure Theory of Law*, op. cit., pp. 355–56.
50 M. Weber, *Critique of Stammler*, G. Oakes (trans, English), New York: Free Press, 1977, pp. 128–29.
51 M. Weber, 'Some Categories of Interpretive Sociology', E. Graber (trans), *The Sociological Quarterly* (1981), 22, 151–80, p. 158.
52 Kelsen, *General Theory of Law and State*, op. cit., p. 177.
53 Ibid., p. 178; Renato Treves, 'Hans Kelsen et la sociologie du droit', *Droit et Société* (1985), 1, 15–22, p. 19.
54 M. Weber, 'The Meaning of "Ethical Neutrality" in Sociology and Economics', in *The Methodology of the Social Sciences*, A. S. Shils and H. A. Finch (trans and eds), New Brunswick: Transaction Publishers, 2011, p. 43.
55 Weber, *Economy and Society*, op. cit., p. 850.
56 Ibid., p. 842.
57 Ibid., p. 858.

Index

Aquinas, Thomas 179
Aristotle 46, 47, 49, 128, 131, 179
Aron, R. 169
associational membership 46–8, 51, 54
Austrian Constitution (1920) 3–4, 36
Austrian Republic 5
Austrian Social Democracy 34
Austro-Hungarian Empire 1–2, 11, 131–2

Balkans: *zadruga* community 182
Basic norm (*Grundnorm*) 7, 9, 78, 82, 83, 118–19, 120, 127–8, 165–6, 191
Bobbio, N. 28, 32, 171
Bodin, J. 117, 120, 132, 133
Braudel, F. 131
bureaucratic system 3, 6, 29, 34, 70–2, 171

capitalism 10, 30, 148, 151, 152
Carré de Malberg, R. 8, 116, 117
Central and East European socialist States 46
centralization and decentralization 12, 113, 114, 171, 185–6, 191
Chinese law 189
civic republicanism 45, 46
civil society and civic friendship 44–54
class struggle 33
communitarianism 45, 46
Constant, B. 31
constitution 11, 133–4; Austria (1920) 3–4, 36; United States 134; Weimar 3, 31, 36
constitutionalism, liberal 28
'copy theory' of knowledge 190
credit rating agencies 133
cultural institutions 133
culture and law 12
custom 12, 48, 63–4, 77, 79, 103, 117, 119, 126, 168; *see also* history, using Weber's and Kelsen's schemas for legal

decentralization and centralization 12, 113, 114, 171, 185–6, 191
democracy 2–5, 11, 129, 133, 134; direct election of the President 3, 31, 34–5; federalism 36–7; *Führerprinzip* and democracy in Weber and Kelsen 27–37; impossibility of direct 4, 32, 35; Kelsenian concept of rule of law and Weberian concept of legal power 34; parliament 28, 29, 31–2, 33, 35–6; political parties 3–4, 29–31, 33, 35–6; proportional representation 33–4, 36; small leading groups 30; within pluralism: Kelsen on civil society and civic friendship 44–54
democratic type of personality 4, 54
demythologizing the political, Kelsen's project of 48–52
Dreier, H. 76
due process 134
Dworkin, R. 134
dynamic legal system 115

education 133
Ehrlich, E. 110, 181–2, 183
England 182

federalism 36–7
feudal law 113, 114
formal rationality and legitimacy of modern law: Weber and Kelsen 163–74; antinomy of form and substance 164; axiological neutrality 163, 165, 167; completeness 165; deductive character

165; formal ('legal-rational') legitimacy of law 167–73; formal legitimation 165–6; formal rationality of law 164–7; identity of law and state 167, 171–3, 174; logical coherence 164–5; methodological specificity 165; natural law 163, 165, 167, 168–70; substantive rationality 166–7
formal/substantive and rational/irrational law 12, 814–15
France 114, 116, 117, 146–7; Napoleonic Code (1804) 183, 187, 189; Revolution (1789) 27, 131, 140
Freud, S. 4
fundamental norm *see Grundnorm*

Geny, F. 181
Gerber, C.F. von 68, 72
German Democratic Republic (GDR) 80, 83
Germany 1–2, 69, 71, 131–2, 146–7; Civil Code 189; National Socialism 2, 32, 126, 179; Weimar Republic 2, 3, 5, 31, 36
Gierke, O. von 68–9, 181, 182
globalized financial system 133
Grotius, H. 117
Grundnorm (Basic norm) 7, 9, 78, 82, 83, 118–19, 120, 127–8, 165–6, 191

Habermas, J. 167
Hart, H.L.A. 183–4
Hellpach, W. 65
Hermes, S. 70, 72, 73, 74
historical economics 10
Historical School of Law 168, 182, 187, 188
historical sociology and natural law 170
history, using Weber's and Kelsen's schemas for legal 179–92; genesis of legal orders: reading Weber with Kelsen 180–6; legal science 180, 181, 186–92; representation of legal orders: reading Kelsen with Weber 186–92
Hitler, A. 2
Hobbes, T. 2, 27, 28, 35, 48, 132–3
human rights and subjective rights: affinities in Weber and Jellinek 140–54; epistemology: types of knowledge interests and ideals 143; functionality of human rights and subjective (public) rights 148–9; genesis of human rights 143–4; human rights as social rights and rights of participation 151–3; law of nature and human rights: legitimacy, obedience or acceptance of legal system 149–51; overview of primary texts and secondary literature 140–3; subjective (public) rights as juridification of idea of human rights 144–8
Hume, D. 71

imputation: Kelsen 7, 11, 76, 165, 173; sovereignty 116–17, 118, 119
in dubio pro reo principle 134
innocence, presumption of 134
international law 36, 113, 114, 129
irrational/rational and formal/substantive law 12, 814–15
Islamic law 182, 188–9

Jansen, L. 79–80
Jellinek, G. 9–10, 76, 111, 172; ethics and morality 131; relationship of law and state in work of Kelsen and 10–11, 125–34; sovereignty, people and territory 129, 132
Jhering, R. von 191
judicial independence 134

Kant, I. 27, 66, 128, 142
Kantorowicz, H. 110
Kautsky, K. 34
Kelsen, Hans 1–2; character of law: Weber and 11–13, 163–74, 179–92; democracy: Weber and 2–5, 27–37; democracy within pluralism: civil society and civic friendship 44–54; *Der Soziologische und der Juristische Staatsbegriff* 6–8, 32, 61, 98–106, 113; formal rationality and legitimacy of modern law: Weber and 163–74; *General Theory of Law and State* 182, 191; *General Theory of Norms* 9; *Hauptprobleme der Staatsrechtslehre entwickeltaus der Lehre vom Rechtssatze* 6, 32, 33, 106–7; legal history 179–92; legal rights: Jellinek and 9–11, 125–34, 145; 'political' work 1; *Pure Theory of Law* 125, 126, 127, 128, 185–6, 190; *Society and Nature. A Sociological Inquiry* 12; *Sozialismus und Staat* 32, 34; state: Weber

and 5–9, 61–83, 98–107, 110–21; state and law in work of Kelsen and Jellinek, relationship of 125–34; *Wählerlisten und Reklamationsrecht* 33; *Wesen und Wert der Demokratie* 32, 33; 'Zur Soziologie des Rechts' 77
Kersten, J. 145
König, M. 140
Kries, J. von 80

Laband, P. 68, 71, 72–3
Lambert, É. 181–2
Landau, P. 68–9
law and State, identity of 8–9, 76, 110–14, 126, 134, 167, 171–3, 174, 179, 191; as explanation for historic emergence of the State 114–21; ideological character of dualist theory 112; monopoly on the legitimate use of violence 111, 112–13, 115; people, territory and public government 111–12; rational legitimacy 111, 114
law and State in work of Kelsen and Jellinek, relationship of 10–11, 125–34; basic norm 127–8; is and ought 125–6; Jellinek and *Allgemeine Staatslehre (General Theory of the State)* 128–30; law, ethics and state 130–2; normative power of the factual 128–32; norms 126–7, 134; State: concept and its elements 132–3; State under rule of law 133–4
legal history, using Weber's and Kelsen's schemas for 179–92; genesis of legal orders: reading Weber with Kelsen 180–6; representation of legal orders: reading Kelsen with Weber 186–92
legal pluralism 174
legitimacy of modern law: Weber and Kelsen 163–74; antinomy of form and substance 164; axiological neutrality 163, 165, 167; completeness 165; deductive character 165; formal ('legal-rational') legitimacy of law 167–73; formal legitimation 165–6; formal rationality of law 164–7; identity of law and state 167, 171–3, 174; logical coherence 164–5; methodological specificity 165; natural law 163, 165, 167, 168–70; substantive rationality 166–7

Leibholz, G. 35, 36
liberal constitutionalism 28
Locke, J. 27
Loos, F. 65
Lotze, H. 65–6
Lübbe, W. 81, 82

Marx, K. 4, 34
Mayer, O. 68, 71, 72
Möllers, C. 76

Napoleonic Code (1804) 183, 187, 189
National Socialism 2, 32, 126, 179
natural law 2, 36, 50, 125–6, 127, 163, 165, 167, 168–70, 179, 187, 190
natural sciences 165, 168, 173
Neo-Kantianism 10, 62, 65, 66, 163, 190
norms 6–7, 9, 10–11, 63, 65, 73–4, 77–8, 110, 126–7, 134; Basic norm (*Grundnorm*) 7, 9, 78, 82, 83, 118–19, 120, 127–8, 165–6, 191; unity of law and state: emergence of state and hierarchy of 9, 113, 114–21

original norm (*Ursprungsnorm*) 171
ought/ought-to-be (*Sollen*); is (*Sein*) and 7, 78, 82, 83, 104, 125–6, 163, 168–70; Kelsen 7, 9, 10–11, 78, 81, 82, 83, 104, 163, 170; Weber 5, 83, 104, 163, 168–70, 172

Pandectism 173, 186, 187, 188, 191
Plato 48–9
pluralism 4–5, 174; Kelsen on civil society and civic friendship: democracy within 44–54; Kelsen's project of demythologizing the political 48–52
political parties 3–4, 29–31, 33, 35–6
Popitz, H. 71
presumption of innocence 134
primitive law 114, 184, 185
private and public law 11, 115
proportional representation 33–4, 36
Prussian Code (1794) 185, 187
public and private law 11, 115

Radbruch, G. 168
rational/irrational and formal/substantive law 12, 814–15
Rawls, J. 45, 46, 50, 51, 52
referendum 29

relativism 4, 44, 51–2, 169, 170
religion 9–10, 49, 78; religious freedom 140
representation, principle of 27, 35
Rickert, H. 65
Roman law 71, 182, 187, 188, 189, 191, 192
Romantic Movement 168
Rousseau, J.-J. 4, 49–50
Russian Revolutions 10
Ryle, G. 79, 80

Schluchter, W. 83
Schmitt, C. 28, 31–2, 33, 35, 36, 53
Schönberger, C. 72
Searle, J.R. 115
separation of powers 133
Smend, R. 35
social contract 49, 132
social welfare 133
socialist economy 115
Sollen (ought/ought-to-be): Kelsen 7, 9, 10–11, 78, 81, 82, 83, 104, 163, 170; *Sein* (is) and 7, 78, 82, 83, 104, 125–6, 163, 168–70; Weber 5, 83, 104, 163, 168–70, 172
Sommerhäuser, H. 66
sovereignty 9, 27, 36, 37, 49–50, 115–21, 129, 132–3, 145–6, 147, 173; Hobbes and Weber 28
Sperber, M. 130
Stammler, R. 169
State, emergence of the 9, 110–21; Kelsen's theory of unity of law and State 110–14; unity of law and State as explanation for historic 114–20
State and law: identity of the 8–9, 76, 110–21, 126, 134, 167, 171–3, 174, 179, 191; in work of Kelsen and Jellinek: relationship of 10–11, 125–34
State, Weber's conception of the 5–9, 61–83; *Anstalt* and *Staat* 69–74; monopoly on the legitimate use of violence 8, 61, 73, 100, 102, 111, 112–13, 115, 173; origin of the sociological conception of *Anstalt* 67–9; 'social relationship' as fundamental category 62–4; state as 'anstalt' 62–4; state as validating idea (*der staat als geltungsvorstellung*) 74–80; validation 64–6,
73–80; *Verband* 5, 6, 8, 9, 63, 67, 71, 73–4
Stegmüller, W. 79, 80, 83
subjective rights and human rights: affinities in Weber and Jellinek 140–54
substantive/formal and rational/irrational law 12, 814–15
Swiss Civil Code 188

terrorism 133
Thoma, R. 62
Thomas, Y. 117
transnational corporations 133
Triepel, H. 33, 35–6
Troeltsch, E. 168

United States 29, 34; Constitution 134
Ursprungsnorm (original norm) 171
utilitarianism 131

Weber, Max 1–2; character of law: Kelsen and 11–13, 163–74, 179–92; 'Critique of Stammler' 64, 73, 75, 166, 169, 190; democracy: Kelsen and 2–5, 27–37; *Der Reichspräsident* 31; 'Essay on Categories' 64, 69–70, 75, 105; 'Essay on Objectivity' 74–5; formal rationality and legitimacy of modern law: Kelsen and 163–74; human rights and subjective rights: affinities in Jellinek and 9–11, 140–54; legal history 179–92; *Parliament and Government* 29; 'political' work 1; *Politik als Beruf* 29; *The Protestant Ethic and the Spirit of Capitalism* 10, 78; *Soziologische Grundbegriffe* 149; state: Kelsen and 5–9, 61–83, 98–107, 110–21; 'The Economy and Social Orders' 64, 73; *Wirtschaft und Gesellschaft* (Economy and Society) 7–8, 28, 61, 64, 75, 99, 101, 180, 187; ('Basic Sociological Concepts') 61, 63, 64, 67, 69, 70, 74, 99, 100–1; ('Sociology of Law') 11, 67–8, 77, 163, 184–5

Weimar Republic 2, 3, 5; Constitution 3, 31, 36
Windelband, W. 65, 66

zadruga community 182
Zingerle, A. 70
Zitelmann, E. 181, 182